D0208007

The Chinese Americans

Other Titles in
The New Americans Series
Ronald H. Bayor, Series Editor

·The Chinese Americans

Benson Tong

THE NEW AMERICANS
Ronald H. Bayor, Series Editor

GREENWOOD PRESS
Westport, Connecticut • London

Library of Congress Cataloging-in-Publication Data

Tong, Benson, 1964–
    The Chinese Americans / Benson Tong.
        p.   cm.—(The new Americans, ISSN 1092–6364)
    Includes bibliographical references (p.   ) and index.
    ISBN 0–313–30544–7 (alk. paper)
    1. Chinese Americans.   I. Title.   II. Series: New Americans
(Westport, Conn.)
    E184.C5T63   2000
    973'.04951—dc21   99–30319

British Library Cataloguing in Publication Data is available.

Library of Congress Catalog Card Number: 99–30319
ISBN: 0–313–30544–7
ISSN: 1092–6364

First published in 2000

Greenwood Press, 88 Post Road West, Westport, CT 06881
An imprint of Greenwood Publishing Group, Inc.
www.greenwood.com

Printed in the United States of America

The paper used in this book complies with the
Permanent Paper Standard issued by the National
Information Standards Organization (Z39.48–1984).

10 9 8 7 6 5 4 3 2 1

For my sister, Vennee

Contents

Photographic Essay follows p. 97.

Series Foreword

Oscar Handlin, a prominent historian, once wrote, "I thought to write a history of the immigrants in America. Then I discovered that the immigrants were American history." The United States has always been a nation of nations where people from every region of the world have come to begin a new life. Other countries such as Canada, Argentina, and Australia also have had substantial immigration, but the United States is still unique in the diversity of nationalities and the great numbers of migrating people who have come to its shores.

Who are these immigrants? Why did they decide to come? How well have they adjusted to this new land? What has been the reaction to them? These are some of the questions the books in this "New Americans" series seek to answer. There have been many studies about earlier waves of immigrants—e.g., the English, Irish, Germans, Jews, Italians, and Poles—but relatively little has been written about the newer groups—those arriving in the last thirty years, since the passage of a new immigration law in 1965. This series is designed to correct that situation and to introduce these groups to the rest of America.

Each book in the series discusses one of these groups, and each is written by an expert on those immigrants. The volumes cover the new migration from primarily Asia, Latin America, and the Caribbean, including: the Koreans, Cambodians, Filipinos, Vietnamese, South Asians such as Indians and Pakistanis, Chinese from both China and Taiwan, Haitians, Jamaicans, Cubans, Dominicans, Mexicans, Puerto Ricans (even though they are already U.S. citizens), and Jews from the former Soviet Union. Although some of these people, such as Jews, have been in America since colonial times, this series concentrates on their recent migrations and thereby offers its unique contribution.

These volumes are designed for high school and general readers who want to learn more about their new neighbors. Each author has provided information about the land of origin, its history and culture, the reasons for migrating, and the ethnic culture as it began to adjust to American life. Readers will find fascinating details on religion, politics, foods, festivals, gender roles, employment trends, and general community life. They will learn how Vietnamese immigrants differ from Cuban immigrants and, yet, how they are also alike in many ways. Each book is arranged to offer an in-depth look at the particular immigrant group but also to enable readers to compare one group with the other. The volumes also contain brief biographical profiles of notable individuals, tables noting each group's immigration, and a short bibliography of readily available books and articles for further reading. Most contain a glossary of foreign words and phrases.

Students and others who read these volumes will secure a better understanding of the age-old questions of "Who is an American?" and "How does the assimilation process work?" Similar to their nineteenth- and early twentieth-century forebears, many Americans today doubt the value of immigration and fear the influx of individuals who look and sound different from those who had come earlier. If comparable books had been written one hundred years ago they would have done much to help dispel readers' unwarranted fears of the newcomers. Nobody today would question, for example, the role of those of Irish or Italian ancestry as Americans; yet, this was a serious issue in our history and a source of great conflict. It is time to look at our recent arrivals, to understand their history and culture, their skills, their place in the United States, and their hopes and dreams as Americans.

The United States is a vastly different country than it was at the beginning of the twentieth century. The economy has shifted away from industrial jobs, the civil rights movement has changed minority-majority relations and, along with the women's movement, brought more people into the economic mainstream. Yet one aspect of American life remains strikingly similar—we are still the world's main immigrant receiving nation and as in every period of American history, we are still a nation of immigrants. It is essential that we attempt to learn about and understand this long-term process of migration and assimilation.

Ronald H. Bayor
Georgia Institute of Technology

Preface

This volume is an interpretive narrative of the Chinese American historical experience since the 1780s to the present. The purpose of this book is to elucidate the impact of political, economic, social, and intellectual trends, both those in the countries of origin and, to a larger extent, those in the United States, on the lives of Chinese immigrants and Chinese Americans. The Chinese American experience, including its contemporary state of affairs, is surveyed in order to explore the intersections of race, class, gender, and sexuality. Equally critical is the examination of how Chinese Americans, in turn, have played active roles in shaping the history of the United States. The narrative focuses on the agency of Chinese Americans through the selective presentation of their "voices."

The expansive story presented here suggests that the Chinese American identity was and is far from being singular, static, or irreversible. The book challenges the assimilationist thrust of some of the previous surveys of this same historical experience. Chinese immigrants and subsequent generations, through the exercise of their human agency, have instead continuously negotiated the boundaries of race, gender, class, ethnicity, sexuality, and nationalism and thus defy any neat categorization of their identity or "place" in American society. Furthermore, Chinese Americans, through their attempts to apply lessons of democracy and equality of humankind, have played a vital role in shaping republican ideology and ultimately have forced the United States to uphold its revolutionary promise.

Though designed to provide readers with a broad understanding of this often historically maligned American ethnic group, this volume, due to the limitation of space, is still somewhat selective in its coverage. Therefore, the discussion focuses on post–1945 developments, particularly those that relate to politicization and the formation of ethnic identity. Readers who are interested in knowing more about earlier historical developments as well as the intricacies of Chinese culture and customs should consult materials listed in the bibliography.

In regard to the transliteration of Chinese names, words, and phrases, it is important to note that *putonghua* (Mandarin), the official dialect in today's mainland China, is quite different in pronunciation from Cantonese, which most early Chinese immigrants spoke. Following standard practice, I use Mandarin, rather than Cantonese, for proper nouns. For such nouns, I have used the *pinyin* romanization system, except in cases where the name or word typically has been spelled in the Wade-Giles system. Cantonese transliterations are offered in parentheses for some Mandarin words.

Acknowledgments

In the course of researching and writing this volume, I have once again been reminded of the multiple debts I owe to friends, professional acquaintances, and family members. It has been a "perilous journey," to quote from one Gold Mountain song, and yet calmness prevailed in the end. The warm embrace of a circle of lifelong friends and even strangers has enabled me to "come ashore, the sooner the better" as phrased in another immigrant song.

I would be a *juk sing* (literally, in Cantonese, a "hollow bamboo"—a useless or ungrateful person) if I failed to acknowledge the nurturing gifts of Linda Trinh Vo and Antoinette Charfouros McDaniel. During a trying two-year stint at Oberlin College, I learned many lessons from them, some of which have made their way into this text. For the photographs that grace this volume, I must thank Antoinette, Linda, Terry L. Abrams, and Haipeng Li, who generously expended their time and energy in this venture. Haipeng also deserves all the credit for checking the *pinyin* spelling of Chinese words and phrases. Though my mentor, the late Gerald Thompson, never read this manuscript, I am grateful to him for urging me to accept this daunting project. The writing of this text also attests to his remarkable influence on my professional life, and I hope I have been able to measure up to his exacting standards.

At Wichita State University, Kenneth R. Spurgeon, in his capacity as a research assistant, helped with bibliographical work and eventually researched and wrote, under my supervision, all the biographical sketches included in the appendix. Many other students, mostly at Oberlin College, have also shared their penetrating insights into the Chinese American world. Students enrolled in Asian American seminars at Oberlin prodded me to reconsider some of my understanding of the literature, and I will always be grateful to them for their efforts.

I dedicate this book to my sister, Vennee Tong, who often wondered, "When will you [I] ever come home?" In my absence, she has taken care of our aging parents. I realize that sometimes I have kept silent about her worthy contributions, but I hope that this dedication can rectify that inexcusable inarticulation.

The Chinese Americans

1

Roots of a Diaspora: Chinese Culture and Society in the Late Qing Period

PRE-QING HISTORY

The Chinese presence in the so-called New World came about through trading connections, particularly those forged by the Manila galleon trade. From 1565 to 1815, Chinese, along with Filipino, sailors and stewards toiled in cargo ships that plied the waters between Manila and Acapulco. By the seventeenth century, some Chinese merchants were trading in Mexico City. These mercantile links had widened by late eighteenth century to encompass the fabled sandalwood trade between Hawaii and China.

The first Chinese to live in Hawaii, experts in sugar production from Guangdong province in southern China, arrived in the early 1800s. The tiny community grew following the recruitment of nearly 200 contract laborers in 1852 for work in sugar plantations. The Chinese presence in mainland United States was first recorded in the late eighteenth century. The first arrivals were three Chinese sailors, known only as Ashing, Achun, and Aceun, who came to Baltimore in 1785 as part of an abandoned interracial shipping crew. From this small, inauspicious beginning the trickle widened in the 1850s into a wave as more than 20,000 Chinese in 1852 alone descended upon California because of the gold rush.[1] Chinese immigration to the United States gathered momentum until anti-Asian immigration laws passed in the late nineteenth century halted further arrivals. The story of Chinese America, however, must begin in late imperial China during the height of the Qing dynasty (1644–1912), the last dynasty before the emergence of the republican nation-state.

The Chinese civilization, one of the longest continuous civilizations in human history, may be "visualized [as] a majestic flowing stream."[2] Its cultural and geopolitical dimensions across time and space have maintained a strong historical presence in the imagination of Chinese, both within mainland China and beyond. Being the site of the geopolitical and cultural roots of the historical Chinese diaspora to Southeast Asia, Australasia, South and North America, China embodies complexities in language, religion, customs, political system, legal heritage, and physical landscape. This land of more than 4 million square miles (including Inner Asia—Mongolia, Manchuria, Chinese Turkestan, and Tibet) and almost 430 million people in the middle of the nineteenth century is indeed a country of dramatic contrasts and diversity.

Scholars typically trace the origins of the Chinese identity to the middle Yellow River basin in northern China nearly five thousand years ago, where some tribes known collectively as the Huaxia had developed a neolithic culture to a somewhat advanced level. The Huaxia tribes then expanded southward to the lower Yellow River and Huai River valleys, where they encountered and absorbed another group of tribes, the Dongyi. By the twenty-first century B.C., the Huaxia had established in Henan the first national state in China, the Xia. This proto-Chinese state and its culture became the foundation for the modern Han Chinese people and culture, which today makes up 94 percent of the population.[3]

In the next centuries the Huaxia people spread to all parts of northern China and established a number of states. In the third century B.C., one state, Qin, through military conquests, successfully unified most of China, including parts inhabited by non-Huaxia ethnic groups. The establishment of this far-flung empire permitted the dissemination of the Yellow River culture to all parts of China for centuries to come.

Recent archaeological findings indicate, however, that this cultural process was not simply a one-way phenomenon of domination by one particular group over the others. Neither was it necessarily a process that began five thousand years ago. In fact, several centers of cultural development, as long ago perhaps as ten thousand years, across present-day China contributed to the shaping of the Han Chinese and its civilization which, in turn, has given rise to regional variations in dialects and customs among the Han Chinese people.

For example, the Yue people, one of the largest, most prominent ethnic groups, which first appeared in history more than 3,000 years ago in the lower Yangzi Valley in eastern China and then spread southward into present-day Fujian, Guangdong, Guangxi, and northern Vietnam, had a language or languages and a culture different from those of the proto-Chinese states in the Yellow River basin of the north. It was this Yue culture that over time contributed primarily to the cultural development of Guangdong, the southernmost province, to which, up to 1965, from 90 to 95 percent of the Chinese in America trace their *gen* (roots). An indicator of how the confluence of peoples and cultures has resulted in variations lies in the realm of surnames. The three most common surnames in China—Li, Wang, and Zhang—are rarely found in Guangdong; however, Mai, ranked eighth in the same province, is not listed among the 100 most common surnames in China. Still, the perception that there is a cultural core area has given the Chinese, both citizens of mainland China and the *Huaqiao* (overseas Chinese), an imaginary claim of a common place of origin.

This element of commonality has been reinforced by the classical distinction made between the Hua or Huaxia (Chinese), which suggests culture and civilization, and the "barbarians," namely those who did not live in China Proper (defined as south of the Great Wall of China and excluding Inner Asia). This sense of cultural superiority, which solidified ethnic pride and defined *zuguo* (the motherland), helps explain the perpetuity of the well-known *Zhongguo*, or "Middle Kingdom" or "Central Cultural Florescence," syndrome.

GEOGRAPHY OF THE MIDDLE KINGDOM

From a physical environmental standpoint, it is understandable why the Middle Kingdom mentality—that China was the center of the world and superior to other civilizations—continued for so long in the popular imagination of the Chinese. The region north and west of China is a vast, relatively empty area of wind-swept desert or grassland country, namely the steppes of Mongolia and the Gobi desert. To the southwest, beyond the Kunlun range lie the rugged, lofty Tibetan plateau and the Himalayas. Directly to the south are steamy, dense tropical jungles; to the east, the forbidding Yellow Sea and China Sea. These formidable barriers kept premodern China (before penetration of the West in early nineteenth century) relatively isolated, although controlled commercial contacts with the outside world were never severed.

Such premodern historical contact, however, remained one way. The cultures of Southeast Asia, Japan, and India only marginally shaped Chinese civilization. Furthermore, China's closest neighbors were either sedentary peoples who consciously chose to emulate Chinese culture—especially the

Koreans, Annamese (Vietnamese), and Japanese—or pastoral peoples, such as the Mongols, Uighurs, and Kazakhs, who occasionally offered a military challenge to China but never a cultural one.

In fact, until the disruptive nineteenth-century contact with the outside world occurred, intermittent visitors to China submitted themselves to the symbolic ritual of the Chinese tributary system. The farther these "foreign devils" stood from the civilizing influence of Chinese culture, the more "barbaric" and lowly they were considered by the Chinese. Thus, the Chinese structured the tributary system to express their cultural superiority. It also stood as an extension of their own internal social and political order. Within this hierarchical structure of foreign relations, China served as the lord and other states as the vassals. Non-Chinese rulers and their subjects presented tributes or gifts to the imperial court as a sign of submission and, in return, they received imperial gifts, trading privileges, and protection. Diplomatic relations, similar to interpersonal ones, also embodied the principle of reciprocity.

Given this limited, unequal contact with the outside world, as well as the awe-inspiring landscape, it is not surprising that historically the Chinese had a strong sense of "place" and that this, in turn, was celebrated in classical literature and popular mythology. Overseas Chinese of the past maintained some level of emotional identification with their homeland—a phenomenon catalyzed by the legal and social discrimination they encountered in host countries including the United States.[4]

China's vastness and highly diversified landscape have also resulted in multiplicity in both socioeconomic life and cultural expression which, in turn, has shaped the diasporic process. First, China Proper, consisting of eighteen provinces, can be differentiated physically and culturally from Inner Asia. Inner Asia, an uninhabitable, arid region, historically has been of marginal economic importance to China, but it served well as a buffer zone against the border "barbarians" to the north and west of Inner Asia.

The topography within China Proper fragments it internally, first along the north-south direction and then again within each half. The most prominent divisive element is a mountainous region, made up mostly by the Chinling range, which stretches across central China from Tibet toward the China Sea. This separates the Yellow River drainage zone of the north from the Yangzi River drainage zone of the south and its coastal valleys. Though both northern and southern China feature major waterways, each area is different.

Northern China's main traffic artery—the Yellow River—brings with it heavy sedimentation which has impeded navigation. In the past, the silt has also led to the danger of a rising riverbed, and when dikes break catastrophic floods occur. Given that, the river's bitter nickname, "China's Sorrow," seems appropriate. The north also features a smooth coastline with few places suitable for harbor development. The Yangzi River, the main southern artery, is far less malevolent; it is navigable all the way, and its many tributaries provide easy access to all surrounding areas. Unlike the north, the south has a rough coastline suitable for ports and maritime trade. Not surprisingly, this transportation network historically kept the south ahead of the north in terms of economic development.

The north is made up of two fairly inhospitable areas: the somewhat arid, vast lowland plain in the east and a highland plateau in the west. The north also suffers from a rigorous climate; relatively dry year-round, it alternates between a very cold winter and a very hot summer. Because of these climatological conditions, the growing season in imperial times was short, and only dry crops such as wheat and millet were cultivated, mostly for subsistence purposes.

Southern China, however, is a contrast to the north; the former boasts of many undulating valleys and hills and an abundance of lakes, rivers, streams, and other waterways. Unlike the north, the south is blessed by adequate monsoon rainfall and moderate variations in temperature. All that, coupled with its primarily leached, noncalcareous soils, resulted in a nine-to-twelve-month high-yield growing season and the farming of such crops as rice, fruits, and beans for the market economy.

The south is further fragmented into distinctive smaller areas, separated from each other by stretches of low but rugged hills. For example, Guangdong, the southernmost coastal province, is shielded from the Yangzi River basin by a mountainous barrier. Fed by numerous rivers, the southern part of this province forms a common delta known as the Pearl River Delta. This delta area of Guangdong is fertile and hilly. In the nineteenth century it was heavily terraced for both subsistence and commercial farming.

Guangdong, because of its unique southerly position and protective coastline, has attracted traders from southern Asia and Southeast Asia since the third century A.D. By the early sixteenth century, Portugese maritime travelers, followed soon by the English, Dutch, French, and Americans, became interested in Guangzhou (Canton), the maritime center, as the gateway to the lucrative coastal traffic in silk, tea, porcelain, and other Chinese goods. Following such exposure to these influences from abroad, which included science, Christianity, and fanciful stories of other lands, America included, the people of this subregion gradually became more receptive to new ideas and change.[5]

China's topography overall lends itself to regional separatism in multiple forms and that, in turn, has made the process of political centralization problematic and, at times, nearly impossible. Centrifugal forces would become more visible at the dawn of the turbulent nineteenth century.

LANGUAGE

The influence of regional separatism is evident in the realm of language. Although racially China is fairly homogeneous—only about 6 percent of the populace is made up of non-Han people comprising more than fifty minority groups—China exhibits a marked linguistic diversity.[6] Such divergences are clearly the result of internal geographical isolation across time.

The spoken language is fragmented into at least half a dozen mutually unintelligible regional dialects, each of which has any number of local variants. Chinese dialects differ significantly in pronunciation but less so in idiom and syntax. Cantonese (also known as Yue), to use one example, is a dialect spoken mostly in the southeast, especially in the province of Guangdong. It has therefore historically been spoken in many communities in the United States. Today there are about 50 million speakers of this dialect within and outside mainland China, including the Sanyi, Sze Yup, and Zhongshan varieties so prevalent among Chinese abroad, especially in the Americas and Hawaii. Other important dialect groups in Guangdong that have made their way to the United States include Hakka and Fujian-derived dialects.[7]

Most dialects such as Cantonese vary dramatically from Mandarin (*putonghua*), the official dialect spoken by most Chinese today. However, all are written alike. Despite the babel of dialects, China is united linguistically via the standard written language which is used by every group and region.

The Chinese written language, which earliest archaeological evidence dates back to the Shang dynasty (1765–1122 B.C.), is unique. The complex characters, today numbering about forty thousand, are not letters, which all Western languages employ, but began as pictures or symbols. The characters are not phonetic representations, but actually ideographs. Many consist of simpler characters; for example, by combining those for sun and moon we get bright, illustrious, or clear. Since a character is an ideograph, it has the same meaning or meanings to all readers though it may be pronounced differently in various dialect regions. Each character also represents a separate word in Chinese. Each Chinese character signifies both the meaning and the sound for a whole word.

Part of the Sino-Tibetan family, which embraces the tongues of Tibet, Thailand, Burma, Vietnam, and Laos, Chinese features only monosyllabic "words" or characters. Since there are more characters than syllables, many characters are pronounced as the same sound or syllable. In short, the language is littered with homophones. For example, the character for east carries the sound "tung." So does the spoken word meaning freeze and roof beam. To differentiate these, tones are used. Every character has a fixed tone. This tonal feature in the spoken language gives Chinese a musical rhythm.[8]

Another significant element in Chinese language is the emphasis on word relations which tends to echo the relational character of Chinese philosophy. Ideas are often presented by compound expressions consisting of antonyms; examples include "buy-sell" for "trade" and "advance-retreat" for "movement." The antonyms are not seen as opposites but as united concepts forming a complete idea. The meaning of each character can be determined only in relation to other words.

All this reflects the focus of Confucianism—the core of Chinese thought—not on the individual, but on the web of human relations. The emphasis here is on the person's moral obligations to others, not on the individual's human rights. The fact that Chinese possesses an extraordinary number of kinship terms suggests an intense concern with family relationships; similarly, the rich body of ethical terms and concepts indicates China's preoccupation with moral values.

The intricacies of the Chinese language have, in the words of an eminent Chinese historian, "the character of an institution, rather than a tool, of society."[9] The language with so many meanings and allusions, simply put, is cumbersome, though paradoxically it has been used to produce a greater volume of recorded literature than any other language before modern times. The mastery of classical Chinese (*wenyan wen*), as opposed to the "vulgar" vernacular speech (*baihua wen*), however, involves long years of learning just to understand parts of the literature. Not surprisingly, written language, at least before the iconoclastic vernacular or plain language movement of the early twentieth century, which swept aside that arcane classical style of writing, remained the province of the scholar-gentry class throughout most of Chinese history and helped, in that sense, to preserve the hierarchical Confucian old order. Some scholars have even gone so far as to argue that the complexity of this language inhibited easy contact with the outside world and kept China fairly isolated from modernity until the Western intrusion in the mid-nineteenth century.

SOCIETAL STRUCTURE

The hierarchical class structure also tended to preserving this old order. The scholar-gentry or scholar-official class was one of the four major classes in the traditional Chinese society. By late Qing, society was highly stratified with status distinctions maintained via the sanctions of ritual and law. The four classes were ranked according to their social value in the following descending order: scholar-officials, farmers, artisans, and merchants. This categorization exalted government service above all other occupations and attached little or no social value to wealth or military valor. It also privileged scholastic achievement but co-opted intellectuals into government service.[10] This class structure also, to some degree, shaped the fortunes of early Chinese immigrants in North America, particularly how host countries received them and how intra-ethnic relations played out.

In late Qing, the scholar-official class, which made up only an estimated 3 percent of the population at the dawn of the twentieth century, was typically outranked in status by hereditary nobles. At the top of the social hierarchy during the Qing dynasty were two groups of hereditary nobles: the imperial Manchu clansmen and certain civil or military officials, including the renowed fighting bannermen. The court bestowed upon both titles and privileges as acknowledgment of certain achievements. Both groups received special allowances of property, food, and money, as well as certain other social and economic benefits in accordance with their rank.

Civil bureaucrats or scholar-officials, some of whom also carried titular nobility, also enjoyed significant prestige. By late Qing the court had devised a nine-rank system for officials, and each rank came with a certain official dress and other symbolic marks of status. Those who belonged to this scholar-official class typically spent years mastering the classics and sat for arduous examinations held at different levels of increasing difficulty with the climax being the metropolitan or national ones held in Beijing.

Those who constituted the lower gentry had passed only the preliminary or first-level examinations, which did not qualify them for bureaucratic office. Students who passed either the provincial or national examination earned the right to be part of the upper gentry and also the necessary qualifications for imperial offices. Some members of the upper gentry became part of this class by passing military examinations or by purchasing academic titles or bureaucratic ranks. On the whole, only a very small fraction of an estimated 1.1 million degree holders during the Qing period held office. Both the upper and lower gentry earned the legal privilege of wearing distinctive robes and caps, exemption from certain types of punishment if convicted of a crime, and avoidance of the labor service tax and other taxes.

The gentry class in China, unlike those in Europe, did not resemble a landed elite. Though most did live in the rural areas and many were landlords, by the early eighteenth century the scholar-gentry often served as the administrative brokers between imperial officials and the local people. Thus, their income came from performing local services such as supervising schools, managing public works and welfare projects, organizing the militia, and mediating legal disputes. Over time, such income progressively replaced landed wealth as the major economic foundation of the gentry class. Before the sociopolitical chaos engendered by the Chinese Revolution of 1911, few members of the scholar-gentry class found it imperative to leave their homeland to eke out a better livelihood. Consequently, very few of them, except those who left to pursue higher education, could be found in the early Chinese immigrant community of nineteenth-century America.

Below the gentry stood three classes of commoners. Peasants ranked higher than artisans or merchants because farming was regarded as a productive contribution to life. Craft and mercantile activities, on the other hand, were considered unessential, unproductive, and frivolous. The overall understanding here reflected the agrarian-oriented Confucian value system. Local variation rooted in urbanization aside, in late imperial times peasants made up at least 80 percent of the population. They labored on the land, experienced limited social mobility, and lived on the margin of subsistence. Because of the absence of primogeniture, or inheritance by the oldest son, Chinese landholdings became fragmented into small plots. On the average, families in southern China owned only from twelve to fifteen *mou* (i.e., two to three acres), which economic historians have deemed insufficient for an economy of scale to occur.[11]

Also, throughout nineteenth-century China, an estimated 30 percent of the peasant families were tenant farmers and another 20 percent were petty landowners, who in addition to working their own land, rented more land to make ends meet. Because of a general shortage of fertile soil, as well as a shortage of capital, rents were high, and rural interest rates sometimes climbed to 40 percent per year.[12] These conditions partly explain the nineteenth-century exodus out of China and the upswing in the diaspora of the laboring class to the Americas.

Probably due to necessity, many Chinese peasants by the mid-nineteenth century turned to the handicraft sector to help supplement their meager family incomes. Small rural workshops and peasant homes processed goods ranging from wine, oil, and sugar to silk, cotton cloth, and iron utensils. Peasant women often played a significant part in these activities and thus enhanced their economic importance to the family.

The class below the peasants—the artisans—though ranked lower in status, often earned as much, sometimes even more, income per capita than did peasants. A wide range of occupational groups came under this class, including craftspeople, manufacturers of commodities, and service-oriented individuals. These artisans and laborers could work as independent operatives or be employed by gentry families, the merchant class, or the state.

By the late nineteenth century, in the wake of early industrialization, a segment of this class had become the new, still small, urban proletariat who worked in shops and factories using low-level technology. Unlike traditional artisans, industrial workers did not enjoy paternalistic relations with employers, and they were driven to maintain high levels of productivity, often living in decrepit urban surroundings. It was this growing urban proletariat class that rose to prominence during China's revolutionary era in the early twentieth century, and their political agitation, in turn, influenced to some degree the worldview of the Chinese in America.

Merchants theoretically ranked at the bottom of the four-class structure. Mercantile activities were stigmatized as exploitative and demeaning. Merchants, in order to secure large-scale businesses, had to cultivate the paternalism and support of imperial officials. So unattractive was this class that many merchants deliberately bought degrees and titles to gain higher prestige and enjoy certain benefits. Following the anti-Qing rebellions of the mid-nineteenth century, which wiped out the financial resources of the imperial government, as many as 50 percent of the official posts were secured through purchase; many of these presumably were bought by the merchant class.[13]

Following the expansion of commerce and industry after the 1870s under the influence of the West, the stigma attached to mercantile activities began slowly to ebb away. Some literati, disillusioned with the demanding scholarly life and encouraged by the burgeoning market economy, threw their resources into Western-style economic ventures. Thus, the boundaries between the classes gradually became somewhat blurred. But the stigma attached to mercantile activity, not to mention governmental supervision of industrialism, never disappeared, as attested to by the need to rationalize such activities in the name of preserving national strength and prosperity. This social attitude, coupled with the promise of mercantile freedom, explains in part why some of the merchant class made their way to the United States in the late nineteenth century.

The four-class structure has recently been shown to be simplistic. It has been argued that there were at least nine distinct cultural groups positioned in relations of dominance and subordination. By applying three variables—education, economic position, and legal privilege—in various ways, the Chinese social spectrum ranged from the classically educated, legally privileged, and economically self-sufficient elite (the most dominant group) to illiterate and dependent commoners (the most subordinate group).[14] This scenario included the emergence of a new, independent merchant class and a small intellectual class—both freed from gentry-like aspirations.

Complicating this picture further is gender. A woman of elite background could be privy to all advantages and still exercise very little influence. Women's subordinate position in society was certainly reflected and asserted in legal statutes, informal social customs, elite and popular literature, handbooks on household ritual, and medical texts. Further, circumstances for women in China were never the same throughout the country, even for those of the same class.

Though Chinese society was stratified, there was no caste system. Theoretically everyone could access mobility, regardless of family, birth, or religion. The Chinese system's emphasis on merit rather than birth and the partial accessibility of education produced a society in which considerable movement between the classes or social groups took place. Consequently, the rural-urban gap in terms of cultural literacy and lifestyles was not as marked as that in some European countries in the nineteenth century, although rapid economic development in urban centers in the late Qing period eventually created social differentiation.

THOUGHT AND RELIGION

Perhaps what held Chinese society together despite the pressure of internal modernization was its pervasive thought or philosophy, which undergirded religiosity. The presence of ethical terms in every area of traditional Chinese culture, including music and the arts, is an indicator of the strong influence of Chinese thought in shaping the Chinese identity.

Traditional Chinese thought, shaped primarily by Confucianism with some marginal influences of Buddhism and Daoism, embodied a strong concern with human relations. This focus could be found in the Five Constant Virtues of Confucianism: *ren* (humaneness or filial piety and submission), *li* (propriety), *yi* (duty), *zhi* (humane wisdom), and *xin* (faithfulness). Of the five, *ren* was the most important since it served as the key to an orderly family and state. Other significant elements of Chinese thought included an emphasis on nature and natural processes, as reflected in the belief in predeterminism of fate by Heaven, a profound of sense of cultural superiority, an awareness and respect for tradition, and a focus on hierarchical order and social harmony—all of which made Chinese traditional society a conservative, precedent-minded one.[15]

Unlike other cultural traditions, the Chinese saw their moral order as one shaped by men and women; the human being, not God, stood at the center of the universe. The ethical system as it existed by the late Qing period did not spring from any supernatural authority, as it does in the case of Christianity or Islam. Buddhism and Daoism, the major two institutional religions in traditional China, offered few major contributions to this ethical system; much of it was, in fact, grounded in Confucianism.

The core of Confucianism in late Qing was the Three Bonds: between ruler and subject, father and son, and husband and wife. These and the relationships between older brother and younger brother and friend and friend constituted the Five Relationships. All five relationships involved subordination, inequality, and nonreciprocal service; for example, a wife was subordinate to the husband but enjoyed virtually no rights.

In this patriarchal construct, the family served as the central unit of society, and all relationships outside it mimicked those inside it. Thus the ruler-subject relationship echoed the father-son tie; similarly, the ruler, who supposedly received the mandate from Heaven to rule, stood in a position of a son to Heaven. The Chinese did not consider the emperor as divine in any sense; rather, in a broad extension of the family pattern, the ruler functioned as the mediator between Heaven and humankind, playing one role as filial dependent to Heaven and another role as paternal exemplar to the people. Thus in Confucianism the cult of Heaven, the family system, and the state constituted a unified entity. Just as critical was the idea that the cosmic universe constituted one entity, without either a beginning or an end, and was not divisible into natural and supernatural realms.

The foundation of this entity was ritual (*li*). Ritual in this context includes all forms of codified social behavior, ranging from simple daily greetings to elaborate state ceremonies and religious offerings. These multiple types of ritual pervaded all aspects of Chinese life. All Chinese, from the emperor down to the merchant, understood and practiced ritual as a way to preserve status differentiation, encourage social unity, and relay tradition. Ritual, in sum, served to mold the identifiable Chinese character in many ways.

It would not be an exaggeration to describe mid-nineteenth-century China as a land of polytheism and eclecticism. Religiosity took on a highly diffused character and served to uphold the moral order as defined by Confucian ethical values. Though the two major institutional religions, Buddhism and Daoism, remained visible in late Qing, far more practiced was a form of popular religion, which involved a syncretic melding of the teachings of Buddhism, Daoism, and Confucianism; the practices of local cults and ancestor worship; the worship of patron gods and spirits via divination and sacrifice: the mystical arts of prediction—astrology, palmistry, and geomancy—and animism. Not surprisingly, Chinese religion did not feature a personal creator external to the cosmos.

Because of the dominance of the rationalistic features in Chinese thought, the motivation for popular religious interest was rooted in pragmatism, not theological absolutism. A woman, for example, would willingly pray to a Daoist deity for the return of her health, but on another day she might approach a diviner to have her fortune told; she would never consider that she had been unfaithful to any religion.

Religion, given its polytheistic and highly diffused character, has served well as an integrative force for Chinese social institutions and organized groups. Ancestor worship, typically carried out at shrines in the home and sometimes also at graves and ancestral halls (for collective observances by extended family and kinsfolk), constituted a cultural universal in traditional China. Through the performance of prescribed, scheduled rites, family members rekindled the memory of the departed kinsfolk and, in turn, integrated the living with the dead in perpetual kinship ties. Living family members also were conjoined as one through such collective expressions. The values of familism—all rooted in Confucianism—became strongly reinforced. Periodic or anniversary sacrifices for the ancestors and elaborate mortuary rites for the recently deceased were customary practices for most Chinese families.[16]

The parallel for family ancestral worship could be found in public religious observances. A communal belief in the appeal to the supernatural for attainment of success and security welded together such organizations as fraternal groups, protective societies (tongs), occupational associations, and local communities. For example, southern coastal, maritime communities actively worshipped the goddess of sailing, Tian Hou. Every traditional trade also had its own patron god, whose birthday celebration constituted a major event with tradespeople, one commemorated typically with festivals and even parades. These celebrations also embodied a specific social function; for the masses, life had always been a constant struggle for subsistence, and so such celebrations served as a mechanism for the affirmation of life through drama, joy, and merriment. In a predominately agrarian economy, shrines and temples dedicated to agricultural deities governing the natural forces such as the Dragon God or Lung Wang (which regulated water) were common. The existence of elaborate annual imperial sacrifices to these deities reflected the primacy of agricultural deities to the well-being of the nation.

Popular religion, however, over the centuries had also appropriated Buddhist concepts such as the transmigration of souls and the law of causal retribution (karma). Most Chinese in late Qing consequently believed that the soul existed eternally, materializing in an endless succession of temporal existences in multiple forms of life. Popular religion also incorporated the Buddhist bodhisattvas, beings who compassionately refrain from entering nirvana to help others, into its pantheon of gods. In general, Buddhism worked well with Confucianism: both emphasize the preservation of a moral order through service, self-control, and selflessness. Also, the Four Noble Truths, the core of Buddhist teachings, impart that life is an endless cycle of births and deaths in a sorrowful world and only the elimination of selfish desires will eliminate pain and sorrow.

The elimination of selfish desire is attained by following the Eightfold Noble Path, which is akin to the Confucian Five Constant Virtues: correct views, attitudes, speech, conduct, occupation, effort, perception and consciousness or self-examination, and concentration. In general, Buddhist morality is based on concrete social values such as love, charity, courage, self-control, and respect for all living matter. By following these precepts, an individual, through multiple rebirths, can gradually move toward Enlightenment, or the ultimate existence, whereupon the painful cycle of life and rebirth can be broken.

Daoism also contributed to the popular religion by way of its mystical aspects of occult magic and the practice of deifying prominent, legendary, and historical figures. Over time, the Chinese landscape became dotted with shrines and temples devoted to a large host of national, regional, and local gods. The Chinese valued Daoist gods for their utilitarian function, much as they approached Confucianism and its moral precepts. It was the moral and magical functions of the cults, not the religious identity, that dominated the people's consciousness and their receptiveness to any given belief.[17]

Daoism advocates spontaneity in union with nature. Followers seek to renounce obligations attached to social relationships and to seek psychological freedom by being oneself naturally. The central principle of Daoism is the independence of each individual—in direct opposition to Confucianism's objective of bringing humans in line with established social conventions.

As is the case with Buddhism, the value system of Daoism echoes Confucian virtues. The social principles of loyalty, faithfulness, integrity, duty, and filial piety constitute the exalted core of Daoism as they do in Confucianism. Daoism, inspired by the Buddhist idea of karmic retribution, developed a system of merits and demerits that reward good behavior with prolonged life and reduce years for wrongful acts.

Much of this eclectic, popular religion was transmitted to early Chinese America. Discriminated against by the larger Euro-American society and forced to exist in segregated spaces, Chinese immigrants fell back on religiosity for emotional sustenance and self-identity. The practice of religion, particularly ancestor worship, also helped this largely bachelor society, the by-product of antifamilial immigration laws, at least until the liberalization of these laws in the mid-1940s, to maintain ties with both nuclear and extended family units left behind in China.[18]

Some of the earliest social institutions erected in American Chinatowns were temples for collective worship. Early immigrants also visited shrines memorializing patron gods, built mostly in the headquarters of mutual aid associations and tongs. Many turn-of-the-century Chinatowns, such as those in San Francisco, New York, and Los Angeles, held anniversary festivals and colorful parades. Of these, the Chinese New Year festival, the only holiday still celebrated by most Chinese in America today, was by far the noisiest and merriest. The fifteen-day celebration typically ends with the dragon dance which commemorates this creature of strength and goodness who carries out the will of the gods.[19]

Another important celebration in both mainland China and Chinese America was Qing Ming or the Pure Brightness Festival. The Chinese considered visits to family tombs a formal and necessary annual rite. Since the Chinese in America lived far away from the ancestral graves or family tombs of their native villages, they visited the local Chinese cemetery on this occasion. Most mutual aid and fraternal associations erected spirit shrines for those who had no loved ones buried in the area.

Women, trained since girlhood, typically have played a prominent role in all celebrations and ancestor worship in China and America. Women have shouldered the responsibility of remembering the death-dates of ancestors, praying to the ancestors for the family's well-being, and often also trying to interpret unfavorable ancestral behavior. They also have learned and carried out the customs and minute details of the rituals necessary for each celebratory occasion.

The belief and practice of popular religion and its eclectic philosophical underpinnings ensured that the country's culture or *tezhi*, its way of life, remained stable and uniform, even though it was saddled with a shaky, unwieldy political system and constantly rocked by internally driven, transforming socioeconomic changes.

THE RISE AND FALL OF THE QING DYNASTY

Until the arrival of the tumultuous Chinese revolutionary era in the early twentieth century, a succession of imperial dynasties governed China ever since the first one, the Shang, nearly 3,565 years ago. In 1644 the reigning emperor, Chongzhen of the Ming dynasty (1368–1644), was toppled by the northeastern Manchus who swept into northern China.

The Manchus arrived in a time of socioeconomic dislocations, a time beset with difficulties "usually associated with the end of a 'dynastic cycle'—eunuch domination of the court, moral degradation, political corruption, intellectual irresponsibility, high taxes, and famine."[20] The masses, dissatisfied with the failure of the ruling house to solve poverty and privation, were on the verge of large-scale rebellion, and the Manchus found allies among the leaders of the Chinese rebel forces. This scenario, repeated again and again throughout the imperial times, was typically interpreted by the popular mind as evidence that the emperor, the Son of Heaven (*Tian zi*), had lost the sacred mandate to rule.

Though the Qing dynasty was a non-Han dynasty, it accepted the traditional Confucian order. Such adaptation gave this ruling house some stability until the era of Emperor Qianlong (1736–1799), whereupon China entered into another dynastic cycle. By then the Manchus' zealous championing of the traditional orthodoxy had become a liability as the winds of change began to sweep through this vast land.

The Manchus never discarded their ethnic identity. They preserved some aspects of their cultural distinctiveness by outlawing intermarriage between Manchu and Chinese, disallowing footbinding for Manchu women, and giving Manchus first preference in official appointments, examinations, and many other areas. In this way, the alienness of the Manchus helped maintain the distance between the rulers and the ruled and that, in turn, kept the sparks of anti-Manchu sentiments alive and led to the downfall of the dynasty in the last decades of its rule.

Below the emperor was the nobility, composed of both those of Manchu and Chinese origins, who, unlike those in Europe, wielded little political or administrative power. As a rule, they were kept fairly isolated from the corridors of power. It was the scholar-official class that populated the multiple levels of governance ranging from the Grand Secretariat, the advisory group to the emperor, all the way down to the lowly district magistrates who collected taxes, settled litigations, and generally maintained peace and order in the locality.

Within district divisions, such as villages, towns, and cities, the magistrate relied on two self-governing neighborhood organization systems called *baojia* and *lijia*. Local residents, including many of the ancestors of present-day Chinese Americans, made up the *baojia* and *lijia* with the former facilitating police control and the latter helping with the collection of taxes. Thus, the

Qing government maintained imperial control even at the local level but without extra officials or additional expenses. For local residents, the *baojia* and *lijia* helped to reinforce pseudo-kinship and familial ties.

Further reinforcing such ties was the lineage tradition. In Guangdong, peasants lived in lineages, which linked all families, regardless of socioeconomic standing, with a common ancestry. A lineage typically owned property and managed temples, schools, and charity projects. Land, in particular, constituted corporate ownership and was rented out to locals who also had a stake in it. Thus, the classic European division between landlord and tenant is not applicable to this context.

However, the political system was, from a Western perspective, fraught with problems. For example, the judiciary did not stand independent of the executive branch. Due process of law did not exist, nor did advice of counsel in a trial. A case often was tried simply on the basis of its moral implications, regardless of the legality factor. Chinese society believed that the law served to uphold social order, not to protect individual rights. Thus, magistrates applied the codified laws in a flexible manner, depending upon the people and given circumstances. Men and women certainly did not stand equal before the law. Because litigation supposedly stemmed from behavior that was not virtuous, even on the part of the suing party, the Chinese, to avoid social disapproval, customarily avoided recourse to law unless absolutely necessary. Much of this, however, was not necessarily transplanted wholesale to the Chinese American world.

When Qianlong abdicated his throne in 1799, the Qing dynasty had already passed its apogee. Although Qianlong began his long reign with spectacular victories in consolidating China's western borders, the later years witnessed the emergence of imbalanced economic development with some regions outpacing others. That unbalance threatened the state, since unequal development, in the absence of political centralization and economic linkages, could lead to conflict. Compounding the situation was a series of expensive, bungled military campaigns, localistic rebellions, and a rapidly rising population without necessary innovation in technology. The next emperor, Jiaqing (1799–1820), inherited a country that was "externally strong but internally shriveled" (*wai qiang zhong gan*). Within the next twenty years or so, the country suffered from serious administrative, military, and moral maladies which the Chinese masses took to be clear signs of a falling dynastic fortune.[21]

Administrative lassitude and ineptness stemmed from the suspicion harbored by the Manchu court toward its Chinese officials. This situation led to a policy of constant mutual checking. Creativity became stymied and officials focused more on currying favor than carrying out directives. Eventually a high concentration of power occurred at the higher levels of the bureaucracy, and, as soon as the leadership faltered, the state was in peril.

Equally problematic were imperial favoritism and widespread corruption. One official, the infamous Heshen, a favorite of Emperor Qianlong, reportedly amassed within twenty years of service, wealth amounting to half of the total state income for the same period. Graft, extortion, and irregular levies became commonplace. A corollary of this was the degradation of the bannermen, who made up the elitist core of the Manchu military power at the beginning of this dynasty. A privileged, lavish lifestyle quickly led to the dissipation of military skills.

At the end of the eighteenth century, a large-scale anti-Qing movement— the White Lotus Rebellion (1796–1804)—broke out. Initiated by the White Lotus Sect, a secret society dedicated to restoring the Ming dynasty, this rebellion cost the Qing government over $200 million, some of which went into the private coffers of military officers. In the same era, a number of other minor uprisings also occurred. The well-known Ming loyalist Heaven and Earth Society (*Tian Di Hui*), also known as the Triad Society (*Sanhehui*), the historical origin of many secret societies or tongs in America, perpetrated a significant uprising in Taiwan in the 1780s. Equally irritating to the imperial government were two Muslim revolts in northwestern China and a series of uprisings conducted by Miao tribesmen in southwestern China. Though the Qing government succeeded in suppressing these challenges, it bore a heavy monetary burden and failed to eliminate the religious, economic, and ethnic resentments. The ineffectual nature of the government's response shook public confidence and badly weakened the economic foundation of the Qing empire.

Exacerbating these convulsive changes was population pressure. The population began to grow in the sixteenth century and more rapidly in the next two centuries. By 1800 the population stood at 300 million, at least a twofold increase since the 1660s. But arable land throughout this period had not increased correspondingly since so much of China consists of arid and mountainous areas. Between 1661 and 1812, arable land increased by less than 50 percent, but the population had increased by more than 100 percent.[22]

Though population growth moderated after the 1770s, a drop in the death rate, mostly as a result of a long period of relative peace and stability, kept the momentum going. Without any fundamental change in the economic system or the impact of an industrial revolution, population pressure became a significant problem. For the displaced, poor, and unemployed, survival often meant turning to banditry or social action antithetical to prescribed conventions.

All of these problems—faltering administration, widespread corruption, degeneration of the military, and the pressures of a rising population—indicated that the ruling power had passed its peak. Ironically, internal economic and social changes, not unlike those taking place in Europe, only served to highlight the ineptness of the state. Since late Ming times, China had experienced a series of intertwined precapitalist changes, including significant urbanization, especially in the lower Yangzi area; the increasing role of a monetary economy; the development of regional and long-distance trade; the emergence of a countrywide market for commodities; more geographical mobility; the expansion of popular literacy; the growing heterogeneity of the gentry class; and the professionalization of some managerial activities.[23] In this context of fluid social relations and gradual disintegration of the old order, the country by 1800 had become vulnerable to both internal rebellion and external invasion. In this milieu, social dislocations intensified and, against such a backdrop, both migration and emigration became viable, even necessary possibilities.

2

Travelers to Gold Mountain: Immigration, Labor, and Exclusion

CONTEXT FOR IMMIGRATION

By 1800 China faced more rapid change and was looking toward to an ominous future. China was too weak militarily to protect itself from Western imperialism, but too strong culturally to surrender the political initiative to Chinese modernizers. In the absence of modernization, its people were forced to look elsewhere for a livelihood.

Early Chinese immigrants in the nineteenth century who chose to journey to California (also known in Cantonese as *Gam Saan* [*Jinshan* in Mandarin], or "Gold Mountain") hoped to strike fortunes in the gold mines of the proverbial *Mei Kuo* (*Mei Guo* in Mandarin, or "Flowery Flag," the Cantonese colloquial term for the United States). But *gam saan haak* (Cantonese for "travelers to Gold Mountain") found only *hek fu* (Cantonese for "taking in pain" or adversity). Prejudice, disfranchisement, and social exclusion marked their daily existence. Life simply became a struggle, one haunted by unfulfilled Gold Mountain dreams.

But before the pressing reality of America confronted them, potential emigrants found themselves caught in circumstances unique to Guangdong, the main source of immigration to America. In Guangdong province a dramatic rise in the population stood as the most fundamental indigenous change. While China's total population increased by 47 percent between 1787 and 1850, Guangdong's for the same period showed a gain of 79.5 percent. One of the five fastest-growing provinces in China, its population shot up to 28,182 from a low of 16,014.[1]

This enormous population growth in southern China led to a struggle for limited cultivable land, a situation compounded by the absence of primogeniture. In Guangdong, the population-land ratio outpaced the national average. The social implications could have been ameliorated if the tremendous economic vitality and social change experienced during the sixteenth to eighteenth centuries—not unlike those that led to the Industrial Revolution in Europe—had developed into full-scale industrialization. The reasons for this failure are manifold.

For one, China's educated elite spent so much of their time and energy trying to attain the status and prestige of the scholar-official class that it had to sideline endeavors that might have fostered economic and technological change. Heavy government exactions, but without an erection of an infrastructure for trade, on private wealth and investments also dampened the spirit of entrepreneurship. Perhaps the most convincing explanation for China's inhibited industrialization was the relative stability of the market demand, which offered little stimulus for radical technological change and attending higher productivity. Even in agriculture, rapid commercialization did little to transform small-scale subsistence farming.

Without rapid capitalist and technological improvements to absorb the dispossessed, any human dislocation took on an ominous note. European imperialism, which precipitated the first and second Opium Wars (1839–1842 and 1856–1860), hampered industrial growth via the costly effects of foreign wars, the drain on the specie through the importation of opium, and general economic competition. As the major point of contact with the West, Guangdong was visibly affected.

In Guangdong, an overabundance of cheap, mass-produced, foreign goods flooded the domestic market, limiting the demand for products of the premodern Chinese handicraft industries. Even though Chinese investment in foreign enterprises in China grew after the 1860s, little of this economic pattern benefited the masses. The rapid growth of the colonized islands of Macao and Hong Kong, as early as the mid-1850s, captured much trade from Guangzhou (Canton, the main port city of Guangdong). By 1870 free trade and competition from other coastal ports exacerbated the unemployment rate for the urban proletariat.

Concomitant with such economic imperialism was the process of the international migration of labor. The global expansion of European and American capitalism had necessitated the movement of workers, capital, and technology across borders so that investors and businesspeople could tap into the natural resources and markets of the underdeveloped countries. The eventual immigration of those from Guangdong to Gold Mountain was part of a larger diaspora that involved as many as 2.5 million between 1840 and

1900. These mostly young, poverty-stricken men, notwithstanding the 250,000 forced into slave labor in the "coolie trade" (the trafficking of contract laborers) of Cuba and Peru, heeded the call of Western capitalists and departed for underdeveloped colonies in Africa, Southeast Asia, Australia, New Zealand, Hawaii, the West Indies, and the United States.[2] Thus, this human migration was the product of transnational connections between colonizing and colonized powers.

Paralleling such disruptive developments was a series of internal uprisings, including the Taiping Rebellion (1850–1864) and the Red Turban uprisings (1854–1864), both of which ravaged the countryside. A government report noted that "ever since the disturbances . . . [the] able-bodied go abroad. The fields are clogged with weeds."[3] The Punti-Hakka interethnic feuds between 1856 and 1870 over fertile delta lands, a bloody conflict that raged across the province of Guangdong, further exacerbated the plight of poor peasant and proletariat families.

Natural calamities compounded the declining conditions. Between 1832 and 1881, at least one major catastrophe plagued the county of Xinning (later renamed Taishan). Located within Guangdong, Xinning was the place of origin for more than 40 percent of first-generation Chinese Americans. Just about every year the people of Xinning, Xiangshan (later renamed Zhongshan, the second most important emigrant community), and surrounding counties faced natural disasters—droughts, floods, snowfalls, typhoons, or crop failures caused by insects or blights. One flood in Guangdong was so severe that, according to one imperial account, the "rivers and the sea and the streams, have joined in one sheet over the land for several hundred *li*" (one *li* equals a third of a mile).[4]

Famines and natural disasters often hit all classes of Chinese society, but the subsistence-based peasantry bore the heaviest taxation. Following the devastating Opium Wars, the financially strapped Qing government, saddled with large indemnities for the recent conflicts, imposed new taxes on peasant farmers, but few could pay, and many lost their lands. Corruption on the part of officials sometimes compounded the financial burden of these families. The turmoil in the economy, coupled with the hostile ecological and climatic conditions, led to destitution and deprivation. Faced with such conditions, some Chinese made the choice to leave their villages for distant lands.

That decision was partly encouraged by exaggerated tales of the riches of America. Since the late eighteenth century those from Guangdong had been exposed to American influences by way of Yankee traders and missionaries. In addition, some of the earliest writings about the United States, dating back to the early nineteenth century, first appeared and circulated in this area. Of more importance were the direct trading links, from the late eighteenth century, between Guangzhou and California. A two-way traffic of lucrative goods ranging from sea-otter skins to Chinese ornate furniture led to the dissemination of news in southern China about the fabled America.[5]

Stories about the discovery of gold in California reached China as early as the summer of 1849, barely a year after the astounding news leaked out of the American Pacific Coast. Most probably Cantonese merchants, with fairly extensive ties to Americans, helped spread this news, and soon local Chinese shared tales of astounding wealth that lay on the other side of the Pacific. Other Guangdong residents heard about the golden hills of North America through friends and relatives who had been part of the earliest wave of prospectors in California. The promotion of the supposed bountifulness of California by captains of foreign vessels, who were interested in expanding their business in human cargo, also captured the attention of locals. Overall, these trans-Pacific connections partly explain why Chinese emigration took place and why most of the Chinese immigrants came from Guangdong.

REVISIONIST HISTORY

Recent scholarship on immigration history has forced a reevaluation of the understanding that the general immigrant experience was one of uprootedness and alienation. Previously, it was understood that individual emigrants, torn from their peasant communities by the encroachment of capitalism, were forced to leave their disintegrating villages for an alienating industrialized environment. As a result of these so-called push factors, they became strangers in a strange land.

In reality, many emigrants, like the Chinese, had already migrated within their homeland and experienced the forces of modernity. Hired hands, poor peasants, sharecroppers, and small landowners, who constituted the majority of the Chinese exodus, had all faced economic pressures and so had to look for new ways to make a living. Prospective emigrants opted to emigrate so as to maintain their status and economic lifestyle and often they did so with the help of a social network of relatives and acquaintances. Forward looking, rather than past oriented, emigrants hoped in the long run to control and improve their lives.

Though the diaspora of Chinese can be conceived as part of the international migration of labor, those headed for Gold Mountain made their own choices regarding their futures. These mostly young Cantonese men (a small minority were Hakkas) departed for America to achieve upward social mobility. The fact that so many came from Xinning, the county that supplied most of the experienced wage laborers for the subregion's market-oriented economy, suggests that some of those who left were not necessarily unworldly victims of Western capitalism. The smaller stream of merchants and artisans, who were already engaged in a premigration network of business connections in China, also flowed to America as early as 1849 in a context of prior exposure to capitalism.

Though adventurous and enterprising, as a result of a long seafaring tradition, these men, who often left their families behind, planned eventually to return to their ancestral villages. During the first decade of immigration to the United States as many as a third of them did so. This phenomenon, known as return migration, also characterized turn-of-the-century European immigration to the New World.[6] Though many Chinese Americans began their stay in the United States as sojourners, or "birds of passage," involved in temporary migration, a large number, for legal, financial, or other reasons, remained in America to live, work, and settle.

THE NATURE OF IMMIGRATION

In the nineteenth century most Chinese sojourners came to America either as contract laborers or as free laborers under the credit-ticket system. The contract laborers went primarily to Hawaii; a few were there as early as the 1830s. Here, the Chinese gradually replaced the native Hawaiian workers in the sugarcane fields. Planters recruited workers by using emigration brokers who offered Chinese free passage to the islands. Chinese laborers signed labor agreements to work for a planter for a term of five years and received in return wages, shelter, food, and medical care. These Chinese laborers, an estimated 50,000 of whom had arrived between 1852 to 1900, however, soon found themselves pitted against other ethnic groups, such as Japanese workers, as a result of an attempt made by planters to control workers by developing an ethnically diverse, but divided, workforce.[7]

Most of the larger number of Chinese sojourners, who went to mainland United States, relied on the credit-ticket system. In this system, a broker loaned money to an emigrant to pay for the voyage, and the emigrant in turn paid off the loan plus interest out of earnings made in the new country. Many emigrants also borrowed from their kinsfolk for the trans-Pacific journey.

Almost all of the early wave of Chinese immigrants were men, even though an estimated half of them were married and many had established families prior to immigration. The situation in Hawaii, however, differed somewhat from that on the mainland: in Hawaii, missionaries and planters encouraged the immigration of women to maintain social control and to prevent "loose morals" in this predominately male populace. By 1900, of the 25,767 Chinese in Hawaii, 13.5 percent (3,471) were females; on the mainland, only 5 percent of the 89,863 Chinese were females.

WOMEN AND GENDER DISPARITY

The glaring absence of women on the U.S. mainland was a unique phenomenon and departed from the immigration pattern of other ethnic groups. The sex ratio for the entire Chinese population in the United States in 1860 stood at 1:186 or 1,784 females compared to 33,149 males. Between 1860 and 1900, the skewed sex ratio did not improve at all; women never exceeded 7 percent of the total Chinese population for that entire period.[8]

Various factors accounted for the disparity in gender and the resulting disjointed households. Patriarchal cultural values, rooted in the hierarchically oriented Confucian ideology, dictated that women be subordinated to men and confined to the domestic realm. Single women did not engage in unaccompanied travel to distant places and married women remained at home. The "thrice obeying" dictates of Confucianism deemed that women should obey their fathers at home, their husbands after marriage, and their eldest sons when widowed. Playing this subordinate role required women to follow the Four Attributes: propriety in behavior, speech, demeanor, and work.

Since early childhood females led a precarious life. The Chinese proverb, "A boy is born facing in; a girl is born facing out," encapsulated the general consensus on the low status of Chinese women. Infanticide, abandonment, and sale into indentured servitude tended to fall on daughters rather than sons. Unlike sons, daughters were typically excluded from education.

Daughters were also considered unworthy of much social investment because after years of careful nurture most of them married and joined other households. Families, however, did see the betrothal of a daughter as an opportunity to display status and dignity through ostentatious dowries for the bridegroom's family. Sons were far more prized because they continued the family lineage, performed ancestral worship, and labored for the family's honor and livelihood. So important were sons that families without male heirs, especially those in the southeastern provinces, sometimes resorted to matrilocal or uxorilocal marriage.

The ultimate symbol of the imposition of subordination on women was footbinding, which symbolized social rank (only women of nobility, gentry, and mercantile background typically had their feet bound), proper upbringing, and erotic appeal, but also restricted women's mobility and reinforced the Confucian ideals of female virtue and isolation. A Chinese merchant in 1855 explained that many men did not bring their wives along with them to America because they had "compressed feet" and so were "unused to winds and waves."[9]

Peasant women, expected to labor inside and outside the home, however, generally did not bind their feet. Work, however, did not result in greater independence for these women. Some women who engaged in the sericulture industry, in which raw silk was produced by raising silkworms, in the Pearl River delta, did enjoy economic freedom and openly resisted marriage. They joined sisterhoods, rejected footbinding, and practiced celibacy. Hakka women in Guangdong were also well known for their rejection of footbinding and their display of self-confidence. These women aside, most performed labor that sustained family life and most found themselves on the periphery of power.

When their husbands went abroad to *Mei Kuo*, or the United States, wives were expected to stay at home and take care of the children, the in-laws, and the home. Some of these *gam saan po* (*jinshan po* in Mandarin) or "Gold Mountain wives" did more than that, however. They toiled in the fields and factories, joined rebel groups, banded together as sisters in the marriage re-sistance movement, and, at the turn of the century, contributed their voices to the rising feminist consciousness in China. This milieu of an emerging sense of self-identity was partly responsible for driving a small trickle of women to go to America to flee gender oppression and to gain a measure of independence. Much more of the female migration was orchestrated by men for profit, especially for the lucrative forced prostitution trade.[10]

Most Chinese wives and daughters, however, were left behind because the upkeep of families abroad was too costly. Moreover, the men thought they would be separated from their loved ones only temporarily. In a culture where the family served as the core of the social order, keeping wives at home also guaranteed that husbands would not forget their kinsfolk in China, would send remittances, and eventually would return to China and continue to support their elderly parents.[11]

Discouraged by the transitory, frontier-like, and inhospitable conditions in America, women deemed it wise to remain in China. Early male immi-grants labored in mines, on railroads, and in the fields—workplaces deemed incompatible with the needs of wives and children. During most of the second half of the nineteenth century, the height of Chinese immigration to the mainland United States before the gates were closed for a long time, capitalists and policy makers discouraged the arrival of women. Considered a temporary labor force, Chinese men were disposable. But the immigration of Chinese women and children would, as feared by the white-dominated society, lead to family formation and a possible mongrelization of the superior Anglo-Saxon race.

Class- and gender based, racist, anti-immigration laws, designed to meet the need for cheap, exploitable labor without threatening the racial homogeneity of America, blocked the entry of Chinese women into the United States. Given the less than civil treatment and the lack of legal protection Chinese immigrants had to endure upon arrival, Chinese women had little inclination to leave a familiar environment for barbarian lands. In an 1852 letter written to the California state government, Chinese community leaders bitterly explained that "if the privileges of your laws are open . . . a better class will come . . . [and bring] their families with them."[12]

THE ENDLESS JOURNEY TO AMERICA

The trans-Pacific journey was a cumbersome one for the Chinese emigrants. Though Qing anti-emigration laws went largely unenforced as early as the mid-eighteenth century, American consular officials in Hong Kong (the port of departure for many Chinese emigrants), who were charged with enforcing anti-coolie laws, placed certain legal barriers on immigration. Following passage of the 1862 Act to Prohibit Coolie Trade, the American consul or his agent, to prevent involuntary travel, examined each prospective immigrant. However, from 1862 to 1871, the certification process, tainted by ineptness, became perfunctory.

The same cannot be said about the Page Law of 1875, which was designed to check the flow of Chinese prostitutes to America, who could, in the mind of the Euro-American society, debase white manhood, health, morality, and family life. Chinese prostitution in America, a function of gender-based immigration laws, flourished well until early in the twentieth century. Chinese men, bereft of family life and denied conjugal ties, sought prostitutes or *baak haak chai* (a derogatory Cantonese phrase for "one hundred men's wife")— as they did opium smoking and gambling—for entertainment. Applied stringently, the Page Law excluded wives and single women with legitimate claims. Immigration officials believed that prostitutes typically posed as wives, sisters, or daughters of sojourners already in America. Officials consequently assumed that all Chinese women seeking entry into the United States were potential prostitutes.[13]

Because of the uneven application of the law by American officials in Hong Kong, Chinese men (at least until the era of exclusion laws), but not women, could proceed with their departure from Asia for America. Following the signing of the Burlingame Treaty (1868) between China and the United States, the Chinese secured the right to open, voluntary immigration to America. The century-old prohibitory emigration law of the Qing government was repealed. The treaty further offered Chinese residents equal protection of all legal rights enjoyed by other foreigners domiciling in the United States, and later, in the early 1870s, U.S. federal courts decided that the treaty also provided for the right to work and live in America.[14] However, anti-Chinese sentiments along the Pacific Coast and their consequences soon made a mockery of the spirit of that treaty.

From approximately 1849 to 1867, *gam saan haak* journeyed to that distant land by sailing on voyages that took from fifty-five to one hundred days or more. The advent of the Pacific Mail Steamship Company's famed China line in 1867 ushered in the age of steamships, which plied the trans-Pacific route until well after the turn of the century. Unlike sailing ships, which held departure until fully booked, steamers offered a schedule and a speedy voyage. The time taken to reach San Francisco shortened from months to weeks. Steamships also could hold more passengers. All that, coupled with a more than threefold drop in the fare, encouraged immigration.

Chinese passengers on the way to America, with the exception of those of privileged background, almost always traveled in the cheaper steerage section. Passengers ate poor, bland food, scrounged for limited water, slept in rickety berths consisting of canvas stretched over wooden frames, and suffered from inadequate ventilation. Sometimes even basic bodily functions proved difficult because of overcrowding. During storms, immigrants curled up in berths, and food, utensils, and people bounced in all directions. Such conditions must have given these travelers little comfort.

As their ship cut across the wide waters of the high seas, they struggled, being unsure of the future and anguished by the separation from loved ones, to hold onto the dream of finding a new start, of shaping unknown beginnings. That guarded anticipation, mixed with melancholy, was reflected in this early twentieth-century Cantonese folk song: "Drifting on a voyage of thousands of miles/I reached the Flowery Flag Nation to take my chances/sorrow is to be so far away from home."[15]

ARRIVING IN AMERICA: IMMIGRATION CLEARANCE

When immigrants first set eyes on the land of their destiny, they were awash in a surge of anticipation. Huie Kin, a male immigrant who arrived in 1868, recalled that the "feeling that welled up in us was indescribable," "to be actually at . . . the land of our dreams."[16] With the exception of those who were smuggled into the United States by way of Mexico or Canada, immigration clearance for most arrivals, however, turned into a nightmarish hurdle.

A gloomy, poorly lighted, two-story shed—known to Cantonese Chinese as *Muk uk* (*Mu wu* in Mandarin) or "Wooden Barracks"—at the Pacific Mail Steamship Company wharf greeted early arrivals in San Francisco, the point of disembarkation for most nineteenth-century Chinese immigrants. Chinese arrivals were held at this overcrowded, unsanitary, and unsafe facility until immigration officials cleared them. In 1910, partly in reaction to Chinese complaints and partly to isolate those with supposed communicable diseases, the government erected a two-story wooden building to serve as the new immigration station on Angel Island out in the San Francisco Bay. A trickle of arrivals entered the West Coast by way of Seattle's immigration station. Those who arrived in New York City were processed at Castle Garden, the immigration depot that operated until 1890, when Ellis Island became the new processing center.[17]

Immigration officials then subjected the Chinese to an extensive examination. This interrogation was protracted because officials believed that almost all Chinese lied to gain entry into the United States. Perhaps many Chinese were guilty of illegal immigration, but only because Chinese exclusion laws forced it underground. By the turn of the century, as racial hostility intensified and loopholes in the laws were closed, the Chinese relied on duplicity to enter the United States in order to reunite families or establish a livelihood and continue the financial support of loved ones left behind in impoverished China.

Typically, a Chinese merchant or one that posed as one would claim American birth (and thus citizenship as guaranteed by the Fourteenth Amendment). He then would claim the birth of a new son (rarely a daughter) upon his return from each visit to China. A potential immigrant could then, after buying that "slot," pose as the merchant's son or daughter and claim entry into the United States. Some Chinese, aware that merchants were exempted from exclusion laws, bought business shares in order to claim they were merchants or bribed merchants to list them as partners. After the devastating San Francisco earthquake of 1906 destroyed most of the municipal records, thus ending a way to verify data supplied by new arrivals, such claims quickly increased.[18]

The purchase of a falsified identity did not guarantee entry. To prepare for this the ordeal of an exhaustive examination, Chinese emigrants studied purchased crib sheets containing information about their "families." Those who failed the initial interrogation could appeal or be reexamined. Throughout this ordeal, Chinese relied on their transnational networks of family, clan, and community across the United States and in China to provide financial backing, immigration advice, crucial witness testimony, and legal counsel. About 10 percent of all Chinese who arrived on Angel Island, however, were eventually forced to return to China. The fraud allegedly committed by these returnees became part of the justification for imposing anti-immigration laws, which, in turn, reflected anti-Chinese prejudices.

NATIVISM IN THE LATE NINETEENTH CENTURY

Anti-immigrant sentiments in the second half of the nineteenth century, though not without precedents, were particularly virulent. Before that period, faith in the process of assimilation, which supposedly would transform untutored foreigners into upright, patriotic citizens, predisposed most Americans to accept new immigrants. In this classic melting-pot thesis, American society would take on a cosmopolitan, unique character as the diverse elements gradually fused and lost their indigenous roots.

Before rapid industrialization and a consolidating national market economy arrived in the late nineteenth century, ethnic groups lived apart from one another, and the majority Anglo Americans remained dominant. The process of assimilation played out rather slowly without much interethnic antagonism. Occasionally, nativist sentiment did break out, most notably during the 1840s when the anti-immigrant Know-Nothing party targeted Germans and Irish Catholics for religious and ethnic persecution.

However, general consciousness of racial and ethnic differences became intensified in the late nineteenth century as spatial and socioeconomic boundaries between communities blurred under the influence of industrialization and economic development. The American national identity's ability to hold the republic together—one rooted in abstract democratic ideals—was called into question. An aggressive movement to forge a homogeneous, national identity rooted in Anglo-Saxon culture soon emerged, and certain ethnic groups, the Chinese included, were deemed unassimilable.

LABORING LIVES

At the height of the anti-Asian movement in the late nineteenth century, the Chinese never constituted more than 0.2 percent of the total U.S. population, and yet they still encountered rabid hostility. The white-dominated society, however, initially welcomed the Chinese as workers and investors for a booming economy.[19] The seemingly imperceptible presence of the Chinese—one shaped by the scattered nature of the early arrivals—rendered them innocuous. But soon nativism reared its ugly head.

Within just several years of the discovery of gold, 24,000 Chinese, an estimated two-thirds of the Chinese in America, were laboring in the mines of the American West. Considered an economic and moral threat, Chinese miners, cooks, and laundry workers toiling in white-dominated mining districts soon came under heavy fire. In 1852 the California state legislature passed the Foreign Miner's Tax, which was ostensibly to be imposed on all miners who did not desire to become citizens. Lawmakers knew, of course, that the Chinese could not gain citizenship since the 1790 Nationality Act reserved that privilege for white persons. The tax, therefore, fell heavily on Chinese miners, and that, coupled with the decline of placer mining (collecting surface gold from streambeds) in California, forced them to venture farther inland. These miners were also encouraged to move farther east by stories of new gold, and then silver, strikes in places as far away as Tombstone, Arizona, and Boise Basin, Idaho. By the 1870s the Chinese had spread to every placer area, and they represented about 25 percent of all miners.[20]

During the mid-1860s, as gold became scarcer, Chinese miners began abandoning the fields. Some of them ventured into fishing, and eventually Chinese fishing activities stretched from the Oregon boundary down to Baja California and also along the Sacramento River delta. A number of them by the early 1870s concentrated on catching and processing shrimp in the San Francisco Bay, and others collected abalone in the waters off the Southern California coast.[21]

A good number of the Chinese—about 5,000—built most of the Central Pacific Railroad, the western half of the ambitious transcontinental railroad that challenged the physical endurance and creativity of these workers. Following the completion of this project in 1869, some Chinese laborers scattered into the hinterlands for agricultural work. They constructed irrigation channels and reclaimed swamplands in California's Sacramento–San Joaquin River delta area. As tenant farmers or sharecroppers they introduced new strains of fruit and grew vegetables for local markets. Some of those involved in agriculture were vendors and labor contractors. Most of the Chinese, however, were farm laborers who toiled in orchards, vineyards, and hop fields.[22]

More significant for the long-term distribution of the populace was the dispersal of Chinese laborers to the rest of the American West and eventually to all parts of the United States. In 1870 Chinese workers began showing up in the salmon canneries on coastal bays and streams from central California to western Alaska. Others arrived in the Pacific Northwest after being recruited to build the Northern Pacific line or to run lumber mills. Some

Chinese, after the end of the initial engagement, moved to Seattle, where they worked in small businesses—laundries, restaurants, and dry goods stores—owned by Chinese merchants. In the early 1870s Chinese workers were recruited, some from Cuba, for plantation work and railroad building in Louisiana, Mississippi, and Florida, mainly to help fill the role left by former black slaves. In Florida, Chinese work gangs also labored in drainage operations, construction sites, and turpentine camps.[23]

White planters and contractors aspired to use Chinese, in addition to their labor, to help control recently enfranchised blacks through their model behavior and "docility." Given whites' fear of "Nigger rule" in the South, sentiments that never resembled the reality, and the absence of Jim Crowism (institutionalized segregation) until the 1880s, this attempt to play one ethnic group off the other to maintain white control was hardly unexpected. Conversely, when Jim Crow laws became established at the turn of the century, and the existence of another race promised to complicate the enforcement of segregation, Florida, at least, dissuaded Chinese from migrating to the state.

Chinese laborers also wended their way to the Northeast, specifically Massachusetts, New Jersey, and Pennsylvania where, in 1870, factory owners used them as strikebreakers in shoemaking, steam laundries, and cutlery making, against disgruntled, mostly Irish, employees. By then, an estimated 500 Chinese lived in New York City. Some of them, independent of any internal migration from California, apparently arrived by way of their involvement in long-running American maritime trades or coastal shipping routes. They were engaged in a variety of endeavors: cigar making, cigar peddling, running boardinghouses and laundries, maritime shipping, and retailing. Boston's small Chinese populace in 1900, a little under 900, also showed the same concentration in service-oriented and self-employed occupations. As a result of this general dispersal, only a little over 60 percent of the total populace in 1920 remained in the West.[24]

In the early 1870s, however, many unemployed Chinese, newly released from railroad work and unable to find work in the exhausted minefields, flocked to San Francisco (*Dai Fow* [Cantonese for "Big City"]), by then a burgeoning city of opportunity. San Francisco's Chinese population zoomed from 2,719 in 1860 to 12,022 ten years later. What happened in San Francisco was repeated elsewhere. Los Angeles's Chinatown, for example, trebled in size from 605 in 1880 to 1,817 in 1890, in large part because of growing sinophobia (fear of Chinese) and concomitant gloomy economic prospects elsewhere in nonurban areas.[25] The growing urbanization of the Chinese population was a nationwide phenomenon during the turn of the century as racial hostility forced them to retreat to Chinatowns, the physically segregated neighborhoods within white-dominated cities and towns. By the end of the nineteenth century Chinatowns were no longer simply transient centers for gold miners and laborers headed for the hinterlands. Chinatowns gradually became not only places of refuge and residential communities but also economic enclaves.

In the 1870s, urban Chinese moved into the manufacturing economy and found themselves relegated to low paying, racially segregated jobs, mainly as factory operatives in woolen mills, knitting mills, paper mills, tanneries, shoe factories, cigar-making factories, and garment industries. Often Chinese occupied the menial positions, while Euro-Americans took the skilled ones— a reflection of a labor market stratified by race. In instances where they held the same job as whites, they often earned less than their white counterparts. In the early 1880s, Chinese men earned one dollar a day as factory operatives, half what white men made per day.[26]

The small number of Chinese women—in 1880 there were 4779 (compared to 100,686 males)—fared even worse.[27] Suffering from both racial and gender discrimination, coupled with inadequate education or untransferable skills and having to meet domestic responsibilities, most Chinese women in the late nineteenth century were restricted to a few occupations. They either did piecework at home for subcontractors—sewing, washing, rolling cigars, and making slippers and brooms—or performed personal and domestic service, namely prostitution and domestic labor. The domestic laborers worked primarily in the role of *mui-tsai* (Cantonese) or contracted girl servants.[28]

Although, by the early twentieth century, women had found work in garment and food-processing factories or sweatshops, they were paid on a piece-rate basis with no hope for upward mobility. They were also paid less than men and suffered from sexual division of labor, whereby they were given the less remunerative tasks. Waged labor, however, was not entirely oppressive. Though women carried a double burden as both wage earners and unpaid household producers, women's earnings and access to social networks outside the family ameliorated to some extent the male authority within the home.

Furthermore, the skewed sex ratio in America transformed gender relations in other ways. The shortage of women slowed down the transplanting of patriarchal values to Gold Mountain, forced men in womenless households to learn domestic skills (even to use them to eke out a livelihood, for example, laundry work), and enhanced the social value of the few Chinese women in the immigrant generation. Chinese women became prized as marital and sexual partners and that, coupled with their contribution as wage earners, led to a slightly more elevated status in America compared to the one they left behind in China. Thus, women's employment in America was as liberating as it was oppressive.

Given the generally less-than-ideal working conditions, some Chinese chose to pursue self-employment in the form of running laundries, retail establishments, and restaurants, which catered to the growing ethnic community and to white customers. Chinese gravitated to laundries because of the minimal capital and language requirements; in 1900, one out of four employed Chinese males in the United States was a laundry worker or owner. Such self-employment occasionally did lead to class mobility as individuals, relying on their managerial skills, accumulated capital and American experiences, and invested in new ventures; however, most self-employed individuals remained mired in self-exploitation and marginal existence. Other Chinese, to avoid intense inter-racial interaction and conflict, hired themselves out as domestic servants, who typically worked for one Euro-American family at a time. However, in Southern cities where African Americans dominated the bottom rungs of the urban economic structure, Chinese found rather limited opportunities in service-oriented establishments and semi-skilled or unskilled labor.

THE ANTI-CHINESE MOVEMENT

By the early 1870s sinophobia had already found expression in the formation of anti-coolie clubs, sporadic boycotts of Chinese-made goods, and anti-immigration laws. In 1870 the California state legislature passed a discriminatory statute that required each Chinese immigrant to provide proof that he or she possessed "good character." The law, with later amendments, also required the state commissioner of immigration to collect from a ship's owner or consignee a monetary bond for every passenger deemed to be a non-citizen, pauper, lunatic, handicapped person, or prostitute. It was presumed, incorrectly of course, that most Chinese would fall into one of these categories.[29]

In addition to state and federal laws, the Chinese had to deal with insidious local ordinances which also sought to impede their livelihoods and ultimately force them to return to Asia. This form of prejudice became prevalent after the passage of the 1870 Civil Rights Act, which among other things was supposed to protect their right to testify in court and forbid the imposition of unfair exactions and taxes. The former removed the legal disability imposed by the *People v. Hall* (1854) decision, where Chinese testimony against Caucasians, as well as that of American Indians and African Americans, on the basis of their racial inferiority, was deemed invalid. The latter provision, coupled with the equal-protection clause of the Fourteenth Amendment, invalidated anti-Chinese state laws. Congress in that same year, however, countered this reversal of fortunes by amending the 1790 Nationality Act so that Chinese would not be covered by the extension of naturalization to African Americans.

To circumvent the Civil Rights Act, local governments passed ordinances that were neutral on their face but could be enforced selectively against the Chinese. In San Francisco, the cubic-air law, implying that the Chinese lived in overcrowded, dirty conditions, forced every residence to have at least 500 cubic feet of air per person. The queue ordinance required the hair of every male prisoner in the city jails to be cut to within one inch of the scalp, a disgrace to Chinese nationals, and the sidewalk ordinance prohibited peddlers from using poles to carry loads on the sidewalk. In Los Angeles local officials required vegetable peddlers, a trade group overwhelmingly dominated by Chinese, to meet certain licensing and regulatory requirements. Outraged by these impositions, the Chinese vendors went on strike, which hurt the larger populace so much that the city rescinded those requirements.

Perhaps the most vituperative San Francisco ordinances were the laundry-related ones. During the 1870s, Chinese owned 240 of the approximately 320 laundries in San Francisco.[30] Considered symbols of Chinese economic success in America, the laundries also reminded whites that the Chinese, far from being mere sojourners, intended to stay. Euro-American proprietors and local newspapers railed against the Chinese laundries, and the embers of smoldering hatred caught fire when mobs in a three-day rampage in 1877 destroyed some of these laundries. In response to this public hostility, the city fathers enacted ordinances designed to harass or force the ouster of Chinese laundries by withholding licensing until they met certain conditions.

The roots of the general animosity may date back to the fifth century B.C., when the military engagement between the "civilized" Greeks and the "barbarian" Persians sparked writings about Asia, a continent supposedly full of exotic, debased, and inscrutable peoples. The Mongol invasion of Europe in the thirteenth century gave credence to the developing Yellow Peril image of Asia. This irrational fear of an "Oriental" conquest found fertile soil in America and grew. In the minds of European settlers, American Indians, the descendants of Asians, stood in the way of progress, of America's evolution from savagery to civilization. African Americans similarly represented a threat to the development of American civilization since their slave labor constituted unfair competition for free workers—an argument that portended claims later made against the Chinese.

Such colonial understandings of nonwhite groups fed into the Yankee traders' construction of the image of China and its people following their arrival in China in the late eighteenth century. The travel accounts of American traders, as well as those of American diplomats and missionaries, described the Chinese as a superstitious, crafty, and dishonest race. In the United States, many Americans learned about these so-called aberrations of the Chinese via the popular dime novels of the antebellum years. The interest in the "Orient" and the "otherness" of the Chinese attracted voyeuristic Euro-Americans to sideshow exhibits of Chinese human "freaks" such as the Siamese twins Chang and Eng Bunker, who were promoted as exotic young boys. Equally exploited as a showpiece was Afong Moy, supposedly the first Chinese woman to arrive in America in 1834, whose dainty features and colorful costume gave credence to the mystic of "Orientalism."

By the early 1870s, as anti-Chinese hostility heated up, the prevailing, inscrutable "coolie" stereotype of the Chinese immigrant began appearing in a number of novels about the California frontier by such writers as Bret Harte and Ambrose Bierce. Fictional works in the "future history" genre, which prophesied an "Oriental" invasion by the mindless, monolithic Chinese mass, such as Pierton W. Dooner's *Last Days of the Republic* (1880), echoed the larger fear of Chinese immigration.

A major factor in the shift from simply negative representations of the Chinese to their exclusion altogether was the unstable economy. Slashed wages and high unemployment characterized the lean years of 1873 to 1878. During this severe recession, American labor groups blamed their woes on the Chinese and their capitalist employers. White workers chafed at the industrialists' recruitment of Chinese laborers and were unpersuaded that the status and occupations of white workers would improve as the Chinese filled the lower-ranking jobs. The fact that the Chinese, in the middle of this recession, had migrated to the heavily populated Northeast, established themselves in New York, Boston, and Philadelphia, and supposedly found work in major industries only heightened the alarm about an impending "Oriental" invasion.

Stories about the "slave-like" nature of Chinese labor whipped up fears about the return of slavery and all of its attending political complications. Though charges of "coolieism" were unfounded, Chinese laborers were still, erroneously of course, compared to American black slaves. Supposedly the physiognomy of the Chinese was akin to that of African Americans—both indicated a level of biologically determined depravity that could taint the purity of the white race.

The supposed similar depravity of both Chinese and African Americans explains the application of the color line in schooling to both racial minorities. In 1854 the local school board in San Francisco provided a "colored school" for black children, and, in 1858, the board passed a resolution institutionalizing separate schooling for whites and blacks. Echoing public sentiments on this issue, the *San Francisco Bulletin* commented: "Then let us keep our public schools free from the intrusion of the inferior races . . . let us preserve our Caucasian blood pure. We want no mongrel race of moral and mental hybrids.[31] Two years later, the California legislation passed a law that established segregated schools and authorized the withholding of public monies from any all-white school that admitted racial minorities.

Though an all-Chinese school opened its doors in 1859, low enrollment and the racial prejudices of officials led to its closing in 1870. In spite of the hostile environment of the ensuing decade, the Chinese community persistently lobbied in the name of fair play for access to educational facilities, citing this as a right guaranteed by their tax-paying status. Success seemed to be in sight when Joseph and Mary Tape, in 1884, won their suit against the school board for denying their daughter, Mamie, a public education. However, school officials circumvented the ruling and established a new, segregated Oriental School. Various California communities, including San Francisco, kept Chinese children in segregated schools until the early 1930s when Chinese civic organizations and leaders fought successfully for the end of segregated schooling. Chinese schoolchildren in the South, however, remained in all-black schools until 1950.

Economic, racial, and cultural reasons clearly forged an American consensus on the undesirability of Chinese immigration. For example, local newspapers often carried news of crowds of young whites at the docks heckling and even pelting new Chinese arrivals. Much more ominous was the agitation fostered by the Workingmen's Party and its demagogue, Dennis Kearney. The Workingmen's Party cry, "The Chinese must go," captured the attention of Californians. Capitalizing on the economic crisis, and aware of the potential political windfall for the labor movement in terms of increasing its influence in state politics, labor leaders lined up behind the anti-Chinese rhetoric.[32]

The political influence of the Workingmen's Party was evident in the California constitutional convention of 1878–1879. Delegates, in a display of intense animosity toward the Chinese, chose in the final form of the document to insert an article that prohibited corporations from employing Chinese and forbade their employment in the public sector. It even called for the expulsion of Chinese from towns and cities or their segregation within prescribed limits. The Chinese were also stripped of equal protection and the right to vote in state elections. Echoes of such nativism were heard on the East Coast. In New York City, labor unions and local politicians organized anti-coolie rallies as early as 1870, and the hostility of organized labor prevented most Chinese from entering the manufacturing sector of the city's economy.

Elsewhere anti-Chinese intolerance stemmed as much from being used to deflect nativism away from certain European immigrants as it did from the perceived economic threat argument. In Colorado in the 1870s, Italian workers in coal mines felt threatened by fellow Chinese workers. Italians feared that eventually they would be displaced by the "cheaper" Chinese or that their pay would be lowered to the Chinese level. Complicating the picture was the social prejudice of Cornish, Irish, and Austrian immigrants against the Italians. Long seen as the most "brutish" of all the European ethnic groups, Italians chose to adopt existing social prejudices toward the Chinese as a way to show their own adaptation to mainstream American society, assert the definition of Americans as "white" persons, and deflect nativistic antiforeign feelings from themselves.

ANTI-ASIAN LAWS AND CHINESE RESISTANCE

The Chinese did try to resist such prejudices, and in so doing, demonstrated a knowledge of American governmental institutions and a remarkable savvy in manipulating them. In the 1850s, taxation on miners elicited protests from Chinese mutual aid associations. The leaders of these associations, through a lobbyist in Sacramento, succeeded in preventing the passage of certain subsequent odious legislation, and they were instrumental in securing protection for the Chinese under the Civil Rights Act of 1870. As the anti-Chinese movement swung into full gear, however, their strategy of petitioning lawmakers became increasingly futile. In exasperation, some Chinese community leaders urged fellow compatriots in China to dissuade potential immigrants from coming to America. For the most part, their resistance now had to take place within the courts of law. This decision to employ American jurisprudence constituted a departure from the traditional Chinese submission to the government's laws and probably reflected selective acculturation into the American way of life.

In 1862 the plaintiff Lin Sing successfully challenged the validity of the monthly tax on Chinese residents in California on the grounds that it violated the Constitution or laws of the United States, particularly the federal power over foreign commerce (in this case, the Chinese). In the next several decades, Chinese litigants pressed this line of attack. When the Chinese in Idaho heard about the Civil Rights Act of 1866 and the subsequent Fourteenth Amendment, which collectively guaranteed every U.S. citizen equal protection under the law, they secured more grounds to fight discriminatory state laws. In several suits they fought against Idaho's head tax, which was levied on every Chinese resident, and the special monthly levy on Chinese gambling houses and brothels. Ultimately they failed, mainly because the courts ruled that because they were not citizens, the Chinese were not covered by the equal-protection clause.[33]

In the late 1870s, the Chinese community in San Francisco questioned the constitutionality of the queue-cutting ordinance, arguing that it undermined the equality of treatment promised to the Chinese by the Burlingame Treaty, the Civil Rights Act of 1870, and the due-process and equal-protection clauses of the Fourteenth Amendment. Almost concomitant with that were suits against that series of laundry ordinances, which concluded with a resounding affirmation that the Chinese, in spite of not being citizens, deserved equal protection of the laws.

The Chinese, however, suffered a severe setback on the question of naturalization. In 1878 several Chinese asked the federal courts to rule that Chinese aliens did fall within the 1870 stipulation, namely "any alien, being a free white person" could become a citizen of the United States. This became necessary since, aside from "white persons," African Americans were the only other group granted access to naturalization. But the courts found that a white person was a Caucasian and since Chinese were not Caucasians, they were barred from citizenship.[34]

The failure to gain citizenship gave the anti-immigrant movement a boost. Since they could not vote, not only were the Chinese unable to deflect the movement against them politically, they also must in the white mind, deserve exclusion from citizenship because of their racial inferiority. Restrictionists however, still had to overcome the limits placed on state power over immigration and the free emigration provision in the Burlingame Treaty. They realized that they had to fight for their cause in Congress itself.

Their first attempt—the fifteen-passenger bill of 1879 (no vessel should carry more than fifteen Chinese passengers to the United States)—was vetoed by President Rutherford B. Hayes because it violated treaty protections. Chinese immigration, much to the joy of restrictionists, however, became a major issue in the national election of 1880 because the Pacific Coast served as the swing vote on several key issues. In an effort to curry votes, both parties called for the restriction of Chinese immigration and an amendment of the treaty.

In response to that, the Hayes administration impaneled a commission to negotiate a new, restrictive treaty with China. The new treaty, however, was a compromise—a testament to the Qing government's late response to earlier numerous pleas for diplomatic intervention from Chinese mutual aid associations in America. Faced with Qing resistance, the U.S. commission secured only restriction of Chinese laborers who had yet to immigrate to the United States; those already present in the country and those of nonlaboring classes could still enjoy free travel and equal protection. The Angell Treaty of 1880 represented a significant departure: class-based restriction of migration had been written into treaty form, and the institutionalization of prejudice against the Chinese gathered momentum.[35]

That momentum was steamrolled by the commission of a series of anti-Chinese outrages. Violence against Chinese was nothing new; it is estimated that almost ninety Chinese miners in the 1850s lost their lives over the contested Foreign Miners' Tax. Spontaneous outbreaks against the Chinese occurred in several California towns in the 1870s, including one failed attempt to burn down Chico's Chinatown. Chinese merchants in San Francisco responded to this wave of violence by pleading in a letter written in 1876 to the city authorities for treaty protections and reciprocity in Sino-American relations: "[B]eing here under sacred treaty stipulations, we simply asked to be protected in our treaty rights."[36] The merchants demanded indemnification for loss of property and lives, but to no avail.

Sustained, organized violence, which took advantage of the absence of political rights and legal protection for the Chinese, took place primarily in the 1880s. In this decade, hostilities broke out in Denver, Colorado; Rock Springs, Wyoming Territory; Snake River Canyon, Idaho; Portland, Oregon; Tacoma, Puyallup, and Seattle, Washington Territory; and many California towns. Though the Qing government protested, U.S. authorities brushed off the protests and denied that the United States was liable for any Chinese losses.

In Congress, opponents of restriction—most of whom represented commercial and religious groups—tried to check antiforeign feelings by emphasizing the contributions of the Chinese to the economic well-being of the country, but to no avail. Congress passed the Chinese Exclusion Act of 1882 by a wide margin, and for the first time in its history, the United States adopted a policy of exclusion based on race and nationality—a measure that laid the foundation for future barriers against other ethnic groups.

The 1882 act suspended the entry of Chinese laborers for the next ten years. Chinese laborers already in the United States as of November 17, 1880, could remain, but they were governed by certain entry and exit regulations. This class-bound legislation did not apply to merchants, diplomats, teachers, students, and travelers (the exempt classes) but did require them to possess documentation attesting to their right to enter. The act, significantly, denied all Chinese, on the basis of race, access to naturalization.[37]

Almost immediately after the passage of that act, the Chinese tried to mitigate its severity. Once again resorting to the mediation of the federal courts, Chinese litigants managed to loosen the regulations governing the entry and the exit of laborers with "prior" resident status and those of merchant background. Because so many Chinese entered following these rulings, Congress in 1884 tightened the regulations. In that same year, the courts, in decisions with far-reaching consequences for family formation, ruled that Chinese children born in the United States were U.S. citizens and that wives and children of Chinese merchants could enter the country (though not those of the Chinese laboring class).

Following the wave of mob violence against the Chinese in the American West in 1885 and 1886, the Qing government, in a move to curtail further loss of lives and property, assented to the revision of the 1880 treaty, including a twenty-year moratorium on the immigration of Chinese laborers in exchange for a guarantee of protection of the Chinese residents already in the United States. Unsubstantiated rumors that China planned to reject the revisions led Congress to push through the rather severe Scott Act of 1888, which prohibited all Chinese laborers from entering the United States, even those who had been here before November 17, 1880, and had the necessary documentation. Though the Chinese challenged the validity of the 1888 amendment via *Chae Chan Ping v. United States* (1888), they failed. In a decision with profound implications for immigration law, the U.S. Supreme Court affirmed that Congress had the sovereign power to exclude aliens, even those previously granted permission to stay.

By the early 1890s, prejudice against the Chinese had expanded to include certain European immigrants. Blamed for the rise of radicalism, a disorderly labor movement, and the industrial depression between 1883 and 1886, Eastern and Southern European immigrants bore the brunt of many Americans' anxieties about the new economic order. In the late 1880s Congress passed laws to reduce the importation of foreign labor under contracts, which supposedly had depressed the labor market.

To further control this immigration wave, Congress passed a new law in 1891 that allowed the federal government to take full and exclusive control of immigration; to exclude certain criminal, immoral, or indigent classes; and to deport those already admitted into the United States if they were found excludable. In step with this sweeping hostility, Congress passed the Geary Act of 1892. Applied specifically to the Chinese, the law required all Chinese laborers in the United States to register for a certificate of residence. Barring that, they could be arrested and even deported.

This new law angered the Chinese; the Chinese vice-consul in San Francisco complained that this system of registration placed the Chinese "on the level of your dogs."[38] The Chinese Six Companies, the umbrella organization for Chinese mutual aid associations, for its part urged the community not to register because the law was unconstitutional. The companies also hired lawyers to bring a test case—*Fong Yue Ting v. United States* (1893)—but the suit ended with an affirmation of the right of Congress to expel or deport, which the Supreme Court deemed to be part of a sovereign state's unconfined power over immigration. This upholding of the new law had a chilling effect on the number of Chinese arrivals: 39,579 had been admitted in 1882; only 472 entered in 1893.[39]

Two years after the passage of the Geary Act, the United States and China concluded the Gresham-Yang Treaty of 1894 in which the tottering Qing government agreed to accept the contents of that act and the extension of the exclusion of Chinese laborers for another ten years. In return for that, the United States allowed the return of domiciled laborers who had left temporarily and who had family or property in the United States. When, in 1900, Hawaii was formally annexed to the United States, Chinese entry into the islands also came under the exclusion laws, which were extended in 1902 for another ten years.

In 1904 China declined to renew the Gresham-Yang Treaty, and Congress made Chinese exclusion indefinite. Thus a long invidious chapter, one that began in the 1870s, of limiting and then excluding Chinese immigration finally came to an inglorious end. It would be nearly forty more years before Congress reconsidered these barriers. Even then, substantial changes would not be made until 1965.

Though the Chinese community had little success in fighting those federal laws, Chinese individuals, by filing writs of habeas corpus, found a way to gain possible admittance into the United States even though they were initially refused by immigration authorities. As many as 85 to 90 percent of the petitions filed between 1882 and 1891 ended with the reversal of the earlier decision to exclude.

Furthermore, Chinese embroiled in civil disputes with whites often resorted to U.S. courts to secure redress. Typically, Euro-American companies or individuals owed Chinese workers wages or money for services rendered or goods delivered. In Idaho, in 1870, four Chinese laborers—known only as Ah Lung, Ah Tung, Ah Hee, and Ah Why—in separate suits sued Robinson, Taylor, and Company for unpaid wages. Given the fact that this company owed, on the average, each man only $15.00 and that in traditional China civil disputes were settled outside the courts by village or clan leaders, it is clear that these Chinese plaintiffs had not only become acquainted with the American judicial system, but also that they probably had absorbed the meaning of Western justice.

Overall, the litigation that the Chinese brought before American courts during the late nineteenth century proved that they never stood idly by while discriminatory laws and their attending violence descended on them. Through their cases Chinese litigants questioned the boundaries of governmental authority and the rights of citizens and noncitizens, and in so doing, contributed to the shaping of American democracy and republicanism.

ECONOMIC DISCRIMINATION AND LABOR PROTEST

Chinese immigrants also challenged the United States to live up to its promise of equality and opportunity by resisting economic discrimination through class alliance within the community and with other ethnic groups. In this way, the Chinese rebuked the perception that they were "docile" and "servile."

The Chinese railroad workers' failed strike of 1867, in which they demanded higher wages and shorter hours from the Central Pacific, is an often told story. Less well known would be the agitation among contracted Chinese laborers in the South. The Chinese protested here against planters and railroad owners who withheld wages or who arbitrarily changed the terms of the contracts. Aware of the growing shortage of Chinese workers following the enforcement of the exclusion laws, farm laborers in California in the 1880s and 1890s also struck time and again for higher wages and for the recognition of their rights as workers, including advances for their labor and better working conditions. The growing consciousness of such rights also pervaded the mind-set of Pacific Northwest–bound Chinese salmon workers, who demanded an advance on their wages before boarding the ships departing for the north.

In Hawaii, aside from individual acts of violence against bosses and plantation property, dissatisfied Chinese workers in 1891 banded together to protest against misleading expectations in their labor contracts. Nine years later, Japanese and Chinese laborers—in a departure from historically rooted interethnic antagonism—collectively struck over the same issue. In so doing, the Chinese and Japanese held out the possibility of forging a class-based consciousness and identity.

Any workforce differentiated by race in terms of both type of work and wages often resulted in ethnic competition and mutual distrust. This was the exact scenario for the Chinese toiling in the salmon canneries of the Pacific Northwest. Chinese salmon workers retained a monopoly on the more skilled and better paying jobs while Japanese, and later Filipino, workers had to struggle to break into this ethnically split labor market. Not surprisingly, the early Chinese, who organized at the dawn of the twentieth century in this subregion, remained intraethnic but not for long. In the face of industrial expansion, employers undermined class-based alignment by turning to other ethnic groups for new sources of labor.

Chinese laborers could not seek the support of the white-dominated organized union movement. Save for isolated cases, such as the admittance of Chinese and Japanese miners into United Mine Workers' locals in Wyoming in 1907 and failed attempts made by the Knights of Labor to organize Chinese laundry workers in New York City in the 1880s and 1890s, the exclusion of Chinese, along with other Asian laborers from national labor unions was thorough and complete. For example, when Chinese cigar workers in San Francisco walked out in 1885, white unions not only offered no help but also accused them of being cocky and misguided.

Because of the fragility of institutionalized organizing, Chinese workers, from farmhands in the San Joaquin Valley to plantation laborers in the Deep South, often relied on co-ethnic labor contractors (who hired workers and supervised the workplace on behalf of white employers) to help them secure the best jobs and sometimes to offer protection against an employer's oppression. Labor contractors also, however, frequently exploited their subordinate co-ethnics by way of excessive profits from supplying food and necessities and lucrative commissions levied for finding them work. In this way, co-ethnic workers became dependent on them, thus forging tight race-based relationships that precluded the emergence of class consciousness. And so racial solidarity triumphed at the expense of class-based alliance among Chinese workers and other ethnic groups.

Meanwhile the exclusion laws led to a sharp plunge in the Chinese population—from a high of 105,465 in 1880 to a low of 61,639 in 1920.[40] This dramatic decline within just forty years is unprecedented in the history of American ethnic groups. Furthermore, exclusion laws, by hindering entry and family formation, gave rise by 1920 to a community of mostly middle-aged men with foreign-born males outnumbering citizen males well into the World War II era. Such facts, coupled with a heavily male-dominated culture, a history of economic and social discrimination, a legacy of white-inflicted violence, and a high degree of cultural difference between the Chinese and the Euro-American society, probably explain why the acculturation of the Chinese occurred rather slowly. Still, the Chinese discovered that their lives, and the communities they built, would nevertheless be subjected to the forces of Americanization, Christianization, and China-centered nationalism.

3

Nationalism and Americanization Before World War II

CHINA-CENTERED NATIONALISM

Even though the 1904 indefinite extension of exclusion laws stymied the flow of immigration from Asia to America, sociopolitical and economic life in Chinese American communities continued to develop and even flourish, thereby refuting the supposedly pervasive impact of assimilation on Chinese immigrants and their offspring. Their ethnicity persisted as a source of group identity and solidarity. Though Americanization and, to some degree, Christianity did shape their fortunes and selfhoods, equally important were the countervailing forces of China-centered nationalism and racial exclusion. These conflicting forces sometimes created a sense of ambivalence for the community's self-identity and its relationship to the larger body politic, even as they reinvented Chinese immigrants, through a continuous, multifaceted nonlinear process, into Chinese Americans.

Perhaps an early example of that process would be the boycott of 1905, which though mainly a large-scale boycott of American goods in China, sprang from events in both the United States and China. Chinese Americans, since about 1900, had regarded these events as portending an organized effort to expel all of them. The law of 1904 that set aside all treaty provisions and the *Ju Toy* decision of 1905 upholding the right of the Bureau of Immigration to carry out arbitrary deportations were both ominous signs of an impending fate. More troubling was the 1903 Boston Chinatown raid, which ostensibly was conducted to force procrastinating Chinese to register in accordance with the provisions of the Geary Act of 1892. The real intent, however, was to eliminate the Chinese presence, as evidenced by subsequent deportations and removal to elsewhere.

By the early 1900s, a China-oriented political consciousness had permeated the Chinese American society to some degree. The humiliating defeat of China in the Sino-Japanese War of 1894–1895, the botched "Hundred Days' Reforms" of 1898 (designed to speed up China's modernization), the expanding European economic imperialism in Asia, the continual discrimination suffered by Chinese immigrants in America, and the sociopolitical changes occurring in Chinese America awakened dormant nationalist sentiments in Chinese at home and abroad.[1]

Ardent critics of the Qing government had made their way to America since the turn of the century to establish parties to promote their respective political agendas. Baohuanghui or the Reform party, established in 1899 in Vancouver by reformer Kang Youwei, sought to establish a constitutional monarchy in China. This party competed for Chinese American support with Xingzhonghui (Revive China Society, later renamed Tongmenghui), which was founded in Honolulu in 1895 by Sun Yat-sen, the proponent of a republican form of government for China. Chinese Americans, whose efforts became part of a larger overseas Chinese politicization, soon offered monetary contributions, financed China-based commercial ventures to modernize the homeland, disseminated propaganda in North America, and even organized a military academy in California to train men for subversive work in China. Branches of both parties mushroomed in the major Chinatowns of North America and eventually in China and Southeast Asia. The political freedom the Chinese in America enjoyed allowed these political parties to develop unhindered. The shift, following the 1904 indefinite ban on Chinese immigration, of mainstream American attention from the Chinese to the Japanese "menace" also facilitated this ethnic mobilization.

TRADITIONAL COMMUNITY ORGANIZATIONS

By the early years of the new century, internal turmoil within the Chinese American community had prepared the way for mobilization. Until 1900 leaders of Sanyi origin (Sanyi or Three Districts refers to the Nanhai, Panyu, and Shunde districts in Guangdong), owing to their economic dominance in the community, controlled the ethnic political leadership via the Zhonghua Zong Huiguan or Chinese Consolidated Benevolent Association (CCBA), or its more well-known name, the Chinese Six Companies.

As an umbrella organization for district associations, the CCBA, loosely established in the early 1860s and then formalized in 1882, galvanized a sense of community that crossed clan and regional lines and provided a collective response to anti-Chinese agitation. Until the establishment of the first Chinese legation in Washington, D.C., in 1878, the CCBA operated as the diplomatic representative for the Chinese in America. Since most Chinese were still foreign born and had yet to plant roots in America, the CCBA often justified its fight against racial oppression on the grounds of defending treaty rights and demanded hospitality and reciprocity in accordance with China's sovereignty.[2]

Serving as the mouthpiece of the Chinese community, and buttressed by the explicit support of the Qing government, the CCBA dominated the internal affairs of Chinatowns. It settled disputes between different associations, contested or sought relief from anti-Chinese laws, acted as a clearinghouse for fund-raising projects, and protected the class interests of the merchants. For example, the CCBA witnessed the changes of ownership and property sales and oversaw the credit-ticket system. The power wielded by the CCBA attested to the Chinese immigrants' need for intracommunity governance, given their exclusion from the political sphere.

Below the CCBA were the benevolent regional and district associations or *huiguan*, in which membership was determined by birth. The two earliest, most influential *huiguan* were the Sanyi huiguan (Sam Yup Association) and the Siyi huiguan (Sze Yup Association). These included people from the same region or district of origin; they often spoke closely related Cantonese subdialects. A small minority that spoke Hakka had its own separate organizations; the earliest was the Renhe huiguan (Yan Wo Benevolent Association), which was founded in San Francisco in the 1850s. Other organizations of non-Cantonese immigrants did not appear until the twentieth century when more non-Guangdong immigrants, such as those from the Fuzhou area and Hainan Island, began arriving.

Visible in America since 1851, a *huiguan*, similar to those in China, erected temples for the performance of sacrificial rites, shipped the bones of the deceased back to China and managed cemeteries in the United States, provided medical services for the sick, and established Chinese schools to teach youngsters a China-oriented curriculum. *Huiguan* leaders also mediated personal or business disputes between members. The *huiguan* in the United States were not exact replicas of those in China. The U.S. *huiguan* were immigrant organizations that functioned in a hostile environment; they must be viewed within the context of the exclusion of Chinese from urban enclaves. Consequently, these *huiguan* adapted and offered uniquely American functions. One of these functions, which indicates the merchant class's control of leadership, was to check the absconding of defaulting debtors, mostly linked to the credit-ticket system, through the issuance of an exit permit. Without the permit, debtors could not purchase their ticket back to China. A second unique aspect of the *huiguan* in the United States was the organization of the CCBA to muster collective strength. By the 1890s, as many as 95 percent of the Chinese in North America belonged to *huiguan*, attesting to its pervasive influence.

Related mutual aid organizations, which included surname or family associations, enrolled members of a common surname without regard to locality of origin. These included the numerically large Li (Lee), Huang (Wong), and Chee (Chinn) groups. These associations could also enroll several surnames, such as the Longgongtang (Loong Kong Association), also called the Four Brothers' Association. In the United States, surname associations, which did not require close blood ties, were more visible than clan or lineage associations, which were organized on the basis of an extensive kinship network with members inhabiting the same area. Because the Chinese populace in the early years remained largely immigrant and semitransient, such networks rarely existed in North America. Present in the United States probably by the 1870s, these surname associations provided charitable services akin to those of the *huiguan* and sometimes even offered protection to members threatened by tongs or secret societies.

Far smaller in size, usually made up of no more than fifty people, were the *gongsi fang* (*fong*), which were composed of patrilineal kinfolk descended from a common paternal ancestor or people who hailed from the same village. The *gongsi fang* offered temporary lodgings, provided social centers, and acted as a source for business loans. Because the exclusion era did not come to an end until 1943, the camaraderie offered by the *fang*'s activities served as a substitute for family life. Not surprisingly, *gongsi fang* disappeared following the repeal of Chinese exclusion laws, although surname associations continue to exist today.[3]

Perhaps the Chinatown organizations best known to Euro-Americans are the fighting tongs, a special kind of secret society. Established as early as 1852, these structured, exclusive socioeconomic organizations struggled for political and economic power within the community. Often pitted against one another and also against the CCBA, tongs sometimes resorted to open warfare to settle scores. They took control of or played a role in running Chinese vice businesses—gambling saloons, brothels, and opium dens. Limited employment opportunities and a low level of acculturation—all products of the anti-Chinese movement—drew Chinese immigrants to these organizations.

These tongs, however, must be differentiated from another group of secret societies which, like tongs, also traced their origins to the Triads, or Sanhei-hui, which originally formed in southern China to spearhead an anti-Qing movement. In America, Triad lodges, including such prominent ones as Binggongtang (Bing Kung Tong), Anliangtang (On Leong Tong), and Xieshengtang (Hip Sing Tong), loosely federated as Zhigongtang or Chee Kung Tong and soon attracted many Chinese laborers, Chinese Christians, and some struggling, middle-ranking merchants.

The composition of the lodges suggests the protective nature of these organizations. Sidelined by the wealthy, powerful merchants who controlled the *huiguan*, laborers, Christians, and small-time merchants gravitated to secret societies for security and employment. Chinese who wished to enter America in violation of anti-immigration legislation came to rely on the mechanism of these secret societies (and sometimes also the surname associations). In this sense, the perpetuation of these societies was an outcome of restrictive immigration laws. However, Triad lodges, fighting tongs, surname associations, and *huiguan* were not mutually exclusive; an immigrant could and often did belong to all such organizations. Because of the political legacy and its marginalized image, secret societies proved to be invaluable allies for mainland Chinese political leaders looking for agents to help disseminate their propaganda.

Augmenting the complexity of the social fabric were the conservative merchant guilds, which had only a marginal role in shaping the early fortunes of the community. Later within the context of the rising nationalist response to Western trade competition in Asia, Chinese chambers of commerce had sprung up by 1910 in major Chinatowns and eventually absorbed these early merchant guilds. Two leading guilds found in cities with Chinese communities were the Zhaoyi gongsuo (Shew Hing Association) for Sanyi merchants and the Siyi-dominated Keshang huiguan (Guest Businessmen's Association).

Far more influential, especially after 1900, were the exclusively male occupational guilds such as those that drew together cigar makers or laundry workers and which often challenged the authority of the CCBA and *huiguan*. Guilds also sometimes monitored workplace conditions and often barred nonguild members from gaining employment in certain industries. In general, guilds, secret societies, and fighting tongs had open membership requirements and, by nature, promoted some economic mobility.

Despite the proliferation of social organizations in Chinese America, the CCBA remained the most powerful one. Its Sanyi leaders, drawn from the minority segment of the Chinese populace, lost credibility, however, when they failed to counter the Geary Act. The community leaders of Siyi origin (Xinhui, Taishan, Kaiping, and Enping districts), who made up almost two-thirds of the Chinese populace in America, now found an opening to challenge Sanyi leadership. Boycotts of Sanyi businesses ensued, and soon the tong wars broke out.

AMERICANIZATION, EQUAL RIGHTS, AND THE BOYCOTT OF 1905

Also competing for Chinese Americans' attention by the turn of the century was a tiny, but vocal, Chinese Christian community—which perhaps accounted for 2 percent of the total population in 1892—that rejected the elitist, conservative nature of the ethnic political leadership and instead embraced more Western-oriented political ideals. Partly because of that stance, and partly because their fellow Chinese saw them as insufficiently "Chinese," they were marginalized in Chinatowns. Chinese Christians had to band together for mutual support and soon established their own schools, missions, and even presses.[4]

Through Reverend Wu Panzhao, more commonly known as Ng Poon Chew, a prolific local journalist and lecturer, Chinese Christians vocalized their opinions in Ng's daily newspaper, the *Chung Sai Yat Po* (*CSYP*), the leading Chinese-language paper in the early twentieth-century United States. The newspaper's editorials called for an anti-Manchu revolt in China and linked that to the Chinese struggle for equal rights in America, and Reverend Ng embarked in the early 1900s on several nationwide speaking tours, trying to make a case for Chinese contributions to the well-being of America and thus the need for immigration reform. When San Francisco residents blamed the Chinese in 1900 for a rumored bubonic plague, and the entire Chinatown became quarantined, leading Chinese Christians, taking advantage of a divided CCBA, led the charge to end this demonization. Overall, through these efforts, Chinese Christians gradually established some tenuous credibility within the community.

Against the backdrop of race-based agitation, the call for a boycott of U.S. goods in 1905 in Canton and Shanghai evoked a response from the Chinese in the United States, whose resentment of the years of ill treatment finally turned into outright anger. The boycott, which lasted nearly a year and drew support from all major Chinese organizations including the Zhigongtang, the Chinese Christians, and native-born Chinese Americans under the aegis of the Zhuyue Zongju (Anti-Treaty Society), represented a significant departure from the previous emphasis on judicial or diplomatic recourse. The boycott, however, petered out when the Qing government, buckling under pressure from U.S. authorities, retracted its support for it.[5]

Nevertheless, the boycott checked certain blatant abuses: raids of Chinatowns became a thing of the past, the processing time for new immigrants was shortened somewhat, calls for a more stringent registration process abated, and the momentum to expel all Chinese residents was halted. The slight turn of fortunes was also reflected in the immigration statistics: in 1905, 29 percent of the immigration certificates approved by American consuls in China were rejected; the following year, only 6 percent were rejected.

The failure of the boycott to reverse the anti-immigration laws, however, reinforced the Chinese Americans' sense of inferiority. Strengthening China through evolutionary or revolutionary change could improve the fate of the Chinese in America, but those engaged in China-centered nationalism could also suffer from conflicting loyalties to both China and the United States.

One fledging organization that may have understood the dilemma of this duality was the Chinese American Citizens Alliance (CACA). Founded in 1895 in San Francisco and originally named the United Parlor of the Native Sons of the Golden State (NSGS), this group attracted both native-born and naturalized Chinese Americans, whose worldview was shaped by American education and exposure to Euro-American culture. Their visibility grew during the exclusion era. By 1900 about 11 percent of the Chinese in the United States were native born; this figure had increased to 52 percent by 1940.[6]

Derisively labeled *juk sing* (literally, in Cantonese, the hollow part of a bamboo stalk—but implying "empty" or "useless") by foreign-born Chinese because of their supposed shallow understanding of traditional Chinese culture, some American-born Chinese objected to the homeland orientation of the traditional associations, which seemed to hinder acceptance by the larger society. In their mind, the continual discrimination suffered by all Chinese stemmed from a miscarriage of Americanization. The cause célèbre for direct action came in the form of the controversial Geary Act of 1892. Chinese Americans realized that the legislation violated their rights as U.S. citizens, and, in 1892, a group of them formed a Chinese Civil Rights League in New York City to raise the political awareness of the community and prepare a test case before the U.S. Supreme Court.

The origins of this particular effort can be traced to the life of Wong Chin Foo, an early proponent of modernity in China. Wanted by the Qing government for preaching so-called heretical beliefs, Wong fled to America in 1873. Arriving at the height of the anti-Chinese agitation, Wong soon took to the lecture circuit. In his talks before Euro-American audiences, and later in his published writings, including those in his short-lived *Chinese American* newspaper (Wong was one of the earliest to use this phrase, signifying his desire for recognition as an American), he tried to end cultural misunderstanding of the Chinese. When he realized that this misunderstanding was the root cause of the racial prejudice, he devoted his energy to educating Americans on the virtues of Chinese culture and customs.

In 1884, two years after the passage of the virulent Chinese Exclusion Act, Wong and a group of naturalized Chinese Americans organized what may have been the first Chinese voter registration association in the United States to increase Chinese participation and influence in American politics. But their efforts came to naught. A Chinese community divided by clan, geographical origin, and dialect, coupled with the exclusion of the Chinese from naturalization (as stated in the 1882 law), derailed their efforts.

Wong and his compatriots moved from raising political consciousness to securing equal rights after the passage of the Geary Act unleashed a furor within the Chinese community. The Chinese Equal Rights League, the organization they had formed, departed from the CCBA's conciliatory approach to interracial relations. Unlike the CCBA whose writings and petitions against anti-Chinese outrages often took on a defensive tone, the Equal Rights League adopted an aggressive posture. It demanded that the United States live up to its banner of democracy and that Chinese be accorded equal rights, including suffrage. Though all these early efforts bore no tangible fruit, they did inspire others, including those in the NSGS CACA, to build on Wong's pioneering role in the Chinese civil rights movement.

On the West Coast, the NSGS/CACA quickly garnered a membership of nearly a third of the San Francisco Chinese populace, and in the next several decades it expanded to other cities inside and outside of California, with local lodges in Oakland, Los Angeles, Chicago, Detroit, Boston, Pittsburgh, and Portland, Oregon. The commitment of the organization to assimilation reflected the class affiliation of its membership, which comprised professionals, white-collar workers, and some businesspeople, most of whom had at least an American high school education.

Before the 1930s, the exclusively males-only CACA (women were not admitted until 1976) scored some successes on the political front. It blocked an attempt made in 1913 to disfranchise Chinese Americans and successfully fought against the original provisions of the National Origins Act of 1924. Designed mainly to curb immigration from Eastern, Southern, and Central Europe, this legislation also restricted Asian inflow by way of the clause that barred the entry of "any alien ineligible" for citizenship. When the Supreme Court ruled in 1925 that Chinese wives of U.S. citizens were ineligible for citizenship and therefore not admissible into the United States, the small opening for Chinese female immigration became even narrower.

The CACA fought back, arguing that the new law unfairly separated conjugal partners, stalled family formation, and perpetuated split households. Chinese men were already barred from marrying Caucasian women by antimiscegenation laws passed in as many as fourteen states with California's as early as 1850. Further discouraged by the 1922 Cable Act, which denied a woman (including an American-born Chinese) her U.S. citizenship should she marry a Chinese alien, a Chinese man now had to go to China to marry a woman whom he could see only infrequently. Congress, in reaction to those arguments, amended the act in 1930 so that wives of Chinese citizens who were married before 1924 could legally enter the United States. In part because of this amendment, the sex ratio began to improve: between 1920 and 1940, the male-female ratio dropped from 7:1 to 3:1. In this same period, the percentage of Chinese women in the United States grew from 12 to 26 percent of the entire Chinese population.

In addition to the fight against discriminatory legislation, the CACA tried to foster a more positive image of the Chinese in the United States through its antidefamation efforts. Sensationalist Yellow Peril literature, which presented erroneous statements about the Chinese, became one of its targets. Another effort to promote the incorporation of the Chinese into the larger society involved the campaign for equal educational opportunities in public schools which highlighted the injustice of segregated facilities. "Segregation does not make for good citizenship," said attorney Kenneth Fung, an officer of the CACA. "Our children, born here . . . should not be subjected to a humiliation that would only breed discontent."[7] Finally, on its own volition, CACA offered English-language classes as a means of Americanizing foreign-born Chinese. Overall, CACA served as a vehicle for members to highlight their patriotism to the United States and their American citizenship through peaceful and legal means of resolving injustices.

Notwithstanding its call for Americanization, CACA joined the boycott of 1905. The boycott, as much as it united the community, also polarized it. The Baohuanghui, *huiguan*, merchant guilds, and CCBA—the faction in favor of constitutional reform in China—backed the demand that the United States admit all Chinese except laborers. Opposing that were those who favored revolution in China and the admittance of all Chinese, including laborers. Those linked to this goal included the Xingzhonghui, Triad lodges, Chinese Christians, and American-born Chinese Americans. When the boycott failed to elicit the espoused aims, each faction blamed the other for the failure.

Still, China-centered politics in North American did blunt the sense of regionalism and clan affiliation and concomitantly sharpened ideological commitment. Rivalries between various types of social organizations by 1912 had become redefined in political terms. Zhigongtang and Triad lodges tended to see themselves as the champions of the common man; the *huiguan* backed a type of oligarchy of the wealthy and the educated. Because the *huiguan* were conservative, they tended to support the reform-oriented Baohuanghui; the Zhigongtang and Triad lodges, however were inclined to back the revolutionary politics of the Xingzhonghui.[8] Class lines overall loomed large and remained so for the rest of the early twentieth century. The failure of the 1911 Chinese Revolution to secure full democracy also meant that political consensus within the Chinese American community remained elusive.

Despite such conflict, nationalism was strong enough to initiate some social change. By the 1910s a far broader segment of the Chinese population in America had become interested in politics. Chinese Americans were swept along with the rising tide of strengthening China through modernization and the practice of democracy in the United States. Barbaric practices inflicted on women, such as footbinding, arranged marriages, polygamy, and prostitution, came under fire. Between 1900 and 1920, the *CSYP* featured numerous editorials and articles arguing that women's emancipation would promote equal rights for all Chinese in America. Educated Chinese Americans also denounced opium smoking and queue wearing and promoted progressive reform in Chinatowns and education, as well as integration into the larger American society.

GILDED GHETTOES

Against this backdrop of rising ethnic pride, major Chinatowns by the late 1900s had witnessed a face-lift as opium smoking, gambling dens, and brothels, which became synonymous with outmoded ways, entered into a long decline even as Chinese leaders encouraged the growing tourist trade that capitalized on the supposed exotic nature of "Orientalism." San Francisco's Chinatown best illustrated this image-making process. In 1890 the San Francisco Board of Supervisors passed the Bingham Ordinance, which would have relocated Chinatown to an area set aside for slaughterhouses, hog factories, and other businesses considered prejudicial to public health or comfort. The courts ruled, however, that the institutionalizing of residential segregation was unconstitutional. After the 1906 earthquake, the city leaders again threatened to move Chinatown. Put on the defensive, leading Chinese merchants realized that they had to shatter the slumlike image of Chinatown.

To that end, a gilded "Oriental city" soon emerged—pagodas and false, curved "Oriental" roofs began to dot the skyline, Chinese pageantry was revived, and thousands of lightbulbs transformed San Francisco's Chinatown into a fantasy land. Tourists who visited this and other Chinatowns, which underwent similar changes, could satisfy their curiosity about Chinese culture at the endless curio and gift shops and partake of unusual delectables in chop suey and chow mein restaurants. During the prohibition era tourists who patronized some of the more elegant Chinese restaurants in New York could also dance to live music. Later during the Great Depression, as a way to drum up business during those trying times, Chinese entrepreneurs opened night-clubs that featured cabaret-style entertainment, which capitalized on whites' fascination with the seductive, submissive "China Doll" image of Chinese women.[9] Of the many highlights in Chinatowns, the most eagerly anticipated was one of these sensationalized tours of underground tunnels filled with fake opium dens, gambling joints, brothels, and sometimes even mock "tong wars" over slave girls. The manufactured image of sin and evil, as well as the spectacle of the exotic, became the prime lure for non-Chinese tourists.

Chinatown was more than just a voyeuristic tourist attraction. This ethnic neighborhood served as home and community for those living in a strange land. Racially excluded from the suburbs, they had to put up with over-crowded conditions and decrepit buildings in downtown districts. Only the Chinese lived in these neighborhoods, although some Eastern European im-migrants and a few Irish women (married to Chinese men) lived in the Chi-natowns of Boston and New York. In New York's Chinatown, where in 1940 the sex ratio was still six to one compared to San Francisco's two to one, Chi-nese men lived together in small rooms and apartments. Living among friends and relatives, Chinese had at their disposal services within walking distance.[10] For Chinese men and women, Chinatown nurtured traditional lifeways even as it functioned as a defensive response to the larger hostility.

As the level of anti-Chinese discrimination increased, the Chinese re-sponded by drawing their ethnic boundaries even closer. Recent archaeolog-ical evidence uncovered in Los Angeles's old Chinatown reveals that acculturation was limited up until its demolition in 1933. Artifacts and struc-tural remains indicate the persistence of Chinese names and burial practices, traditional leisure activities, China-made food items, and ethnic-dominated settlement patterns as indicated in land use and traditional architecture. Fur-ther, Euro-American businesses never became part of the ethnic enclave's economy.

Self-employment, residential segregation, and low acculturation collec-tively did not occur by happenstance. The changing geographical distribution of the Chinese between 1900 and 1940 partly prompted the development of Chinatowns into so-called gilded ghettoes. Although only 33 percent of the Chinese population in 1900 resided in cities with 100,000 or more inhabitants, that figure had jumped to 71 percent by 1940. In 1940 the Census Bureau classified 91 percent of the Chinese population as urban.[11]

The urbanization of the Chinese population was no coincidence. Suffering from low reproduction resulting from gender-based immigration laws, Chinese communities in smaller cities or towns shriveled. Also precipitating this shift was the flight of the second generation from small Chinatowns. Striving to distance themselves from the negative image of these neighborhoods, second-generation Chinese shared these sentiments: "I have not cared much about Chinatown. It seemed such a dingy, dirty place. I went there as little as possible and think I was rather ashamed of it."[12]

Shaped by such societal forces, Chinatowns in Western cities, including Butte, Montana; Boise, Idaho; Rock Springs, Wyoming; Denver, and Salt Lake City, were slowly disappearing between 1900 and 1940. By 1940 only twenty-eight cities with Chinatowns remained, and many of these consisted of only a street, a few stores, and several hundred Chinese residents. Euro-American hostility pushed the remaining few out, and soon many flocked to metropolitan cities in search of jobs in an ethnic labor market.[13] In these cities, Chinatowns, with the notable exception of Seattle which still served as a way station for seasonal cannery workers toiling in the hinterlands, became a base for small ethnic businesses.

LABOR AND THE ETHNIC ECONOMY

Clearly, before the 1940s, Chinese were clustered in an ethnic economy holding down mostly low-wage dead-end jobs. In 1920, 58 percent of those gainfully employed were in the service industries, mostly restaurant and laundry work, compared to only 5 percent of native-born whites. Educated, second-generation Chinese women were underemployed and worked primarily in clerical, domestic, and sales jobs.[14] Immigrant (first-generation) women, however, either toiled in garment sweatshops or worked for little or no wages in small, family-run businesses where the line between production and family life blurred. The role of wives, and some daughters, in this family-based economy became more visible following the gradual reversal of the skewed sex ratio, an outcome of the 1930 amendment to the 1922 Cable Act. Few Chinese, male or female, could be found in agriculture, manufacturing (except in the garment industry), or transportation.

The ethnic economy in Chinatowns was also characterized by the dominance of people from the same district or ancestral village in a specific occupation or business. Partly because immigrants came from within a small geographical area, with many related by in-group marriages, and partly because of chain migration, members of the same district or county shared this sense of regional solidarity. In-group mutual aid and support, which immigrants relied on to make the trans-Pacific adjustment, cultivated this sensibility.

People originating from the Hua Xian district during the interwar years, for example, dominated the meat and grocery businesses in Northern California. Doumen people predominated in the growing of asters and chrysanthemums in the San Francisco peninsula. Because many enterprises tended to rely on relatives, friends, and family members as low-cost labor, kinship ties became reinforced.

The 1940 U.S. Census reveals that over 60 percent of the Chinese were manual laborers. Even American-born Chinese with some Western education did not escape this fate; 59 percent of them, according to that census, worked in manual labor.[15] Most of the rest identified themselves as either managers or owners of small businesses engaged in self-exploitation—working long hours with limited returns. In a sense, the gainfully employed Chinese were mostly laborers and merchants.

The case of laundrymen speaks to this lopsided occupational distribution. In 1870, of the 46,274 gainfully employed Chinese, only an estimated 3,653, or 8 percent, were laundry workers. By 1920, however, of the 45,614 in all occupations, about 12,559, or 28 percent, were laundrymen. The number of Chinese-owned laundries steadily climbed during the interwar years. Chicago boasted only 209 laundries in 1903, but twenty-five years later it had 704. In 1910 an estimated 4,600 Chinese laundries could be found in New York City; by 1933, that figure had climbed from 6,000 to 7,500 one-person businesses.[16]

Like countless Chinese men who arrived in America during the exclusion era and were deprived of a normal family life, laundrymen were overwhelmed by loneliness, illness, poverty, and despair. The life of Sin Jang Leung exemplified the plight of such laundrymen. The son of a Gold Mountain sojourner in Taishan, Leung, in an example of chain migration, came to the United States in the late 1930s at the behest of his father. Hoping to attain success, Leung found in New York City only arduous, repetitive labor and little rest. "I really didn't want to work in a laundry, but what could I do?" he recalled in frustration. "I was a newcomer. I didn't know the language. Where could I go?" Leung also suffered from racial prejudice, a phenomenon he attributed to the fact that Chinese Americans "look quite different—our eyes, hair, forehead, everything!"[17] Years of endless toil eventually resulted in tuberculosis, and he finished his years as a down-and-out gambler whose ties to the extended family in China had long been severed.

CLASS-BASED RESISTANCE AND THE CHINESE MARXIST LEFT

But many Chinese laundrymen did find some measure of self-fulfillment through class-based resistance, trying to claim their rights as productive members of their adopted land. In the 1930s Chinese laundries in New York City were forced to lower prices as a way to compete with increased mechanization in white laundries, which had already driven some Chinese laundries out of business. In retaliation, white laundry operators banded together as a trade organization and set minimum prices for laundry work. When Chinese laundries ignored these new rates, they called for a boycott of Chinese laundries. They later persuaded the city authorities to pass an ordinance levying a heavy license fee and requiring one-person laundries applying for a license to post a thousand-dollar bond. Clearly this bond requirement was designed to drive struggling, small Chinese laundry operators out of the business.[18]

As in previous instances, Chinese laundrymen turned to the CCBA for mediation. When the CCBA appeared incapable of effecting change, the laundrymen organized their own independent laundry association—the Chinese Hand Laundry Alliance (CHLA)—a fairly democratically run organization. More than 2,400, or about a third of all Chinese laundrymen in New York City, joined this association. With the help of white attorneys, the CHLA argued before city authorities that the bond discriminated against small laundries and, in the end, persuaded the authorities to reduce the bond to $100.

The CHLA still faced the formidable, hierarchically organized Chinese power structure headed by the CCBA which considered the CHLA's activism to be defiance of its authority. For the sake of survival, the CHLA now tried to forge an alliance of sorts with the Chinese Marxist left. By the early 1930s the Chinese Marxist left, through the Chinese Communist party (CCP) of the United States and affiliated front organizations, had established itself in San Francisco and New York City.

In San Francisco, the Marxist left, through such front organizations as the Chinese Workers Mutual Aid Association and against the backdrop of the depression, organized laundry workers, garment workers, maritime workers, and others, but with limited success. Slightly more successful was the organization of the unemployed. As the depression deepened, some of the unemployed joined the San Francisco–based Marxist left group, Huaren Shiyi Hui, which attempted to aid the unemployed by demonstrating for relief aid from the CCBA and the U.S. government.

Buoyed by New Deal legislation (the federal government's attempt to reinvigorate the economy), which granted organized labor the right to conduct collective bargaining and to demand better wages and working conditions, some Chinese workers, independent of socialist influence, broke into the labor movement. Chinese maritime workers in New York organized as Lien Yi, originally a political arm of the anti-Communist Guomindang (KMT), found acceptance from the National Maritime Union in the early 1940s. Earlier Chinese female garment operatives in San Francisco went on strike for 105 days in 1938 and through sheer determination gained a foothold in the International Ladies' Garment Workers' Union (ILGWU). Though some Chinese did gain membership into a few mainstream labor unions, the color line nevertheless persisted.

In New York City, the Chinese left faced a similar situation. Compounding the situation was a language barrier; many of the early leftists were Mandarin-speaking intellectuals, but the vast majority of the proletariat spoke Cantonese. Organizing workers was also stymied by the lack of class consciousness. Kinship ties and the absence of a clear division of labor between the proprietor and employee, a common feature of small-time businesses, ensured that class conflict would be minimal. That same absence characterized trade guilds like the CHLA, which exhibited division along family, clan, village, and geographical lines rather than class. Thus the average Chinese worker felt alienated from classical Marxist doctrines.

Workers could have overlooked the ideological agenda of the left if they had desperately needed leadership to help overcome the economic downturn of the 1930s, but this was not the case. Though the Chinese unemployment rate in major cities was significant, Chinese Americans, compared to African Americans, Mexican Americans, and others, did not suffer as severely. The segregated ethnic economy and available community resources—the outcome of Chinese exclusion and enduring discrimination—cushioned the Chinese from the full weight of the depression. Chinese American women, who held mostly protected service-sector jobs, also did their part to compensate for any loss of income by their husbands and fathers who were concentrated in hard-hit production jobs. Further, in spite of historical antecedents, the U.S. government did not exclude the Chinese from unemployment relief or any other New Deal federal programs. No wonder the Chinese left made little headway within the community in the 1930s.

KMT, THE LEFT, AND THE TO SAVE CHINA MOVEMENT

The competition of the anti-Communist KMT against the background of a rising tide of Japanese aggression in East Asia in the 1930s, complicated the picture. After the KMT had purged the Communist wing in its party and established a national government in Nanjing in 1928, it began to strengthen its control over Chinese overseas communities as chauvinistic nationalism rather than revolutionary social change began to take over. The Nationalist government tried to cultivate political loyalty and solicit financial contributions for the war against Japan. To those ends, Chinese consulates influenced the local leadership to reinforce orthodoxy in Chinese schools, and KMT agents infiltrated Chinese trade guilds, family and district associations, and labor unions. For example, when unorganized Chinese maritime workers in New York threatened to go on strike in 1936, the pro-KMT Chinese Seamen's Union drew many of them in at the expense of the Marxist left.[19]

The Marxist left, however, found an ally in the laundrymen. They shared some common ground. Both groups took a stand against racial discrimination and domination by traditional authorities in the Chinese community. What riveted them together, however, was common disapproval of the KMT's policy of nonresistance toward Japan. Led by Chiang Kai-shek, the Nationalist government insisted on *annei rangwai* (first pacification [of Communists and local warlords], then resistance). In waging a civil war and ignoring Japanese military aggression, the KMT increasingly earned the wrath of Chinese at home and abroad.

The disapproval it garnered was not limited simply to the Communists and its allies. Soon after the Japanese army's invasion of Manchuria in late 1931—also known as the Manchurian Incident—Chinese Americans, led by the CCBA, organized a *jiuguo* (to save China) movement. Major Chinatowns organized national salvation associations, which backed anti-Japanese rallies and "rice bowl" parties (large-scale events that feature parades and entertainment to raise funds), rallied the community to boycott Japanese-made goods and lobby for a U.S. embargo on all materials heading for Japan, and launched an intensive fund-raising campaign to support China. Chinese Americans also supported aviation clubs and schools to train pilots for the Chinese air force. Chinese American women, for their part, participated in fund-raising, propaganda, civil defense, and Red Cross work. Such national salvation work gave women an opportunity to develop their leadership skills and gain confidence and respect as active participants in a political movement. As women gained entry into the public sphere, the goal of women's liberation, of full equality, became less elusive. Such expressions of China-centered nationalism also suggest that traditional parochialism was breaking down.[20]

RESHAPING THE "ORIENTAL" IMAGE

This nationalistic fervor within the Chinese American community also involved efforts to gain the sympathy of the mainstream society, which was for the most part disinterested in the Sino-Japanese conflict. By portraying Japanese and Japanese Americans in a negative light (and conversely Chinese in a positive one), Chinese American patriots hoped to shatter the image of the "Oriental," an Asian of indistinguishable and degraded ethnicity. In so doing, the Chinese American image, and status, in the United States hopefully would improve.

Soon after the 1931 Manchurian Incident occurred, the Chinese in Walnut Grove, California, to give one example, distributed KMT-produced English publications castigating Japan's actions throughout this area located in the Sacramento River delta. Since both Chinese and Japanese here were either farm laborers or sharecroppers or tenants, they depended on the favor of white landowners and farmers for their own survival in Walnut Grove. Living under racial subordination, the Chinese saw the war crisis as an opportunity to push the Japanese farther down and secure the support of the local white elite. Nationalism and interethnic conflict served as the conduit for economic betterment.[21]

The *Chinese Digest* (1935–1940), a weekly newspaper published in English by American-born Chinese, like the Chinese in Walnut Grove, tried to mobilize nationalism and interethnic strife to counter racial lumping. The *Digest* sought to dispell the common stereotypes of the Chinese, such as the "sleepy Celestial enveloped in mists of opium fumes," a reference to Fu Manchu, the paragon of Chinese evil depicted in British author Sax Rohmer's popular Yellow Peril novels. To contradict the prevailing stereotypes, the *Digest* portrayed the Chinese as "average Americans" who "drive automobiles, shop for the latest gadgets and speak good English."[22] The *Digest* clearly projected a vision of Americanism that included Chinese Americans but excluded Japanese Americans, rendered here as the racialized Other. To validate this socially constructed understanding of American nationalism, the *Digest* manipulated race. It name dropped white public figures who supported the national salvation movement and quoted from or used Euro-American accounts to buttress the depiction of the victimization occurring in China.[23]

Racist sterotypes commonly used against Chinese Americans were also now adopted to create a certain unflattering image of the Japanese. In one article, contemporary China was described as "internally disorganized by swiftfooted, ubiquitous little Japanese soldiers in steel helmets.[24] This subtle depiction of the Japanese as subhuman and the unspoken comparison to insects—like mindlessly obeying ants—is reminiscent of certain stereotypes that plagued the Chinese in America.

The devious image of Chinese Americans moved off center stage when the self-effacing, asexual Charlie Chan, an oppositional racial archetype, emerged. Unlike Fu Manchu, who embodied yellow power, Charlie Chan affirmed white supremacy. First appearing in the novels of Earl Derr Biggers and then in feature films, Chan, through faithful servitude to the needs of the white society, gained upward mobility, having risen from houseboy to the middle class. A benign detective who spoke pidgin English with pseudo-Confucian aphorisms, Chan derived his moral authority from his "foreign" heritage, thus denying the American side of his identity. In this sense, both Fu Manchu and Charlie Chan shared the burden of alienness—Fu Manchu was Yellow Peril gone wild, and Chan was Yellow Peril contained.[25]

An extension of the "friendly Chinese" image of Charlie Chan was that of a humble, gentle people, which was popularized by Pearl S. Buck's *The Good Earth* (1931). A novel that showed the perseverance of a Chinese family in the face of adversity, it projected to American readers a humane characterization of the Chinese. Emotionally moved by this portrayal of the Chinese, Americans, already informed about the Sino-Japanese war raging in Asia, came to see the Chinese as a noble people victimized by the despicable Japanese.[26] As the war plodded on, sympathy for the Chinese perceptibly grew, and the threat of the Yellow Peril shifted in the white imagination to the Japanese Americans.

For Chinese Americans, the war reinforced the belief that creating a stronger China would improve their current subordinate status in the United States. Otherwise, as Zuo Xueli, a woman who spoke at one patriotic rally in San Francisco, warned, "[I]f we don't take immediate steps to defend and preserve our country [China], then I fear the future standing of the Chinese in America will be even lower than the blacks."[27] Given that belief, Chinese Americans were quickly drawn to the anti-Japanese movement. After the forging of the KMT-CCP united front, one established following the outbreak of the Sino-Japanese war (1937–1945), the CCBA, the KMT, and the Marxist left's allies collaborated, though uneasily, in relief associations under the umbrella organization, the Chinese War Relief Association, which coordinated the fund-raising efforts of about 300 Chinese overseas communities throughout the Western Hemisphere.

Such nationalist endeavors were not unique to the Chinese. Other immigrant groups in America, including the Jews and the Irish, engaged in a homeland-based political movement. But unlike the Jews and Irish, the Chinese, as a result of persisting cultural and language barriers, could pursue such activities with little or no interference from U.S. authorities. The vibrancy and long lifespan of the China-oriented movement were outcomes of the unremitting mainstream hostility toward the Chinese.

IDENTITY DILEMMA AMONG THE SECOND GENERATION

The fact that even Chinese with American citizenship engaged in such pursuits underscores that the phenomenon of assimilation fell far short of embracing this second generation. Despite the pervasive presence of American socializing agents such as public schools, churches, civic organizations, and the popular media, the progeny of the immigrant generation stood outside of the mainstream society.

Their racial origin—the visible physical characteristics of their bodies—set young Chinese American men and women of the early twentieth century apart from the larger society. They suffered social segregation, economic discrimination, and legal handicaps because of their perceived physical and biological differences. "They refused to take me in because I was Chinese," remembered David Young, who eventually was admitted into the local grammar school in San Francisco only because he was mistaken for a member of another ethnic group.[28] Chinese Americans also found themselves barred from public facilities including movie theaters and swimming pools.

Chinese American youth played sports on a segregated basis, usually with or against other Chinese or Asians. Their involvement in sports did, however, defy Orientalist stereotypes that perceived Chinese American males as unmanly, asexual creatures and Chinese American females as meek China Dolls, who were submissive and powerless. Their participation in popular American sports such as baseball, football, basketball, and even prizefighting suggested progression toward assimilation into American society, but they were still under the shadow of "racism's traveling eye."[29]

These second-generation Chinese Americans, however, had attended public schools and Christian churches where they learned about American values including equal rights and personal freedom. Taught by their teachers and church elders to accept that Chinese ways were backward and un-American, these youths ran headlong into an intergenerational conflict with their parents who adhered to a more traditional culture. Often parents demanded that their offspring learn the Chinese language and the culture of the old country by attending a local Chinese school. Both at home and in Chinese schools, Chinese Americans were exhorted to defer to filial piety and the authority of their elders but simultaneously suppress their individual aspirations.

These American youths, however, were generally indifferent to this teaching. Their indifference was the outcome of seeing America as their "home"; China remained "foreign" to them. By the mid-1920s Chinese American youngsters sported American accoutrements; Chinese girls, for example, bobbed their hair, wore sleeveless dresses, and emulated the popular flapper image of the day. Many openly rejected their parents' culture and considered themselves modern. In 1924 Flora Belle Jan of Fresno explained, "My parents wanted me to grow up a good Chinese girl, but I am an American and I can't accept all old Chinese ways."[30]

Young Chinese women, more so than their male peers, had to struggle to assert their independence. For them, gender refracted the influence of race and ethnicity. Though expected to abide by patriarchal restrictions on their movement, education, career, and matrimony, some chose to assert their individuality. These American-born women wanted the freedom to pursue a career, choose their own spouse, and base their marriage on love rather than family arrangement.

The working-class lives of women performers in Chinese American nightclubs reflect this generational shift. Their lives spanned a period of change in American women's roles. By the early 1900s, urbanization and industrialization, augmented by widening educational opportunities, gave rise to the "new woman" phenomenon. Less tied to patriarchal constraints and keen to pursue individual self-fulfillment, Euro-American "new women" of both middle-class and working-class backgrounds discovered economic mobility and their sexuality. Unlike white women, Chinese American women faced both racial and ethnic barriers in their struggle to be new women. Chinese performers, struggling against racist images of Chinese women as modest maidens and biologically alien "bow-legged creatures" incapable of dancing and singing, had to contend also with Chinese proscriptive standards of propriety which took a dim view of public displays of immodesty.[31]

Similarly, educated, American-born middle-class Chinese women, inspired by Christianity's message of equality with men in the spiritual world, and emboldened by the spirit of the new woman, resisted Confucianism which discouraged the self-development of women. Concomitantly, Chinese American women were drawn into civic participation, which the church actively encouraged for all women. The American-born women who founded the Square and Circle Club in San Francisco in 1924 exemplified how Chinese American women used Western ideas about the female claim to social leadership to address the needs of the Chinese American community through fund-raising and direct service.[32]

Caught in an identity crisis—being pulled simultaneously in the direction of both Chinese and American cultures—young Chinese American women and men sought a way out. Many felt that the two cultures were worlds apart. In an era when cultural pluralism had yet to make its mark in popular consciousness, a synthesis of both was not an option. Thus, they had to choose one over the other. Until late adolescence, most leaned toward embracing the American side of their identity.

When they moved into adulthood and began job hunting, however, they felt the full weight of racial prejudice. Of the 19,470 Chinese males in California gainfully employed in 1930, 7,773 or 40 percent were in domestic and personal service. Eight years later little had changed. (Information on Chinese females is unavailable.) In 1938 the Oriental Division of the U.S. Employment Service in San Francisco reported that most firms discriminated against the Chinese, including American-educated citizens. In that year, 90 percent of the agency's placement were in the service sectors. Some states, such as California, had laws barring the employment of Chinese Americans in certain fields, such as financial administration, law, dentistry, veterinary science, medicine, architecture, and realty to name a few. Further, Chinese were shut out from jobs that required union membership because they were barred from joining unions.[33]

Though few expressed any desire to follow in the footsteps of their immigrant parents' unrewarding jobs, many in the end moved into these very same occupations. David Chin, himself the owner of a laundry in New York, bemoaned that "even if you had an education, there was no other work than in a laundry or restaurant."[34] When writer Jade Snow Wong was still a senior at Mills College, her vocational counselor bluntly told her that she should not waste her time looking for employment in white-owned firms and should concentrate on Chinese ones.[35]

Compared to their male peers, Chinese women, suffering from sexism in addition to racism, fared even worse. Already denied college education by their parents who instead favored investing in their sons' upbringing, most American-born Chinese women ended up in clerical and sales jobs, sometimes helping out in the family business, or in self-employment. The few who secured higher education did only marginally better. Wong herself in the end chose to pursue writing and ceramics, fields in which she would not have to compete with men or be judged by her race. Even Chinese women who entered sex-typed professions like teaching or nursing encountered difficulty. Either they labored with little recognition or discovered that advancement was reserved for whites. Although the fortunes of these second-generation women were an improvement over those of their mothers, who were still overwhelmingly locked in low-paying, unskilled work, equal opportunity eluded them.

Mired in a socioeconomic milieu that relegated them to a subjugated position, second-generation Chinese Americans eventually realized that the future of American-born Chinese was fraught with uncertainty. Their claim on American citizenry was tenuous. Some began to consider China, that "alien land," as a potential place where they could apply their skills and knowledge. Others held onto their faith in American democracy and its promise of liberty and fair play. This divergence in vision became apparent in a 1936 national essay contest sponsored by the Ging Hawk Club, a women's social club based in New York City, entitled "Does My Future Lie in China or America?"

As revealed in the submitted essays, those who argued that their fortunes and self-identity lay in China acknowledged that racism in America largely turned them into cynics of American democracy. Disenchanted by the injustice they grew up with, they urged, as did Kaye Hong, second-prize winner of the contest, fellow Chinese Americans to "go west . . . to China." Conditions in China also attracted them to consider making a life there. A war-torn China wanted all the human resources it could muster for rebuilding. Consequently, the Nationalist government advertised widely in the United States for aviators, engineers, agrarian specialists, teachers, and translators, among other highly sought personnel. This campaign was somewhat effective; an estimated 20 percent of the American-born Chinese went to China in the 1930s.[36]

Though second-generation Chinese Americans attributed their return to China to the racial prejudice they had encountered, many employed the rhetoric of nationalism—the moral imperative to rebuild the homeland—as the main justification. China advocates placed the collective interest ahead of personal happiness. Their labor in China would free it from the shackles of imperialism and hopefully end prejudice against the Chinese in America.

The fact that this "go west . . . China" movement swelled to a crescendo in the 1930s was no mere coincidence. Persisting racism, compounded by a prolonged economic downturn and the immediacy of the Sino-Japanese war, served as catalysts for this ethnic identification. For the second generation, identification with the Chinese culture stemmed from their marginalized status in America. Given the social and economic isolation imposed on them, Chinese Americans had to see themselves primarily as "Chinese" rather than "American." Thus, the absorption of Chinese immigrants into the mainstream society was never progressive or even irreversible.

Still the dilemma of being pulled in different directions, of a "double consciousness," to borrow African American scholar and activist W.E.B. Du Bois's phrase, never receded.[37] This dilemma stemmed from the multifaceted nature of the assimilation process. Though they adopted the cultural behavior of the mainstream society—also known as behavioral assimilation or acculturation—they did not necessarily experience entry into the institutional activities and general civic life of that society or access structural assimilation. Becoming Chinese American clearly was not simply linear or teleological.

WORLD WAR II AND CHANGING FORTUNES

During the years of World War II, Chinese Americans experienced some tentative progression into mainstream life. Japan's surprise attack on Pearl Harbor and the ensuing U.S. entry into the military conflict meant that China and the United States were on the same side waging a war against totalitarianism. Because of this allied relationship, American images of Chinese, already undergoing revision since the 1930s, began to change even more rapidly. In place of negative stereotypes, the American mass media extolled the Chinese as polite, moderate, and hardworking. Even before the smoke from the bombing of Pearl Harbor had cleared, the December 22, 1941, issue of *Time* magazine explicitly differentiated the Chinese "friends" from the Japanese. The facial expressions of the Chinese, according to this article, were more "placid, kindly, open"; those of the Japanese were more "dogmatic, [and] arrogant."[38] In this environment, Chinese Americans found an opening for sociopolitical and economic gains during the war years and beyond. The Chinese American experience stood in dramatic contrast to the Japanese American one, which encompassed blatant racial discrimination in the form of incarceration in American concentration camps.

In response to the rallying cry for all Americans to back the fight against fascism, Chinese Americans, both men and women, bought war bonds, rationed necessities, volunteered for civil defense work, and raised funds for the Red Cross. No less profoundly "American" was their involvement in the armed services and the war industry. During the war years, 13,499 Chinese, or 22 percent of adult Chinese males, were drafted or enlisted in the armed services. Over 20 percent of the 59,803 Chinese adult males served in the U.S. Army, and a smaller percentage joined the other services.[39] Unlike African American inductees who were placed in segregated units, Chinese Americans were integrated into the military. Though they did not avoid racism, and sexism in the case of the women, Chinese American men and women had their worldview expanded and self-confidence boosted as a result of their wartime service.

Equally transformative was working in wartime industries. Because of a labor shortage, since so many men were away at war, and new federal laws against discrimination, jobs became readily available for racial minorities and women. Suddenly Chinese workers could escape the dead-end, low paying operative, manual labor and service jobs that they had been locked into for so long. In 1942 an estimated 1,600 Chinese Americans, of a total populace of 18,000 in the San Francisco and Oakland Chinatowns, worked in the defense industry, mostly building cargo ships and tankers. Chinese engineers, technicians, and skilled workers also found openings at the Seattle-Tacoma Shipbuilding Corporation, the shipyards of Delaware and Mississippi, and the airplane factories on Long Island, New York. Within a decade, between 1940 and 1950, the number of Chinese who held professional and technical jobs—deemed part of the primary sector of the labor market—had more than tripled. "To men of my generation," recalled Charlie Leong of San Francisco, "World War II was the most important historic event of our times. For the first time we felt we could make it in American society.[40] Chinese American women, in a break with ethnic traditions that circumscribed women's involvement in the public sphere, also increased their presence in all the aforementioned occupations and also white-collar clerical positions.

This turning point, however, marked only one stage in a long process of change. The specter of racism, and sexism, had yet to disappear. The contradiction between the rhetoric of waging a war against Nazi racism and the persistence of anti-immigration laws became obvious to both Chinese and non-Chinese. Furthermore, Japanese propaganda pointed out this American hypocrisy. The propaganda also made it clear that the United States was hardly different from the European colonial powers and had little intention of respecting Chinese sovereignty or independence. In the face of this attack on American credibility, and given the fact that China was an ally of the United States, the campaign for the repeal of Chinese exclusion laws began to gather momentum.

The law that Congress eventually passed in 1943, however, was more symbolic than substantive. While it did repeal thirteen anti-Chinese immigration laws, and allowed Chinese residents to become naturalized citizens, it set an admission quota of 105 Chinese persons per year. Applicants for naturalization had to present documentation to verify their legal entry into the United States and demonstrate their fluency in English and knowledge of American history and the Constitution. As a result of these regulations, only 1,428 Chinese between 1944 and 1952 became naturalized.[41] The repeal also stopped short of rejecting race-based restriction of immigration. As amended shortly thereafter, the law stated that any person of half or more Chinese "blood" from anywhere in the world would be included in this annual quota of 105. The entry of Chinese into the United States continued to be regulated on a racial, rather than national-origin, basis.

In spite of the shadow cast over the liberalization of immigration for Chinese, which in 1946 was extended to Filipinos and Asian Indians, the repeal did constitute a new era for Chinese American history. After suffering nearly a century of racial exclusion, Chinese Americans now could at the very least consider the possibility of making a claim on political equality and making America their homeland.

4

New Ties and New Lives in Cold War America

SOCIOECONOMIC CHANGES IN THE POSTWAR YEARS

Chinese American participation in the larger society during the years of World War II brought about changes that reverberated long after the end of the war, which, in turn, created fissures within Chinese America. World War II clearly was a transforming experience for Chinese Americans, regardless of gender or class background. As a result of their military service and contribution to the wartime industries, Chinese Americans altered the previously skewed dominant perception of themselves. Consequently, white hostility toward Chinese declined, some 7,700 Chinese received citizenship between 1941 and 1945, and the exclusion laws were rescinded. The repeal of the exclusion laws, though compromised by a quota on yearly admissions, led to a gradual rise in female immigration and a subsequent balancing of the sex ratio.[1]

Even as families were being reunited, a significant number of young American-born Chinese men and women, having been exposed to wartime patriotic propaganda and emboldened by new economic opportunities, were leaving behind their ties to the family-based economy and forging new lifeways connected to the white-dominated society. However, this was not an unqualified success; Chinese Americans in the 1950s still routinely complained about stymied occupational advancement owing to racism. One postwar study shows that one-third of the 337 respondents cited discrimination as a serious barrier for upward mobility.[2] Still, as some Chinese Americans established their independence away from Chinatowns and old sociopolitical structures, Chinese America became transformed. Over the next several decades, class-based lines rooted in differentiation of occupation, socioeconomic status, English language proficiency, generation, and place of origin—all of which were never absent before 1945—would further polarize this ethnic community and reconfigure social and political links within the community and with the mainstream society. In sum, the Chinese American identity became less definable and more complicated.

An obvious remaking of the face of Chinese America as a result of the rippling effects of the wartime boom and postindustrialization after the war was the redistribution of occupations across gender lines. Of the 36,000 gainfully employed Chinese Americans in 1940, only approximately 1,000 worked in professional and technical positions. A decade later, in 1950, some 3,500 held such positions in a workforce of 48,000. By 1950 Chinese men were not only employed as service workers, operators, clerks, and sales personnel, but also as managers, officials, white-collar professionals, and proprietors.[3]

The war also held the door open for women to increase their share of the labor market. Within the same decade, the number of women in the workforce nearly tripled from 2,800 to 8,300. About a fifth of the wage-earning women were factory operatives, and some were either clerical workers or sales personnel, but a significant minority were also mechanics and professionals in the private sector. By 1950 over 1,150 held professional or technical jobs compared to only 200 ten years before. Racial discrimination, however, continued to block Chinese American women's access to white-collar jobs. The labor participation rate of Chinese women in 1960—30.8 percent—was higher, however, than that of their white female counterparts.[4]

Chinese Americans were able to hold onto the gains made during the wartime years because of specific larger forces unleashed by a post-1945 economic boom. The general demand for necessities and luxuries, coupled with the war-enforced savings of millions, kept factories operating at full capacity. More new jobs opened up in defense-related industries when the Cold War between the United States and the Soviet Union precipitated a rush to increase American military power. Furthermore, the federal government embarked on an expansion of the bureaucracy to implement the multiple parts of President Harry S. Truman's Fair Deal program, supposedly a continuation of the New Deal of the 1930s. Part of the Fair Deal agenda involved massive infrastructure development, including new highways, airports, public power projects, and other facilities. As the federal, state, and local governments raised their level of involvement in national economic life, prosperity filtered slowly downward, though mostly to the white middle class.

RECONFIGURATION OF CHINATOWNS AND SUBURBANIZATION

The occupational mobility enjoyed by Chinese Americans, particularly that of the educated, second-generation cohort, eventually depleted the existing labor force in small Chinatowns. That, coupled with the rapid introduction of technological advancements, forced remaining Chinese entrepreneurs to innovate or move into another venture. For example, mechanization in the form of steam laundries and laundromats drove many old-time Chinese hand laundries out of business in small towns and led to their concentration in cities. Other laundry operators turned their attention to the restaurant enterprise, partly because newly arrived co-ethnics preferred to work in restaurants since they could earn more in fewer working hours. By 1960, for example, only half of Chicago's Chinatown's 430 laundries that had existed in 1950 remained in operation. Handicapped by the absence of economy of scale in an age of corporate consolidation of economic and financial resources, Chinese-owned cafes and restaurants that once served mainly Euro-American food folded as fast-food chains took off in popularity. The ubiquitous independent Chinese vendors and grocery stores similarly were made anachronistic by modern supermarkets in cities.[5]

In the 1950s, a housing boom occurred when the economically revitalized Euro-American middle class fled downtown neighborhoods for the suburbs. Middle-class Chinese Americans joined the exodus to suburbia, and Chinatown businesses seemed set to enter a decline. Chinese restaurants, however, did innovate. Some followed the dispersion of Chinese American families by relocating to the suburbs. Others turned themselves into chop suey and chow mein establishments and introduced the "take home" trade catering to suburbanites, working in the downtown districts, who could pick up the food on the way home.

Despite such innovations, Chinatowns in as many as twelve cities between 1940 and 1955, disappeared. In the postwar period, federally funded highway building and slum clearance for new public housing also contributed to the demise or contraction of Chinese neighborhoods. Changing land use patterns and concomitant land values determined the future of these ethnic ghettos. Philadelphia's Chinatown became physically smaller when the authorities turned the main street into a thoroughfare to help connect the city with New Jersey. Similarly, Pittsburgh's Chinatown was obliterated by the laying of a modern expressway. In 1955 the last surviving block of Los Angeles's Chinatown was demolished to make way for the widening and opening of roadways in connection with the building of the Hollywood Freeway. In other instances, for example, Chicago, the encroachment of the central business district into Chinatown—an outcome of urban expansion and the rezoning of land use—forced the relocation of the ethnic neighborhood. But the life cycle of remaining Chinatowns was considerably extended by the arrival and settlement of new immigrant families.

Working-class and immigrant Chinese families who could not afford residential mobility discovered that Chinatowns, in the wake of "white flight," had turned even more into segregated neighborhoods. Thus, even as some Chinese Americans increased their share of the economic pie or, in other words, experienced incorporation into American society, others faced the continuation of physical and social segregation and remained excluded from mainstream life. Chinese Americans, despite enjoying some success in challenging race-based and gender-based occupational barriers, were still routinely denied access to high-paying jobs. Equally important was that, fifteen years after the end of World War II, for every $51 earned by a white male, Chinese males earned only $38 according to one California labor report, in spite of the fact that college graduates were 24 percent more likely to be found among Chinese males than among their white peers.[6]

POSTWAR IMMIGRATION LAWS

In the immediate postwar years, a major departure from the restrictive, national origins–based immigration policy, adopted since the swelling of the nativist tide in the 1920s, began to emerge. The goodwill generated by the Allies' victory over fascism nudged Congress to pass in 1945 the War Brides Act, which permitted the spouses and children of U.S. citizens of the military to gain nonquota visas during the next three years. However, veterans of Asian ancestry, including Chinese, had to wait until 1947 when an amendment to the law finally included them in the provisions. The liberalization of immigration laws also came closer to fruition with the 1946 act that allowed Chinese spouses of U.S. citizens to bypass national-origins quotas and enter the country as "nonquota immigrants." Although the law applied only to marriages after its enactment, a subsequent amendment allowed wives to gain nonquota entry regardless of the date of marriage. An additional act, also passed in 1946—the G.I. Fiancées Act—permitted 5,000 alien fiancées of U.S. servicemen, including Chinese, to enter the United States within the next three years.[7]

The 1946 acts, along with the 1947 amendment, led to the entry of an unprecedented number of Chinese women into the United States. Along with that came a change in the arduous process of immigration clearance. In 1948 thirty-two-year-old Leong Bick Ha, after a fifteen-year separation from her husband, had not performed well at her immigration interrogation. After being held on Angel Island for three months with no sign of an impending release, Leong decided to hang herself. More than 100 Chinese female detainees protested with a day-long hunger strike. The resulting adverse publicity and public pressure eventually forced the Immigration and Naturalization Service to terminate its policy of detaining Chinese arrivals.[8]

Mostly wives forcibly separated from their husbands by previous immigration policy and new brides whom Chinese American soldiers had married in China, this new influx of female immigration in the 1940s helped raise the total Chinese population in the United States from around 77,000 in 1940 to more than 117,000 by the end of the decade. About 89 percent of the over 12,000 Chinese immigrants who entered the country between 1945 and 1953 were females. Between 1954 and 1960 almost 15,000 Chinese women were admitted into the United States.

Overall, during the first two decades after the end of World War II, 70 percent of the 53,044 admitted Chinese immigrants were women, and of that, an estimated 65 percent entered as wives of U.S. citizens. Also a visibly dramatic change was the balancing of the sex ratio: by 1960, it stood at 1.3 to 1 compared to 2.8 to 1 in 1940. The preponderance of younger age groups among new post-1945 immigrants—which meant the presence of a cohort at its reproductive peak—facilitated the gradual adjustment of the previously skewed sex ratio. From 1947 to 1956, for example, 76 percent of the total admitted fell within either the age group of 15 to 29 or 30 to 44.[9]

Clearly, this systematic effort to upgrade Chinese immigrants and their descendants—namely to confer citizenship on those of Chinese ancestry—stemmed from the globalization of American power, particularly its emergence as a superpower in the Pacific, and the worldwide rejection of colonialism, imperialism, and racism after the end of World War II. To counter perceived rising Soviet Union hegemonic influence in the Pacific, the United States sought allies among East Asian powers, including Japan and the Guomindang (KMT) government in exile in Taiwan. A shift in U.S. immigration policy could solidify these developing trans-Pacific diplomatic ties.

A massive reaction against colonialism, imperialism, and racism—provoked by the recent fight against Nazism and wartime and postwar nationalist movements afoot in Asia to overturn old imperialist powers—paved the way for Americans to gradually accept a change in immigration policy. Americans were compelled to reexamine the concept of the American identity in relation to their shortcomings as a nation. Nationhood was now less linked with any single ethnic derivation, and more tied to abstract values such as freedom, democracy, and equality. The postwar confrontation between Western democracy and communism also constantly reminded Americans of the national discourse to uphold self-determination and equality worldwide. Tolerance of cultural pluralism was gradually turning into a tenuous shared belief.

IMMIGRATION LEGISLATION AND THE COLD WAR

The Cold War, however, preserved residual suspicions of so-called un-American or alien behaviors or attitudes. Supposedly internal as well as external dangers loomed. Partisan politics—Republicans and Democrats were locked in a contest to outmatch each other's attack on Communist subversion so that each could gain the political upper hand—only spread the hysteria. Consequently, in the name of safeguarding the republic, Congress passed the Internal Security Act (McCarran Act) of 1950 which empowered federal authorities to deny entry to or deport aliens who had been Communist party members or belonged to Communist front organizations. Resident aliens with such affiliations could be denied citizenship. The act also authorized the president to order the attorney general to round up and detain persons considered national security risks, a measure that recalled the internment of Japanese Americans during World War II.[10]

When the Korean War broke out in 1950 and brought Chinese and U.S. troops into direct military conflict, the loyalty of the Chinese in the United States came under scrutiny. Apparently the federal government used the McCarran Act against Chinese of radical or progressive persuasion. One such case involved Kwong Hai-chew, a Chinese sailor of permanent residence status, who following his return from a prolonged stint on board an American merchant ship, was detained and denied reentry on grounds of his alleged ties to the American Communist party. Though Kwong was a labor activist—he had been president of a Chinese seamen's association and was involved in the white-dominated socialist-influenced National Maritime Union (NMU)—the prosecution could not offer substantive proof of his alleged "red" connections. Yet it took seventeen years of persistent litigation to bring about a reversal of the decision to deport him, one that hinged simply on an accusation of guilt by association.

The new emphasis on national security—mirrored in the large-scale investigation conducted into the loyalty of more than 6 million federal employees beginning in 1947 and Senator Joseph McCarthy's virulent claim that "Commies and queers" existed in the State Department—increased the momentum to revise and recodify the multitude of immigration laws in existence since the early twentieth century.[11] This process clearly reflected the belief that controlling the gates of immigration would stave off any possible internal subversion.

The resulting McCarran-Walter Immigration and Nationality Act of 1952, passed over the veto of President Truman, was in many ways a regression for immigration policy reform since it retained the national-origins system. The new legislation also discriminated against potential immigrants of Asian ancestry since only a token 2,000 visas were set aside for all nineteen countries that fell within the so-called Asia-Pacific triangle. Small quotas, on the average 100 per year, were set for each of the nineteen countries. In contrast, Northern and Western Europe received 85 percent of the annual admissions.[12] Furthermore, unlike other quotas which were set according to the country of birth, these quotas were ancestry categories such as Chinese, Japanese, and Korean. Asians regardless of their country of birth or residence had to qualify under those limited categories. In a sense, this legislation perpetuated the legacy of restriction and expressed isolationist nationalism.

However, the McCarran-Walter Act was progressive in other respects. The legislation not only permitted persons of all races to become eligible for naturalization by explicitly abrogating the 1924 "ineligible for citizenship" clause, but also demolished the long-standing principle of Asian exclusion. Through this 1952 legislation, other Asian nationalities and permanent residents, such as Indians, Filipinos, and Koreans, could also now enjoy similar immigration rights, which, in turn, has contributed to the escalating Asian inflow, doubling its share of all legal immigrants from 6 to 12 percent between 1950 and 1960.[13]

The 1952 legislation also dramatically expanded the selective system of "family and skill screening" which now gradually replaced the "ethnic screening" in force since 1924. The screening here refers to the multiple categories of admissions. One of these—covering spouses and unmarried minor children of U.S. citizens—was not limited by the yearly numerical quota. Other categories or classes, however, fell under the preference system, whereby each class received a certain share of the available quota visas for that year, and those applicants who met the criteria for the highest preference standing received the first available visas until the number assigned to their preference class had ran out. The 1952 law assigned the highest preference to immigrants who possessed urgently required technical or professional expertise and their immediate family members. Secondary preference went to the parents and adult children of U.S. citizens. Spouses and unmarried children of permanent resident aliens received third preference; siblings (and immediate relatives) of U.S. citizens followed next.

FAMILY FORMATION

Aside from the first preference, the other categories, along with the right to attain naturalization, engendered chain migration. New citizens of Chinese ancestry resorted to this preference system to reunite their family members. Thus, in the postwar period, the legal immigration flow was sustained more by family reunification preferences and by kinship networks than by economic cycles and deliberate recruitment. The immigration regulations of the Chinese government, however, also governed the rate of this flow. For example, C. Ng's daughter (name unknown) brought her father to America in the early 1960s but only after repeated attempts. Other members of the family had to remain behind in China as "hostages" so that Ng and his daughter would continue to send remittances, of which the Chinese Communist government apparently took a large percentage as a form of punishment for the Ng family's landed class background. For some mutilated Chinese families, the prohibitive cost of reunification prevented emigration. Orchard worker Wong Yow lost all of his investments on mainland China after the 1949 revolution and had to wait for nearly another twenty years before he had accrued enough savings to bring his wife over in 1968, thirty-three years after their marriage.[14]

Despite this preference system and the attending racial quotas, the number of Chinese admissions in the 1950s was quite high. Several factors accounted for this phenomenon. As mentioned earlier, family reunification provisions in the 1952 act allowed Chinese with U.S. citizenship or even those of permanent residence status to bring in spouses and children without being subjected to any numerical quota. Additional visas were also extended, using the provisions for political refugees under the Displaced Persons Act of 1948 (further amended in 1950), to an estimated 5,000 Chinese students and professors who could or would not return to mainland China because of financial reasons or fear of persecution following the fall of the country into the hands of the Chinese Communist Party (CCP) in 1949. Visas were also extended to Chinese maritime workers and visitors who were trapped in America.[15]

More Chinese refugees fleeing the rule of the Chinese Communist government—more than 2,000—were admitted following the passage of the Refugee Relief Act of 1953. Another 2,000 Chinese who had secured the necessary clearance from the Nationalist government received visas for entry into the United States. Congress further unraveled the racially based quotas when it passed the Refugee-Escapee Act of 1957, which enabled federal authorities to grant some visas independent of quota restrictions and to admit more refugees including some from China. As a result of all these additional routes of entry, some 32,000 Chinese were admitted into the United States—a figure that far exceeded the annual ceiling imposed by the 1952 legislation. Between 1962 and 1965, more than 15,000 refugees from Communist China, who had fled to nearby Hong Kong, were admitted under special provisions as refugees. Finally, the fact that more Chinese entered the country than left to return to Asia meant that, in the postwar period, the total population grew at a constant pace.

The growth of the total population and the gradual balancing of the sex ratio clearly promoted family formation among Chinese Americans. By 1960 the proportion of married persons for the Chinese—59.8 percent—had nearly caught up with that for the total U.S. population, which was 69.1 percent.[16] However, the percentage of split households for the Chinese remained higher than that for total population. Clearly, this was the lingering outcome of the separation of families as a result of the Communist takeover of China. Because most of the new female immigrants were of childbearing age, however, the birthrate jumped dramatically several years after the passage of the War Brides Act. Whereas the birthrate for the Chinese was the lowest of all ethnic groups in 1940, by 1960 it had outpaced that for Euro-Americans. Because of past exclusionary laws, however, the number of native born did not surpass that of foreign born among the Chinese until 1960. When nativity is examined by sex, the number of native-born women in that year was still significantly lower than that for men, which was a consequence of the gender-biased exclusion laws before 1943.

NEW EDUCATED MIDDLE CLASS

Though the postwar immigration wave was characterized by an overwhelming influx of wives and children, it was also marked by a significant number of young people, both men and women, enrolled in colleges and universities, who arrived either on their own or under government-sponsored or private programs. When the Communist victory occurred in 1949, some Chinese students were stranded in America. Those who relied on family support and those who held scholarships from the defeated Nationalist government found themselves cut off from their financial support. The U.S. government recognized this problem and enacted special regulations in 1951 to allow these students and scholars to accept employment in America, and soon after those who had entered before 1950 were allowed to change their nonimmigrant status to that of permanent residence.

The presence of these stranded students and scholars prompted an increase in the professional and technical category: the percentage jumped from a mere 2.5 percent in 1940 to 6.6 percent in 1950 to 20.3 percent ten years later—an overall tenfold increase within twenty years—for gainfully employed Chinese males. This increase could be attributed in part to the 1944 repeal of the 1879 California constitutional provision that forbade the employment of Chinese by any corporations, state, municipal, or county governments. By the early 1960s, the Chinese had made significant inroads into the professions of medicine, science, engineering, and teaching. In 1961 a survey conducted by the Chinese Taiwanese embassy revealed that more than 1,300 persons of Chinese descent were on the faculties of eighty-eight American institutions of higher learning, including ninety-eight faculty members in Harvard, Princeton, and Yale.[17]

This intelligentsia, along with other Chinese refugees escaping from Communist rule and, beginning in the late 1950s, the arrival of significant numbers of students from Taiwan and Hong Kong to pursue higher education, altered the occupational distribution and diversified the Chinese American community in terms of place of origin and language. Many of these political refugees hailed from provinces outside of Guangdong, the ancestral origins for most Chinese Americans before 1945. Most, unlike earlier immigrants, were urbanites and typically spoke Mandarin, which was considered a marker of respectability. Such class and regional differentiation gave rise to gradual distinctive residential clustering as seen in New York City.

In New York City, there were harbingers of what came to be known as "uptown" Chinese and "downtown" Chinese.[18] The uptown Chinese comprised the newly arrived and displaced Mandarin-speaking group. Many other members of the early uptown Chinese were the monied segment of the populace and, as far as possible, disassociated themselves from the traditional core of Chinatown. Many of those who had earned advanced degrees in the 1940s or 1950s, although suffering from some initial downward mobility because of the deficiency in their command of the English language, found professional jobs. Some of the most prominent Chinese Americans come from this rank, including the architect I. M. Pei, Wall Street financier Jerry Tsai, and Noble Prize winners in physics Yang Chen Ning and Lee Tsung Dao. Perhaps more representative of the displaced Chinese was Rose Chiayin Tsou. A native of Shanghai, she arrived in America in 1947 to study library science. Uncertain of the political climate in the future following the establishment of Communist rule in China, she chose to stay in America. Eventually she and her husband opened a restaurant in Eugene, Oregon. Her social circle, reflecting her language and educational background, included Mandarin-speaking business and professional groups.

As soon as these privileged Chinese had established themselves in America, they sent for their family members, thus consolidating and expanding the social networks that undergirded the emigration from Asia. Typically, early uptown Chinese in the 1950s did not live in the old ethnic ghettos. Aside from their upwardly mobile status, which enabled them to join the white flight to the suburbs, changes in the law facilitated their exodus. In 1947 the Supreme Court ruled that restrictive covenants in title deeds—which for so long had kept Chinese and other Asians out of white-dominated neighborhoods—were unconstitutional. This encouraged some Chinatown residents to leave the ethnic enclaves, especially as local governments gradually lifted those restrictions. Five years later, the California Supreme Court struck down the alien land laws, which had barred noncitizen Asians from owning land, and soon similar legislation in other states was also repealed. Thus those with economic means now theoretically could settle on land outside Chinatowns. Of course, de facto discrimination did not disappear completely. Nearly twenty years after that judicial decision, moving into a white-dominated neighborhood could still spark flames of racial hatred. Sam Sue, who grew up in Mississippi, recalled that the day before his parents planned to close the deal to buy a house in a white neighborhood in 1966, an irate Euro-American resident threatened to burn down that house. Sue's family had to wait nearly five years before they could build their own house on the outskirts of the town far away from any whites.[19]

Chinese America in the postwar years witnessed the emergence of neighborhoods separated from one another by class divisions as taking up residence in the outlying areas of Chinatowns came to mean a higher socioeconomic status. This flight from the inner cities seemed to parallel the larger white outmigration to the suburbs. But because of residual prejudice and for pragmatic and emotional reasons, many Chinese Americans, as did some other ethnic groups, reclustered in neighborhoods adjacent to old Chinatowns. As a result, uptown Chinese could continue to maintain networks of kin and compatriots and, in so doing, preserve (and transmit to the next generation) ethnic values, behaviors, family patterns, gender roles, food preferences, and even sociopolitical choices. The poorest, who made up part of the early downtown Chinese, however, remained in the core area of Chinatown.

WORKING-CLASS IMMIGRANTS

The uptown Chinese were quite different from the downtown Chinese, who, in the 1950s and 1960s, included recent, uneducated immigrants from the rural, southern Chinese working class (including refugees who came by way of Hong Kong) who gravitated to the old core of Chinatown to seek work and living quarters. Some older, native-born Chinese could also be found living in this old neighborhood. Most of the downtown Chinese spoke very little English, and they worked for low wages in dead-end jobs, typically as manual laborers and in service-oriented industries.

These downtown Chinese families, though newly reunited, were immediately consumed by the struggle to survive. The sudden arrival of so many women and children placed severe strains on the male-dominated Chinese community, particularly in the areas of employment, health, and delivery of social services. Suffering from poverty and continuing residential discrimination, many families resorted to living in dilapidated dwellings in the ethnic ghettos. A good number of these families were forced to live in former bachelor quarters, which often consisted of one- or two-room apartments, or hotel rooms, all typically with very limited kitchen and bathroom facilities. In fact, by the late 1960s, Chinatowns had become a frequent topic of sensational newspaper exposés; one article described San Francisco's Chinatown as an "impoverished prison . . . behind the picturesque and colorful Grant Avenue facade."[20]

In sum, the absence of a change in economic status precluded residential mobility, which supports a class-bound theory of residential location. Chinatown crowding, which early Euro-American commentators ascribed to cultural predilection, clearly stemmed from economic constraints. For example, dwelling density in San Francisco declined in the postwar years as Chinese Americans secured increasing opportunities for residential mobility.

However, some people stayed in Chinatowns for reasons of convenience to workplaces, social networks, and ethnic-oriented commercial establishments. For those who lacked skill in the English language, Chinatowns offered language (and cultural) security. A class-based theory of residential location may be insufficient to explain the lack of residential mobility.

GOLD MOUNTAIN WIVES, WAR BRIDES, AND GENDER ROLES

Living on the margins, Chinese women had to work in co-ethnic restaurants and sweatshops to supplement their husbands' meager incomes. Almost all of these women toiled for endless hours in dangerous and unsanitary workplaces, earned below the minimum wage, and rarely received any health or vacation benefits. A typical life story would be that of Dong Zem Ping. Separated from her husband for years, Dong had to pose as a war bride after the end of World War II, gain entry into the United States. Since she possessed limited English language and job skills, she had to work in a garment sweatshop, which also became her site for child care. As told in her recollections, the physical toll she endured exacted a heavy cost: "Many times I would accidently sew my finger instead of the fabric because one child screamed or because I was falling asleep on the job."[21] Through her onerous labors, however, Dong was able to help support her family of four children and later, in a classic case of chain migration, send for her China-born son, her parents, brothers, and even their families.

Gamsaanpo, or Gold Mountain wives, like Dong were generally disappointed with their new lives in America. During the war, many who had lost communication with their trans-Pacific husbands found themselves emotionally abandoned without financial support. After the war most came to the United States full of hopeful anticipation of a better life, but they soon discovered that the dream of securing a share of *Gam Saan* soon turned into *hek fu,* or adversity.

Not only did Chinese wives have to deal with the cultural gap, proscribed economic opportunities, the language barrier, and the emotional cost of trying to survive, they also had to face the challenge of sharing a household with their husbands, whom they had previously seen only during the husbands' sporadic visits to China. In this postwar period of reunification, wives complained of social incompatibility, clashing goals and values, and very often, the meager household income. Many spouses quickly became disenchanted with their husbands' endless working hours and hard physical labor, for which they received pitiful sums of compensation. "I used my tears to wash my face every day," said Lee Wai Lan, who arrived in the United States in 1946.[22] She soon discovered that her husband, who now had a white mistress, lived in a dirty house and could offer her little security. Lee, in an attempt to put that behind her, found manual work in a Chinese restaurant and soon saved enough to start her own restaurant. Some other Chinese spouses, fed up with the daily grind, chose to return to China. Though many other immigrant women like Lee managed to find self-fullfilment, some apparently failed to cope with the pressure of daily survival: the percentage of female suicides rose from 17.5 percent in the 1950s to 28.3 percent in the 1960s.[23]

Young Chinese "war brides," who generally married more acculturated and educated Chinese men, fared better than the "separated" immigrant wives in their adjustment to life in America. Most had already been exposed to some aspects of Western culture while still in China, and these young women, upon their arrival in America, slowly adapted, guided by their Westernized husbands, to the new material culture. Some even fairly quickly learned English. They wore trendy clothing, groomed their hair in the latest styles, and adopted Caucasian names. With these newly developed life skills, they were able to find employment outside the ethnic ghettos.

For both war brides and separated wives, stabilizing conjugal ties with their husbands was fraught with difficulties. Chinese men who had spent years living in an all-bachelor society had acquired recreational habits such as gambling and patronizing prostitutes that provoked heated conflict in these reunited families. Wives also had to accept the loss of control over the household budget which they had managed while residing in China. In the United States, women resisted the practice of sharing or relinquishing their authority to their male spouses, particularly over the issue of household finances. In some households, however, a more egalitarian division of work did emerge; men bereft of their spouses' domestic skills before 1945 continued to use the skills they had acquired during their wives' absence. Women, however, did not necessarily abandon their labor in the domestic realm. Though many had stepped into the wage-earning sphere, they still lived with the burden of being an unpaid household worker under male authority, and, in that sense, labor remained both liberating and oppressive. Clearly both wives and husbands were forced to grapple with a new gender division of labor.

REBELLIOUS YOUTH AND EDUCATION

Equally disruptive in Chinese American family life was the intergenerational tension between the parents and children who had just joined their fathers in America. Like their recently transplanted mothers, sons and daughters were disillusioned with their fathers' small businesses or dead-end jobs. Having been brought up in China in comfortable surroundings made possible by the remittances sent home by Gold Mountain fathers, these youths rebelled against the "slavish" nature of their parents' occupations. In addition, English language deficiency and persistent racial discrimination blocked their own aspirations for occupational mobility. As a result, a good number of them became malcontents and engaged in antisocial behaviors. Increased juvenile crime, though partly rooted in poverty, also stemmed from this general breakdown in family life.

Juvenile delinquency and the antisocial behaviors demonstrated by young people, especially among the foreign born, probably could have been minimized if educational opportunity, considered the main route for achieving socioeconomic mobility, had opened up across racial and class lines. In California the legislature, in 1947, repealed racial segregation from the California Education Code. This terminated de jure segregation in public education and also the policy of allowing local school districts to establish separate schools for nonwhite youngsters. However, segregation did not immediately recede into the distant past. Euro-Americans who disliked racial integration could and did move into so-called better neighborhoods, and school boards resorted to gerrymandering housing patterns to determine school district boundaries.

Accessibility to education was also compromised by the inability of the public school system to cope with the large-scale entry of newly reunified families after the end of World War II. After 1950 more U.S.-based parents, fearful of the impact of Chinese Communist rule and the Korean War on their children's futures, filed papers to send their foreign-born children to America. In San Francisco alone, some 1,500 immigrant boys and girls within a seven-year period (1948–1955) with little or no English language background swelled the ranks of the school-age populace and placed a heavy burden on Chinatown schools. Special classes—known as "opportunity classes" at the elementary level and "Americanization classes" in the secondary schools—had to be set up quickly to immerse these immigrant youths into life in America through lessons in English, citizenship, and geography.[24]

By 1952 Chinatown schools could not longer absorb the onslaught of the massive number of newcomers, and social problems began to manifest themselves. Compounding the situation was the fact that immigrant children often contributed to the household income by working long hours with little rest or sleep. Others had to work to help pay off the recent trans-Pacific passage. A local school survey conducted in 1952 in San Francisco reported that more than 50 percent of these immigrant children held after-school jobs, and school officials were convinced that many of them had flouted child labor laws on the maximum number of working hours per week for minors.

NATIVE-BORN CHINESE AND THE REJECTION OF THE CHINESE CULTURE

The entry of a large number of Chinese female immigrants in the two decades after the conclusion of World War II produced a new generation of native-born Chinese. These Chinese Americans, who grew up in the 1950s and early 1960s, like their predecessors in the 1930s, also suffered from racial and gender discrimination.

Of mixed racial ancestry, Betty Ann Bruno, whose mother was Chinese Hawaiian and whose father was Irish Dutch, partly grew up in California. She remembered that the swimming coach at the local high school prevented her and her siblings from using the swimming pool because the coach mistook them for children of Mexican immigrant farmworkers. Both in high school and in college, Bruno dated white men whose parents, because of antimiscegenation sentiments, forced them to break up with her. Clearly such feelings had not receded in spite of the California Supreme Court's 1948 ruling that miscegenation laws were unconstitutional. It would take nearly another twenty years before most other states repealed their miscegenation laws. After college, Bruno went to Washington, D.C., to work, where she tried to rent an apartment. The landlord had been very cordial on the telephone, but when he met Bruno in person, he told her that the apartment was no longer available. As a result of such blatant racist experiences, Bruno internalized self-hatred; she avoided identifying herself as Chinese or Hawaiian until she was middle-aged and remembered wishing she "was born looking different than what I [she] was."[25]

Rebelling against their parents' traditional, family-centered values and worldview was a way for many native-born Chinese American youth of the postwar years to assert their own selfhood in a climate where their ethnicity remained a liability and where the mainstream youth culture extolled consumerism and rebellion against conformist family life. Ben Fong-Torres, whose Spanish part of his name resulted from his father's having used fradulent papers to gain entry into the United States, grew up to become a journalist. In Amarillo, Texas, he hung out with fellow white schoolmates and drank root beer floats and listened to pop music on the jukebox. This was Fong-Torres' "way to feel Americanized."[26] Similarly, Bruno remembered how she wore "bobby socks, had the long sloppy joe sweaters, and learned to drive when I [she] was fifteen and ate at the drive-in . . . and did everything that everybody else did."[27]

Throughout his life Fong-Torres tried to juggle pursuing his personal desires and ambitions and fulfilling his filial duty to his parents—a dilemma encountered by many young Chinese Americans. In his youth, Fong-Torres dated a white female student but eventually broke off the relationship because he feared the wrath of his parents, who had not attended his free-spirited sister's betrothal to a white artist. Later he deliberately chose to attend a college close to his parents' restaurant so that he could help them by working there on weekends. The juggling resulted in Fong-Torres's writing that he wished he could explain to his parents "the conflicts we [he and his siblings] all felt, growing up both Chinese and American . . . we were torn between obligations to the family and the freedom we naturally wanted."[28]

For some young Chinese Americans, the estrangement from their parents' generation was exacerbated by the silence and secrecy engendered by the "paper-son" scheme. Because of the exclusionary laws, some parents, particularly fathers, used false identities and hid the truth even from their own children and extended families. Wong Gun Chown, the father of scholar Charles Choy Wong, had secured a slot as a son of a bona fide American citizen, and entered the United States in 1936. When Wong senior returned from a two-year visit to China in 1949 he falsely reported that he had sired two more sons (in addition to two real sons) to create new slots for sale. Wong's wife and second son, Charles, entered the country in the 1950s, but not before the duplicity had been exposed during the authorities' interrogation of the wife. In a tragic twist of fate, that exposure led immigration authorities to turn down the visa application of the eldest son who, soon after, committed suicide. This memory of a fractured family haunted Charles Choy Wong for years and probably was the cause of the emotional distance he felt from his father. Apparently, Wong junior discovered the story of his illegal family name and fractured identity during the confession program implemented by the Immigration and Naturalization Service.[29]

CONFESSION PROGRAM

This confession program, initiated in 1957, was ostensibly designed to allow Chinese paper sons and "ghosts" an opportunity to clear up their family immigration histories, which had become contorted because of earlier false claims. This program, however, actually had its origin in the Cold War fear that the fraudulent entry of some Chinese immigrants had allowed the entry of some Communists. In March 1956, agents of the Immigration and Naturalization Service (INS) conducted a series of raids to seize illegal immigrants on both the east and west coasts. Chinese American leaders protested and, probably in an attempt to strike a chord with the capitalist-minded Eisenhower administration, stressed that the raids had resulted in losses of up to $100,000 weekly to merchants there.[30]

Against that backdrop, Congress enacted the confession program, which allowed those who had gained entry through fraudulent means to regularize their status if a close relative—spouse, parent, or child—was a citizen of the United States or a permanent resident alien. Many Chinese Americans, unwilling to implicate their relatives and friends, and historically distrustful of immigration authorities, avoided the process altogether. Although other Asian groups had also resorted to undocumented migration, the Chinese engaged in this more because of their large numbers and longer presence in the United States. This postwar program consequently evoked a general panic in Chinatowns.

Equally discouraging for those who contemplated confessing was the absence of an assurance that if a confessed Chinese was eligible for an existing statutory remedy—such as the person being able to qualify for the preference system or showing proof of extreme hardship and good moral character— the paperwork would be processed in a timely fashion. Those deemed qualified for any of the remedies usually had to give up their citizenship status and wait a number of years before they could apply for and receive permanent resident status. Meanwhile their occupational mobility was circumscribed since they had no immigration status. Furthermore, they had to limit their political participation for fear of being deported on the grounds of "subversive activity." As it turned out, many were not eligible for any statutory remedy and were accordingly deported.

THE CHINESE MARXIST LEFT AND COLD WAR POLITICS

The authorities deported some Chinese Americans because they had been members of either progressive or labor-related organizations, including the Chinese American Democratic Youth League (CADYL) and the Chinese Workers' Mutual Aid Association (CWMAA). These organizations did harbor some Chinese Communist sympathizers, but many of the members of these organizations had also participated in the struggle to gain democratic rights in the United States, such as working in election campaigns for progressive candidates and mobilizing support for the passage of a fair employment practice act in California.[31]

The Marxist Left, through its publications and contacts with affiliated organizations like the Chinese Hand Laundry Alliance (CHLA), captured the attention of political dissidents and Chinese of all walks of life. Many common Chinese men and women had become disillusioned with KMT corruption and totalitarian rule which had, in turn, resulted in economic ruin and social dissipation in China over the last several decades. By the end of 1947, the situation in KMT-held territories in China had deteriorated so much that even some Chinese American businesspeople—generally considered to be the most politically conservative segment of the community— gave their support to a new North American–based united front organization. The Overseas Chinese League for Peace and Democracy in China, founded in late 1947, tried to promote democracy and oppose American involvement in the civil war raging in China.

A few other Left-oriented organizations tried to promote nonintervention in Chinese domestic issues. The CHLA sent telegrams and letters asking U.S. congressional members to vote against military aid for the crumbling Nationalist government. The Chinese section of the NMU persuaded U.S. maritime workers to boycott a shipment of war-related supplies to Chiang Kai-shek's regime. The Chinese Left also organized a number of speak-outs against Chiang and the U.S. military presence in China. When the 1948 presidential race heated up, Chinese Americans opposed to U.S. involvement in China backed the Progressive party candidate, Henry Wallace, who had criticized that U.S. policy. As the conflict in the homeland drew to a bloody conclusion, intraethnic support for the Marxist Left became ignited somewhat, only to be doused by the combined counterattack of KMT elements and the U.S. government.

When the Korean War broke out, FBI agents and immigration officials increased their surveillance of the Chinese community. The resulting intimidation became so strong that even some moderate Chinese newspapers had to fold because of canceled subscriptions and advertisements. In this milieu, KMT supporters, through its China Lobby (a conservative network consisting of Euro-American congressional members, military officials, businesspeople, and journalists), pressured Congress to offer more assistance to the KMT government in exile in Taiwan. Aside from that, KMT forces and their allies, which included the powerful House Un-American Activities Committee, eventually focused on unraveling the so-called Communist conspiracy at home that supposedly had caused America to "lose" China. Scholars affiliated with the think tank, the American Council of the Institute of Pacific Relations, and China experts in the State Department were villified in congressional hearings, including various Chinese American progressives such as Chen Hansheng, Y. Y. Hsu, and Chu Tong. The U.S. Justice Department began applying the "guilt by association" principle even more loosely when it indicted even those who sent money to relatives and acquaintances on the China mainland. U.S. intelligence, with the aid of customs officials, also blocked the entry of any goods suspected of originating from mainland China or even Hong Kong businesses linked to the mainland. Not surprisingly, remittances to relatives in China, which had amounted to $7 million in 1948 plummeted to $600,000 within a year and continued to drop.

The Chinese Left in the United States almost collapsed under the weight of all this deepening scrutiny. Some established organizations, including the CWMAA, went defunct, and others, such as the CHLA, suffered a dramatic drop in membership. Some other organizations chose to drop progressive-sounding names and revamp their missions in order to stay afloat. The CADYL changed its name in 1954 to the more innocuous sounding Chinese American Youth Club (CAYC) and shifted its emphasis to educational, cultural, and social activities.

REVIVAL OF KMT CONTROL

Because of the general political hysteria, interest in Chinatown organizations declined sharply, even in those with little connection to the Marxist Left. That, coupled with ongoing red-baiting, held the door open for a small, selective group of community leaders to control Chinatown's political and social structures until the diplomatic relations between the United States and the People's Republic of China (PRC) were normalized in the 1970s. Meanwhile, KMT agents cajoled the Chinese Consolidated Benevolent Association (CCBA) to form anti-Communist leagues in each Chinese American community. Apparently, CCBA and other pro-KMT Chinatown organizations even went so far as to assist the Immigration Office and the Justice Department in pinpointing Chinese Communist members or sympathizers.

The hostile climate dampened interest within the Chinese community for progressive, left-oriented political activities. Chinese Americans now felt compelled to demonstrate their commitment to Taiwan's government as a way to convince mainstream Americans that they believed in American democracy and that they were "not Communists, but democratic, freedom-loving people," to quote Ruby Chow of Seattle.[32] Victimized by the West's skewed image of Red China and suspected as a potential fifth column of the PRC, Chinese Americans tried to counter that image by taking part in the Guomindang anti-Communist campaign. Chinese American involvement in Guomindang activities received the stamp of approval from the Taiwanese government which, until the 1980s, never gave up the idea of "patriotic overseas Chinese" or the principle of jus sanguinis—that a child's citizenship is determined by its parents' citizenship. Since the Taiwanese government held this ambivalent attitude toward assimilation into mainstream American society, some Chinese in America could still see themselves as part of a larger China-oriented political sphere, even though the PRC had very early renounced its claim on the loyalty of overseas Chinese and encouraged them to take up citizenship in the receiving countries.[33] In the 1950s Chinese America's interest in the politics of their ancestral homeland was compelling for a number of other reasons. This situation could be clarified, perhaps, by comparing Japanese immigration after 1945 to that of the Chinese in the postwar years.

Both mainland China and Taiwan continued to send immigrants to the United States in significant numbers after 1945, unlike Japan, whose flow of immigration was small. As a result, Chinese communities in North America have continuously augmented themselves, both in terms of the number of fellow compatriots and cultural (and ethnic) consciousness. Because these new arrivals had just resided in a country marked by tumultuous events, their political sensibilities were at a heightened level. Furthermore, the unceasing instability in China—the civil war, the rise of Communist rule on mainland China, the socialist transformation, the 1960s chaotic Cultural Revolution, and the continuing political tensions between China and Taiwan—kept the attention of the Chinese in America riveted on China-oriented politics. Japan's political stability, in contrast, has done little to sensitize Japanese Americans to their connections to the ancestral homeland.

NEW SOCIAL ORGANIZATIONS

It would be incorrect to assume that all Chinese in the United States became embroiled in China-oriented nationalism in the postwar period. The diversity of the community itself, with different segments of the populace at different stages of acculturation into the mainstream society, has precluded the KMT from exerting complete influence on all social groups of Chinese America. The existence of American-born Chinese, a displaced intellectual class, the small merchant elite (or *giaoling*), and a dwindling sojourner generation (or *lao huagiao*)—which collectively is admittedly a simplification of the social structure—has led to the proliferation of new organizations. Old Chinatown organizations, with their deeply rooted traditions and ingrained leadership, simply could not accommodate all these different groups. New organizations, the outcome of a reinvigorated flow of immigration, sprang up after the war. These included alumni and professional associations, sports and social clubs, and new non-Cantonese associations.

New non-Cantonese associations mostly had membership requirements based on geographical locality of origin and dialect-group affiliation. Those established during the 1940s include New York's Fujian Tongxianghui and San Francisco's Meixi Fujian Tongxianghui, both of which drew together Fujianese who hailed from Fuzhou, who were primarily maritime workers who settled in American port cities. Those who hailed from Chaozhou organized their own Chaozhou Tongxianghui in New York around 1956. Though they provided services akin to those of the Cantonese associations, they exerted little political influence in large part because of their small memberships.[34]

Perhaps encompassing a growing percentage of the Chinese American populace, especially in the postwar years, would be the alumni associations. Membership in these organizations is determined by matriculation at the particular institution. Since most schools in China drew a high proportion of their students from the surrounding geographical area, these organizations do resemble locality associations insofar as locality of origin is concerned. Unlike locality associations, however, alumni groups tend to be a more recent phenomenon.

The outcome of the higher percentage of foreign-born Chinese with middle school and higher education in the postwar period, alumni clubs can be divided according to the locality of the schools. Institutions in the Pearl River delta, which attracted surrounding Cantonese-speaking people, such as Lingnan and Zhongshan (Sun Yat-sen) universities and Peizheng (Pui Ging) and Taishan middle schools, have alumni clubs in Chinese communities across North America. Universities and schools outside the Pearl River delta, particularly those in eastern and northern China, include such well-known institutions as Beijing (Peking), Yanjing (Yenching), and Jiaotung (Chiaotung). Because the alumni of these reputable institutions are spread all over the globe, the world headquarters of some alumni clubs are in Taipei. When students from Taiwan began settling in the United States in the mid-1960s alumni clubs of Taiwan tertiary institutions, such as Taiwan and Chengkung universities, began to surface. Such clubs are so active that in California there is even an umbrella organization called the Zhongguo Da-zhuan Xiaoyou Lianhehui (Federation of Alumni of Chinese Universities and Institutes). Finally, a few alumni groups in the United States cater to those who graduated from Hong Kong institutions such as Hong Kong University and Chinese University of Hong Kong.

IMMIGRATION REFORM IN THE 1960s

Although the two decades following the end of World War II witnessed changes in the place of origin of emigration, population size, occupational distribution, class alignments, growth in ethnic economy, and the flourishing of sociopolitical life, even more dramatic shifts occurred after significant immigration legislation was passed in the mid-1960s. Before John F. Kennedy entered the White House, Presidents Harry Truman and Dwight D. Eisenhower had tried to push, respectively, for the ending of the national-origins system and the imposition of quotas without regard to race, national origin, creed, or color. However, both leaders failed. President Kennedy shared his predecessors' desire for immigration reform and recognized the need to end the national-origins system. Kennedy consequently called for the repeal of race-based exclusion for the Asia-Pacific triangle. Kennedy's rationale for this lay in his recognition of the interdependence of nations in the growing globalization of the world economy. By the early 1960s, the transnational movement of workers, refugees, and their families had become one of the many global exchanges of capital, commodities, and information across national boundaries.[35]

Immigration reform in the mid-1960s was probably conceived more to promote economic development both at home and abroad than to rectify past injustices committed against Asian immigrants. The Kennedy and Lyndon Baines Johnson administrations certainly downplayed the impact that immigration reform would have on new Asian arrivals. Senator Edward Kennedy, a key figure in shepherding the reforms through the Senate, assured Americans that "the ethnic mix of this country [would] not be upset" and that the reform would "not inundate America with immigrants [from] . . . the most populated and economically deprived nations of Africa and Asia."[36] President Johnson, though critical of the race-based exclusion for the Asia-Pacific triangle, considered reform a necessary correction to repair historical errors made in regulating Eastern and Southern European immigration, but he was fairly silent about how Asian immigrants figured into this plan.

Given the minimal attention paid to the exodus from Asia to America, it is not surprising that the 1965 amendments to the McCarran-Walter Act of 1952 (though the 1965 bill became known as the Immigration and Nationality Act, it was in effect a series of amendments) were less than far-reaching in transforming immigration provisions for Asian arrivals. The legislation abolished the national-origins quota (along with the legislation for the Asia-Pacific triangle) system on July 1, 1968. As of that date, each sovereign country in the Eastern Hemisphere, regardless of its geographical size, received a quota of up to 20,000 per year. The applicant's quota is charged to his or her country of birth, no longer to his or her nationality or race. The Chinese now had a quota of 20,000 per year instead of 105 per year. Since the 1965 bill placed a much heavier emphasis on family reunification (reunification preferences were now ranked over occupational ones) and most of the visas were therefore reserved for relatives, policy makers did not expect that Asians in America, who had low rates of immigration prior to 1965, would be able to take advantage of the new law.

New categories for admittance were also established under these new amendments. Two occupational categories helped aliens fill jobs for which qualified U.S. citizens were not available. Additionally, under the nonpreference category, an alien who invested $40,000 in a business could qualify for immigration to the United States. Furthermore, Congress made available a process for the adjustment of status for people who originally entered as nonimmigrants—such as students, temporary workers, and tourists—and then who later applied for permanent residence. Since these categories were available to applicants of all countries, Asians were not given any advantage over other nationalities. The Chinese, however, could take advantage of a new refugee category that reflected Cold War politics, namely, the "seventh preference" for persons fleeing a Communist or Communist-dominated country.

In spite of the expectations of policy makers and their inattention to Asian immigrants, the 1965 law worked in ways that the sponsors probably never expected. First, the amendments were out of step with the general pattern of immigration. Between 1946 and 1965, only 57 percent of all immigrants that entered the United States came from Europe, and by the early 1960s, the percentage had dipped far below that figure. Fewer Europeans arrived because Western Europeans who enjoyed a high socioeconomic status saw no reason to emigrate. The Irish, the one Western European group that sought entry in large numbers, found it difficult to do so because too few recent legal Irish immigrants were available to provide the close blood kin to generate chain migration. And, of course, Eastern Europeans who wanted to flee Communist repression simply could not do so easily. Of the 4.83 million persons legally admitted between 1946 to 1965, an increasing percentage were Asians: the figure rose from 6 percent of all legal immigrants in the 1950s to 12 percent in the 1960s.

Second, Congress failed to appreciate the impact of chain migration. Growing numbers of Asians (and Latin Americans, since there was no cap on the number admitted from the Western Hemisphere until the 1965 law placed one at 120,000 annually) had arrived since 1945, and as soon as these had attained permanent resident status, a whole cohort of relatives became eligible for immigration under the second preference category. When these received U.S. citizenship, as a large number of them did within the minimum five-year waiting period, more persons became eligible for admittance under the preference system. This process continued with the bestowing of citizenship or permanent residence on each new cohort of arrivals. Since 1965 this chain migration has accounted for the vast majority of all nonrefugee admittances.

Third, the 1965 act, though it places an annual global ceiling of 290,000, is applicable only to those subject to numerical limitation. Legal immigration, which hovered around 250,000 annually in the 1950s, rose to about a third of a million annually in the 1960s, and by the mid-1970s it had reached nearly half a million annually. This pattern of consistent growth was clearly a reversal of the slowdown since the 1920s. More unanticipated would be the reversal of the direction of the emigration; instead of a wave from across the Atlantic it was and still is a wave from Asia and Latin America.

By 1960, as revealed in census data collected in that year, there were

236,084 Chinese (including those in Hawaii), which was a 67.4 percent increase since the figure for 1950. The sex ratio had change dramatically as male dominance dropped from 65.5 percent to 57.4 percent. These changes notwithstanding, some demographic facts remained somewhat the same. Most of the Chinese population was still concentrated in the West: 60.6 percent of them lived in just four Pacific states, namely California, Washington, Oregon, and Hawaii. Still reflecting the bachelor-immigration pattern, Chinese males were significantly older than Chinese females, with a median age of 30.9 years for males and 25.2 for females. Also reflecting the prewar immigration patterns, males predominated among the elderly.[37]

By the mid-1960s, obvious changes had occurred in Chinese America, particularly in the areas of educational and occupational attainment, gender roles, geographical dispersal, and reconfiguration of the ethnic economy. Overall, there was a movement toward acculturation into mainstream life, even though marginality remained a critical phenomenon, particularly for newcomers. In the post-1965 era, Chinese Americans, along with other Americans of Asian descent, would encounter numerous new challenges such as the reemergence of nativism, increasing intraethnic diversity, and the rise of panethnicity or an Asian American worldview. Yet because the growth of the Chinese American community is part of the larger unparalleled migration flow, the social meanings of race, ethnicity, and American identity will be further refracted by the overall changing racial and ethnic makeup of the nation.

Scene inside Chinese American grocery store at the end of the nineteenth century. Courtesy of San Francisco History Center, San Francisco Public Library.

Chinese Equal Rights League membership certificate of Wong Chin Foo, founder of the organization, 1897. Courtesy of San Francisco History Center, San Francisco Public Library.

Chinese American operator at the Chinatown Telephone Exchange, 1939. Courtesy of San Francisco History Center, San Francisco Public Library.

Chinese American boxing exhibition at Rice Bowl party in 1938, possibly in Chinatown, New York City. Courtesy of San Francisco History Center, San Francisco Public Library.

Captured Japanese submarine used symbolically during a U.S. Navy recruitment exercise in Chinatown, San Francisco, 1942. Courtesy of San Francisco History Center, San Francisco Public Library.

Crowded kitchen in a Chinatown, San Francisco, apartment, circa 1940. Courtesy of San Francisco History Center, San Francisco Public Library.

Chinese women in mainland China transporting goods to a factory, 1995.
Courtesy of Haipeng Li, Oberlin, Ohio.

Free market economy in mainland China, which is part of the changing context
of emigration, 1995. Courtesy of Haipeng Li, Oberlin, Ohio.

1996 Annual "Take Back the Night" March at Washington State University in Pullman—designed to raise awareness of violence against women—included the participation of Asian American and Pacific Islander student organizations on that campus. Courtesy of Asian Pacific American Student Center, Washington State University, Pullman.

Christmas potluck for Asian American and Pacific Islander student mentors at the Asian Pacific American Student Center, Washington State University in Pullman, 1997. Courtesy of Asian Pacific American Student Center, Washington State University, Pullman.

Chinese lion dance which was part of the Independence Day celebrations in Washington, D.C., July 4, 1998. Note the involvement of non-Chinese as dancers. Courtesy of Haipeng Li, Oberlin, Ohio.

Chinese market in Chinatown, San Francisco, 1999. Benson Tong Collection.

Gift store along Grant Avenue, the thoroughfare where Chinese-owned businesses cater to tourists in San Francisco's Chinatown, 1999. Benson Tong Collection.

Chinese language and cultural school in San Francisco's Chinatown, 1999. Benson Tong Collection.

The Chinese Consolidated Benevolent Association building in the Asian Pacific Historic District, San Diego. Courtesy of Antoinette Charfouros McDaniel.

Ying On Labor and Merchant Association building, completed in 1928, in the Asian Pacific Historic District, San Diego. Courtesy of Terry E. Abrams.

5

Socioeconomic Mobility and the Ethnic Economy

THE IMPACT OF IMMIGRATION REFORM

Since 1965 the rapid, unceasing flow of *xin yin min* (in Cantonese *San Yi Man*: "new immigrants") to the United States has transformed the socioeconomic mobility of Chinese America and the nature of its enclave economy. As the population turns increasingly heterogeneous and polarized by class lines rooted in differentiation of human and monetary capital, education, language, political affiliation, place of origin, previous exposure to Westernization, and cultural preference pattern, the wage-earning labor force has become less clustered within just a few sectors.

Though a significant number of Chinese Americans have experienced economic incorporation into the larger society, many have not become integrated into the mainstream society. In fact, some have not even undergone cultural assimilation (change of cultural patterns to those of the dominant society), let alone structural assimilation (large-scale entrance into the cliques, clubs, and institutions of the dominant society). In a sense, some new Chinese immigrants, especially those from Taiwan and Hong Kong, have defied the argument of some contemporary social scientists that economic upward mobility is a function of integration into the larger society. To understand this phenomenon, some background information about immigration after 1965 is necessary.

Since the mid-1960s, immigration reform has initiated several significant shifts that depart from the previous pattern of Chinese arrival and settlement before World War II. First, from the 1940s to the 1970s, the majority of the Chinese population were native born, reflecting the maturation of the progeny generation of the early twentieth century. By 1980, however, the majority of Chinese were foreign born.

Second, family immigration has characterized Chinese American life since the mid-1960s reforms went into full effect in 1968. Most of the new Chinese immigrants after 1968 came as nuclear families. In the 1990s, immediate relatives—who are not subject to the numerical limitations of the preference system—remain a substantial proportion of the total immigration to the United States. For example, among a total of 708,394 immigrants admitted into the United States in 1993, 251,647 or 35 percent were immediate relatives of U.S. citizens.[1] This family-chain migration has had an impact on the acculturation of immigrants. Since newcomers are part of a larger ethnic social network, they are dependent on its support. The Chinese community has had to respond to the needs of these newcomers, and in the process, the ethnic identity remains intact, even strengthened.

Finally, newcomers after 1965, unlike those before, include a significant number of white-collar professionals, and many arrive with their families seeking to settle permanently rather than sojourn as single men.

MIGRATION AND CONDITIONS IN CHINA

Although the Chinese migration pattern after 1965 has undoubtedly been reshaped by revised U.S. immigration policy, it has also been affected by the changing conditions in the context of exit. Following the Chinese Revolution of 1949, mainland China slipped into a period of repressive Communist rule that placed a clamp on exit from and entry into the country. Chinese citizens became increasingly resentful of their unrealized potential. Apparently those with *hai-wai-quan-xi* (relatives abroad) were treated as enemies of the People's Republic of China (PRC). They were suspected of having committed or being capable of committing treason in support of the Nationalist government or American imperialists.

One interviewee, identified only as Mr. Peng, recalled that he and the rest of his family lost countless opportunities for advanced education and job promotions because his wife's brother had fled to Hong Kong and then later immigrated to America. Embittered by this experience, Peng remembered that after the end of the Cultural Revolution, he "simply could not take it another time. This world is large—why should I be in China to make a living?" Sometime in the early 1980s, his daughter, who had married a Chinatown worker and later became a naturalized U.S. citizen, managed to get the whole family out of China.[2]

Clearly, in the wake of continual turmoil and political repression in China, the Chinese suffered from a national identity crisis. They came to appreciate the wide gap that existed between aspirations and the means to attain them in China, and they began to see emigration as the most effective means of fulfilling their wish for a better future. Furthermore, the remittances sent to China by newly arrived Chinese workers in America were seemingly convincing testimony that there was an abundance of opportunity in the United States.

IMMIGRATION AND GLOBAL RESTRUCTURING
AFTER 1965

In 1981 the 1965 act was amended—to bring it in line with full normalization of relations with the PRC—so that mainland China, like Taiwan, would receive a separate yearly quota of 20,000 immigrants. As a result of that, the total immigration from both "Chinas" rose from 25,000 in 1981 to nearly 40,000 in 1985. By then the PRC government had adopted an open-door policy and initiated national economic reform. The PRC government gradually lifted the barriers to emigration, although those with exceptional professional skills and higher educational degrees or holding sensitive positions in government or scientific research institutions are prevented from emigrating. Most applicants today still face a laborious screening process.[3]

Chinese entreprenuers and investors in Asia also secured an additional opportunity to emigrate following the passage of the Immigration Act of 1990 which was drawn up to help supply the United States with skilled workers and attract needed capital. This legislation in some ways reverses the postwar trend emphasizing family reunification because it encourages the immigration of skilled workers by increasing the number of visas for such workers from 58,000 to 140,000.

By then global restructuring—rapid global economic integration—had weakened America's postwar dominance of the world economy. Capital from the United States, as well as that from other developed nations, found its way to less-developed countries to take advantage of comparatively lower labor costs and accessibility to resources. Furthermore, developing countries in Asia have penetrated the global economy by manufacturing for export to developed countries like the United States. The result of all that for the United States in the 1980s was stagnation, stymied productivity growth, high inflation, rising unemployment, and economic dislocation. The worst recession since the Great Depression of the 1930s hit the United States in the early 1980s. Overall, the restructuring, coupled with rising productivity rates, has led to a contraction in the number of jobs in traditional production and goods-processing industries. To compensate for that, American capitalism has reorganized by focusing on the information processing and microelectronics industries and the service sector, thus increasing the number of high- and low-waged jobs. Some existing manufacturing industries, however, have innovated through task routinization (which further fragments the division of labor and deskills the workers), thus enabling them to use unskilled labor from the readily available pool of immigrant workers.[4]

To meet the challenge of global restructuring, the United States, as did many industrialized nations, chose to lure new human and physical capital by lowering the immigration bar for capitalist newcomers. The 1990 law not only more than doubled the yearly number of skill-based visas but also earmarked 10,000 of them for those willing to invest at least $1 million in a new business that employed at least ten workers. Additionally, the law provides for an annual lottery that enables the admittance of 40,000 persons per year.

Since 1965 an increasing number of immigrants of Chinese descent have come from the ex-British colony of Hong Kong. In 1986 Hong Kong's quota was increased from 600 to 5,000 persons. In anticipation of the return of the British colony Hong Kong to the PRC in 1997, the 1990 act also allowed for an increase of the quota for Hong Kong to 10,000 and then revised up to 20,000 in 1995.[5]

Some of the more than 850,000 Chinese who arrived in the United States between 1965 and 1990 had entered via new refugee provisions. In 1980 the Refugee Act was enacted to broaden the definition of a refugee beyond that of a person fleeing from a Communist-dominated country as a way to reflect the end of the Cold War. The revamped definition now encompassed those who, for fear of persecution on account of race, religion, nationality, membership in a particular social group, or political opinion, were unable or unwilling to return to their country of origin. This change in the definition has enabled more Chinese, including those originating from non-Communist lands like Hong Kong and Taiwan, to enter. The passage of the Chinese Student Protection Act of 1992, legislated in the wake of the Tiananmen Square massacre of 1989, allowed 48,212 students from mainland China already present in the United States to become legal immigrants.

DEMOGRAPHIC STATISTICS

As a result of all those new avenues of immigration, the number of first-generation Chinese immigrants now far exceeds the number of native born. The U.S. Bureau of Census estimated, in 1990, that 63 percent of the Chinese population were first-generation immigrants. This high percentage is predicted to be sustained far into the next millennium. In fact, it is likely that this percentage would be even higher if a severe backlog—the result of a high demand for visas from China—had not developed for preference categories, with the wait for some being as long as eight years.[6]

From 1980 to 1990, mostly as a result of immigration (a high rate of natural increase also played a secondary part), the Chinese population in America doubled from 806,040 to 1,645,472. Of that total, 253,719 were born in Taiwan; 152,263 were born in Hong Kong; and the rest trace their ancestral origins to mainland China. Among Asian Pacific American (APA) groups, including those from Samoa, Guam, and other Asian Pacific islands, the Chinese for the period between 1980 and 1990 were not the fastest growing. Outpacing the Chinese would be the Vietnamese, Korean, and Asian Indian. In 1990 Chinese Americans, however, constituted the largest APA population: 22.6 percent of all Asian Pacific Americans and about 0.7 percent of all Americans. In terms of total numerical increase, Chinese Americans were definitely ahead of the other APA groups and, more significantly, in the 1980s made up the third largest group of legal immigrants to the United States, exceeded only by those from Mexico and the Philippines.[7]

When all the APA groups are taken into consideration and measured against other groups in the United States, several salient facts emerge. Although APAs made up only 2.9 percent of the total U.S. population in 1990, it had increased by a little more than 95 percent from 1980 to 1990, growing from approximately 3.7 to 7.3 million. African Americans constituted 12.1 percent of the total population in 1990 but saw a net gain of only 13.2 percent during the previous decade. Hispanics, which composed 9 percent of the total population, grew by 53 percent during the 1980s. Finally, whites, which made up 80.3 percent of the total U.S. population accounted for a meager increase of 6 percent during that decade.[8]

Asian Pacific Americans are one of the fastest growing groups in the United States today. Social scientists and scholars predict that the APA population will continue to see rapid growth well into the next century with a projected growth of at least 17.9 million by the year 2020, which would be a 145 percent increase from 1990. A large percentage of this group will be made up of Chinese Americans.[9]

GEOGRAPHICAL DISTRIBUTION

In terms of geographical dispersion, Chinese Americans, as well as other APA groups, continue to maintain bicoastal immigration with only marginal representation in the Midwest and South. Another continuity is the choice of state for residency. The top three states of intended residence for Chinese between 1990 and 1993 in descending order were California, New York, and New Jersey. Numerically most Chinese in 1990 lived in California, New York, and Hawaii. Chinese Americans, like other APA groups, are gravitating to the states where co-ethnic communities, shaped by historical recruitment of Asians for labor, are already well established.

Reflecting its historical legacy, contemporary Chinese America has also remained highly urbanized. Among immigrants from mainland China and Hong Kong, the top three metropolitan areas of intended residence in 1991 in descending ranking were New York, San Francisco, and Los Angeles. The preferences for immigrants from Taiwan were a little different: Los Angeles, New York, and San Jose.

To some extent, the divergence in city preferences that still persists today reflects the composition of the migration flows and the concomitant occupations desired. The Taiwanese flow includes a significant number of highly skilled or professional workers. Many of them have chosen to settle in Los Angeles and outlying areas because of the availability of opportunities in high-technology and aerospace industries and its Asia-Pacific business environment. However, much of the recent exodus from mainland China and to a lesser extent Hong Kong consists of either those of middle- or working-class background with little human capital (education, job experience, and English proficiency); therefore, flocking to New York or San Francisco to take advantage of a burgeoning ethnic economy, knitted by kinship networks, which offers jobs and small-time business opportunities is to be expected.

Urban residence has been the choice for most newcomers because entry-level jobs are far more accessible in large cities. Moreover, Chinese immigrants converge on cities to take advantage of the social and economic support of their ethnic community. Finally, the family-chain network character of Chinese immigration also helps to maintain the pattern of settlement since subsequent arrivals simply concentrate in cities where existing kinship networks are already in place. Sometimes a concerted marketing campaign by Chinese realtors and developers has led to the growth of a Chinese-dominated neighborhood or suburb; an example would be Monterey Park, California, where, as of 1990, 37 percent of the population were Chinese compared to only 15 percent in 1980.[10]

A departure from the past, which stems from population pressure on old Chinatown, lies in the rapid takeover of outlying areas of Chinatowns that used to be heavily white rather than concentrating in the core and then dispersing later. Examples include Flushing in Queens for New York and Monterey Park for Los Angeles (some have spilled over into Alhambra, Westminister, and Garden Grove), both of which feature substantial numbers of Taiwanese immigrants; and the Richmond district for San Francisco, where Hong Kong newcomers have converged after 1965.

Within urbanized areas, residential choice varies according to the group in question. Taiwanese immigrants tend to settle in suburban communities, but most new mainland Chinese and those from Hong Kong, at least initially, converge in inner-city neighborhoods. This discrepancy can be ascribed partly to the socioeconomic status factor. Taiwanese immigrants, given their higher education and better paying jobs, can disperse to suburbia; mainland Chinese immigrants, with less human capital and resources, have to concentrate in Chinatown to access the co-ethnic support system. However, residential patterns are tied not simply to higher socioeconomic status but also to factors associated with bonds of family and kinship and the economic enclave. Those who have left Chinatown rarely sever the social relations rooted in the enclave. Residential dispersion has, in effect, resulted in decentralized ethnic enclaves or satellite Chinatowns, with strong political, economic, and social ties to the original enclave. Thus residential decentralization has not necessarily led to cultural assimilation.

EDUCATED, HIGHLY SKILLED IMMIGRANTS

Statistically, the Chinese in the United States seemed to be highly successful; in 1990, almost twice as many Chinese than whites were employed in white-collar work, including professional, managerial, and technical positions. However, such statistics are less impressive when occupational distribution based on nativity is taken into consideration. The percentage of native-born Chinese in white-collar occupations in 1990 was higher than that of the white population: 77 percent compared to 59 percent. Foreign-born Chinese, however, do not enjoy the same advantage. For them, the bipolar occupational structure, or the clustering of workers in professional and managerial occupations as well as low-paying service sector jobs, has occurred with relatively few in between. This bipolarity has been the outcome of a bimodal distribution of educational background. For example, 31 percent of the adult immigrants from mainland China in 1990 have college degrees, but 16 percent of them have less than a fifth-grade education.[11]

The overall employment profile for Chinese in the United States is partly rooted in immigration policy. The third category of preference visas—members of the professions or those with exceptional ability in the sciences or the arts—and the sixth preference—skilled and unskilled workers that are in short supply—have offered a window for many educated, skilled Chinese who did not have relatives in the United States.[12] In 1969, 21 percent entered in the categories for professionals, and 61 percent entered in the family categories. Admittedly the proportion who entered via the professional and occupational categories did decrease after the mid-1970s but only because of a 1976 law that required all professionals to first secure a job offer from an employer. Furthermore, by the 1980s, professionals were resorting to family preferences to petition for the entry of their relatives, thus swelling the number entering through the family provisions. By 1985 only 16 percent entered in the professional categories compared to 81 percent as family members.[13]

In spite of the steady decline of those entering under the professional provisions, the absolute number of professionals and executives has increased, particularly those from Taiwan. For example, though more than twice as many immigrants from mainland China entered in 1989, Taiwan had more occupational immigrants. The following year, 83 percent of the PRC immigrants entered under family preferences while 42 percent of the Taiwanese came under occupational categories reserved for highly skilled individuals and their families. By 1990 some 36 percent of all gainfully employed Chinese were engaged in managerial and professional occupations, of which a significant number were foreign born. The high percentage of professionals and managers reflects a larger trend; for example, one third of all engineers with a doctorate working in American industry in the 1980s were immigrants, and of that pool, about a quarter were Asian Americans or Asians.[14]

A number of these highly skilled Chinese immigrants, encouraged by the reputation of American higher education, entered the country on a F-1 visa (student) and pursued graduate studies, but many hoped to remain in the United States by adjusting their status to permanent residency. For example, between 1961 and 1981, only 15 percent of the 86,000 persons of Taiwanese nationality who went overseas to study returned, and the large majority of these immigrated to the United States.[15]

Chinese professionals and managers in Asia have become interested in relocating to America partly as a result of the fallout from global restructuring. To maintain cheap labor policies, Asian countries have restricted social spending and consequently jobs in the public sector. Furthermore, the homelands are still in the throes of expanding employment in the private sector and opportunities are limited. Nevertheless, these countries have Westernized their higher education in the scientific and technical fields, thus increasing the pool of highly skilled, but unemployed, labor.

ARRIVALS FROM TAIWAN AND HONG KONG

Highly skilled workers in Asia have also been lured to immigrate to the United States by certain country-of-origin-specific reasons. In Taiwan, an authoritarian regime continues to be in control of the island republic. Complicating the political quagmire is the unabated threat of a military attempt by the PRC to regain control of the island republic. The number of Taiwanese who applied for visas to come to the United States jumped dramatically after Taiwan left the United Nations in 1971 and, again, after President Jimmy Carter established diplomatic relations with mainland China in 1979 and concomitantly terminated official ties and a mutual security treaty with Taiwan. The specter of an imminent PRC takeover has continued to cast a pall of uncertainty over the island republic. Immigrating to the United States, a politically stable country committed to anti-Communism, appeals to many Westernized Taiwanese. David Tsai, who was born in China but fled with his family to Taiwan after the 1949 Communist victory, observed that those who emigrated were "looking out for the future and also for their children," as they did not want them "to be brought up in war." Recent outward direct investment from Taiwan, concomitant with the migration flow, has grown so rapidly that it somewhat shook confidence in its currency during the 1980s and sent unemployment and underemployment rates spiraling upward.[16]

Likewise, the then impending handover of Hong Kong to the PRC in 1997 has encouraged brain drain and capital flight. According to the findings of one research study conducted in 1988, 38 percent of the surveyed managers and professionals revealed that they were prepared to leave in the coming nine years.[17] The Tiananmen Square massacre of 1989 exacerbated the uneasiness felt by Hong Kong residents—many of whom used to be mainlanders who had illegally escaped Communist rule—and thus played a part in accelerating immigration to America. Clearly many were worried about losing personal freedom and the free enterprise system after Hong Kong was returned to China. Additionally, a smaller migration outflow from Hong Kong, as well as from Taiwan, can be ascribed to the perceived need to have children educated in the United States, where the bar for entrance into college education is much lower than in Asian countries.

Hong Kong residents contemplating emigration tend to be young, educated, middle- or upper-middle-class people. Thus Hong Kong emigrants, unlike those from mainland China, tend to be more urbanized and more frequently exposed to Western culture. Generally they have transferable work experience, and some possess necessary monetary capital. Thus some Chinese, in a refutation of the conventional understanding of emigration as the outcome of "income differentials" (people move from low-income areas with abundant labor force to high-income areas where labor is scarce), emigrated more to enjoy political stability and secure the future well-being of their families rather than because they were mired in poverty and unemployment in their place of origin.

OCCUPATIONAL BARRIERS

A number of immigrants who fall into the professional category experience downward mobility upon arrival in the United States because of a poor command of English, the lack of transferable skills, a difficulty in securing professional licensing, the absence of American middle-class "cultural resources" (values, mannerisms, lifestyle, and symbols), and racism. The fact that the percentage of recently arrived Chinese immigrants employed in the professions is generally far below their share of college graduates is indicative of this dilemma. It is not uncommon for former doctors, teachers, accountants, and engineers to take jobs as janitors and waiters when they first arrive. In China, Tom Wing Wah had been a professional with a college degree in physics. When she arrived in the United States in 1976, she initially worked on an assembly line in a factory. She recalls, with a tinge of bitterness, "We are college graduates, but we are working in sewing or electronics factories. We all have taken a big step backwards in our profession or work."[18]

Even those who never experienced any occupational downgrading or who eventually secured a job that fell into the professonal or managerial category often encountered ethnic or gender stratification at work that relegated them to the less prestigious jobs within a given industry. They face barriers for promotion into management positions or suffer from the "glass ceiling." For example, even though Chinese and other Asians are well represented in high-technology professional positions in the Silicon Valley—an estimated 21.5 percent according to one early 1990 study—only 12.5 percent of them were in management positions.[19] Another contemporary survey of the same area reveals that 66 percent of the respondents claimed that their promotion was blocked because of their race.[20]

Of course, other factors exist for the glass ceiling. In one 1987 study, 238 Chinese San Francisco respondents of highly educated backgrounds ascribed the glass ceiling to corporate culture, management insensitivity, and weak language proficiency, in addition to racism.[21] However, there is no doubt that race remains a formidable barrier. The "victims" of a bipolar understanding of race relations, Chinese Americans are not promoted as frequently as African Americans through affirmative action programs, and yet they are not considered as desirable as white executives. Asians are regarded as the highly successful minority group—the "model minority"—and so the question of a glass ceiling seems moot. But Asian Americans are also not regarded as aggressive enough to exercise effective leadership in the workplace.

The workplace environment lately has become even more hostile since discrimination based on workers' English language proficiency, accent, and desire to speak another language has become a common phenomenon. The arrival of a significant number of newcomers who possess varying levels of English language proficiency has been matched by the growing trend of language discrimination. Prospective Chinese employees in the past were disqualified because they failed to pass employment tests that demanded English proficiency even though such proficiency was unnecessary for success in the particular job. Chinese employees have also been subjected to English-only rules in the workplace even though they are sometimes not justified by business necessity. Others have been reprimanded or even fired because of their accent.[22]

Chinese Americans are fighting these biases by adopting certain advancement strategies, such as participating in business-sponsored social functions, cultivating mentors, improving their interviewing skills, and educating employers about existing social biases against Asians. Some Chinese Americans have even resorted to judicial or legal processes to seek redress for their grievances.

For example, in 1988, Angelo Tom, a fifth-generation Chinese American who had worked at the U.S. Department of Housing and Urban Development's (HUD) San Francisco regional office for nearly a decade, was turned down for promotion to the position of supervisor of his unit. The woman chosen for the promotion had less experience than Tom. Before Tom was considered for this promotion, qualified Asian Americans had previously been rejected for upper-management positions in HUD's San Francisco office. HUD alleged that Tom, like the others before him, lacked leadership or interpersonal skills and was too technically oriented for the new job. At the U.S. Equal Employment Opportunity Commission (EEOC) hearing, witnesses refuted that allegation. The presiding administrative law judge agreed and awarded Tom back pay, a retroactive promotion, and attorney's fees.

Chinese American women and men are still less represented in the more prestigious professions—physicians, judges, dentists, and lawyers. In addition, they typically still receive lower wages than white men; in 1990, highly educated Chinese American and other Asian men who worked full time earned about 10 percent less than white men, even though the former were much more likely to have a graduate degree. Chinese and other Asian women fared even worse; they earned about 30 percent less than white men with similar backgrounds.[23] Chinese women, on the whole, receive less economic return than Chinese men, even though their labor force participation leaped from 44.2 percent in 1960 to 59.2 percent in 1990. To some degree, this gender differentiation in income earnings is rooted in the fact that there are more men than women in the professional and managerial class, even though in 1990 nearly a third of the Chinese American women were in the professional or managerial class.[24] In the earlier cited study of 238 respondents, 39 percent of them were women and nearly all reported sex discrimination and work-family conflicts as significant barriers for upward mobility.[25]

These gender-determined socioeconomic patterns most likely have somewhat reshaped gender relations between middle-class women and men. Chinese female professionals, given their earnings, need not depend solely on their spouses for economic survival. Their contribution to the family income has offered them some leverage to negotiate for more male participation in household labor. One study of Taiwanese immigrants in New York revealed that the degree of male spouses' involvement in household labor differed considerably along class lines; those in the professional class bear a larger share than those in the working or small-business classes. These conjugal relations however are not egalitarian in sex-role arrangements because women still perform more of the household task than their husbands. Furthermore, professional women generally cannot rely on female, co-ethnic social networks for material and emotional support because most of them live in white-dominated, suburban neighborhoods.

THE SELF-EMPLOYED AND ETHNIC ENCLAVE ECONOMY

A second group of identifiable participants in the labor force would be the self-employed. Some of the self-employed Chinese in the United States were once professional people in Asian countries. Frustrated by blocked economic opportunities in the United States and handicapped by language difficulty, some chose the path of small-time, ethnic-oriented business ownership. For example, some Chinese subcontractors work for large, high-technology firms in the Silicon Valley producing component parts ranging from circuit boards to graphics cards. Many of these subcontractors once worked as engineers or low-level managers and became tired of being passed over for promotion and decided to leave their mainstream careers. In sum, self-employment has been a way for some Chinese to get around labor-market barriers.

The growing Asian American population, a source of labor and an untapped market for goods and services, lures potential Chinese entrepreneurs into this form of economic adaptation. Apparently, in the Chinese enclave economy, there is a strong interdependency among co-ethnic suppliers or owners and customers—known as ethnic integration—particularly in the finance, insurance, and real estate industries and the service sector. An indicator of this is that, in San Francisco county alone, there were in the early 1990s 9,028 Chinese firms serving a Chinese population of 127,140, which averaged to about one Chinese firm per fourteen Chinese people.[26]

Social scientists have also argued that ethnic entrepreneurship is a manifestation of the national restructuring of capitalist development. By reinvesting capital, recruiting marginalized labor, and increasing the number of small firms so that production and marketing can be more flexible, ethnic entrepreneurship can be considered as a specific response to changing circumstances in U.S. urban economies.

After Korean Americans, Chinese Americans have the highest self-employment rate of any immigrant group. One 1987 government report enumerated 89,717 Chinese-owned firms in the United States, reflecting a 286 percent increase between 1982 and 1987 compared with a 14 percent increase for all firms in the entire country.[27] Chinese American entrepreneurship is represented in just about every venture. Aside from the conventional mom-and-pop grocery stores, gift shops, laundries, and restaurants, entrepreneurs are involved in larger ventures such as clothing manufacturing, publishing, banking, jewelry, fast foods, legal and insurance services, medical equipment, designing and manufacturing, fashion designing, and high-technology industries. Since the 1960s the ethnic enclave economy has dramatically diversified from small-scale service operations into the manufacturing, wholesale, consumer, and professional trades.

Most Chinese American businesses are small and involve minimal capital. A number of these businesses rely simply on personal family savings and money borrowed from a network of kinship ties. However, it is not uncommon for Chinese entrepreneurs to take out loans with banks, often Chinese-owned banks, such as the Cathay Bank, the United Savings Bank, and the Bank of Canton. Certainly there is no shortage of Chinese-owned banks; between 1979 and 1992, seventeen new ones opened in Los Angeles. Their clientele is made up predominately of Chinese and other Asians; unlike certain immigrant ventures before 1945, such as laundries and restaurants, they do not necessarily depend on nonethnic customers to survive.

Many of these ventures have opened new opportunities for immigrant workers. In New York City, for example, Chinatown's restaurants employed, in the early 1980s, nearly 15,000 workers, mostly men. Some 20,000 immigrant Chinese women found work in some 500 factories in the Lower East Side of Manhattan, the extended Chinatown area.[28] Admittedly, many of these jobs involve long hours and pay very little. However, some working-class newcomers, with little education or English language competency, are satisfied with these wages, which are comparatively higher than those in mainland China for the same type of work. "I found a job washing dishes in a Chinese restaurant," said an unidentified Chinese male cook. "I received $300.00 for my wages in the first month. You know that a professor in Taiwan could not even earn that kind of money. I would have liked to have come earlier if I knew that it was so easy to earn big money here."[29]

Testimonies such as these have been used by certain scholars to point to the existence of a reciprocal relationship within the ethnic enclave whereby both employers and employees benefit from their involvement in this economy. Rejected by the host or mainstream society, members of a given ethnic group retreat into own communities where they can rely on ethnic solidarity to offer security, protection, and economic advancement. According to this enclave-economy theory, the low-wage labor force enables small enterprises to compensate for the lack of economy of scale.[30] Chinese entrepreneurs, however, are clustered in these marginally profitable, highly competitive, and labor-intensive enterprises precisely because they lack capital and skills. As a result of these circumstances, most businesses turn in rather low net profits and constantly run the risk of going under.

The enclave-economy theory does not point out another downside of Chinese immigrant entrepreneurship: it has contributed to the strain of urban race relations. These entrepreneurs, especially those who run large operations, exploit disempowered non-Chinese labor, including undocumented immigrants; compete over urban space with non-Asians, forcing real estate values and rents to climb; and engage in exploitative retail trade (such as opening liquor stores in poverty-stricken neighborhoods).

Ethnic entrepreneurship also involves class and gender exploitation. Workers are typically paid below minimum wage level and their jobs rarely lead to upward mobility. The involvement of female family members in these establishments probably has reinforced their isolation from the larger society. As unpaid family labor, wives and daughters remain dependent upon husbands and fathers for economic support and stay unattuned to other gender-role paradigms in the larger society.

TRANSNATIONAL CAPITAL

Many Chinese enclave establishments are hardly isolated from the dominant economy; they transcend ethnic lines in their business activities, and their circle of customers and employees has enlarged to encompass non-Chinese. Thus the enclave economy is not unconnected to the larger world.

Some Chinese immigrants in the United States, especially owners, executives, and investors of major transnational businesses, have established bases in the American economy as a way to move their capital gradually out of politically unstable Hong Kong or Taiwan (or even Southeast Asia) and eventually immigrate to the United States. Most have entered the United States either through the investor migration provision or by being intracompany transferees. Although intracompany transferee is a nonimmigration status, such visa holders can apply for immigration after the operation of the subsidiary is proven to be sustainable.[31]

The entire process of upgrading from nonimmigrant to immigrant status became more expedient for business owners or investors when new legislation in 1990 allowed intracompany transferees to apply directly for an immigration visa under a special category with an annual quota of 40,000. Of course, some business immigrants, including professional ones, have entered America via family categories.

Because of the loopholes, some Chinese subsidiaries in the United States are designed to obtain legal residency rather than to do business as illustrated in this story of an unidentified Chinese immigrant. "I owned a toys [*sic*] factory in Hong Kong. . . . Then, we moved to Los Angeles. In order to maintain my L-1 visa and apply for immigrant status later, I have to import a certain amount [of toys] . . . regularly from Hong Kong to show my business is doing well."[32]

A good number of Chinese owners have also relied on their family members, often second-generation members who are pursuing studies in the United States, to identify and establish their transnational operations ranging from real estate investment to hotel chains. Mr. Lee, the second son of a watch manufacturer in Hong Kong, recalled his immigration to America as part of his father's business strategy: "I was studying at U.S.C. [University of Southern California] then, so he asked me to do marketing as a part-time job. In only a few years, I was able to establish a solid business, so my father decided that after graduation I should settle in Los Angeles and continue the operation."[33]

The involvement of this new wave of privileged immigrants has revitalized Chinatown's economy and given it the character of structural duality. Aside from an enclave protected, somewhat stabilized, sector serving a mostly ethnic clientele, such as restaurants, grocery stores, and service-oriented establishments, there is an enclave export sector, such as the garment and high-technology industries, that services unstable demands generated by the larger consumer market, both within the United States and abroad.

Some of these privileged Chinese immigrants do not even have to depend on the ethnic economy. Hong Kong hotel tycoon Lawrence Chan is president of Park Lane, which owns hotels around the world, including some in the United States. A few wealthy Hong Kong immigrants have bought many of the posh downtown office buildings in San Francisco; others have taken control of formerly white-owned retail chains.

ATYPICAL IMMIGRANTS

In sum, the privileged Chinese in the post-1945 era, who drive Mercedes cars and converse in Mandarin or Cantonese in American cities, do not fit the typical portrait of the "good" immigrant, who is poor and grateful to be in the land of opportunity and who moves through the expected stages of incorporation and economic and geographical mobility. The Chinese of the early labor immigration of the late nineteenth century and early twentieth century took two or three generations to penetrate the middle class. But the immigrants since 1965, in the minds of white Americans, have moved quickly and directly into middle-class status. A white resident of Monterey Park, California, offered some observations on this monied segment of the new wave of Chinese immigration: "Before immigrants lived in their own neighborhoods and moved into ours after they learned English, got a good job, and became accustomed to our ways. Today, the Chinese come right in with their money and their ways. We are the aliens."[34]

The resentment expressed here was rooted in the overturning of the traditional pattern of ethnic stratification. In the mid-1980s white residents (and some established Japanese American and Latino residents) in Monterey Park began to feel threatened by the physical markers of the burgeoning ethnic economy, such as new condominiums, the growth of new ethnic-oriented stores with their Chinese signs, and the increasingly congested streets. These markers of a visible Chinese presence reminded them that this community was no longer theirs to control. Soon anti-immigrant nativism reared its ugly head.

Local politics in Monterey Park became centered around the issue of economic development and lines were drawn within this fractured community. In 1986 the Monterey Park city council passed an English ordinance that made English the city's official language. Then an antidevelopment movement mounted by longtime residents successfully removed pro-development members from the council. Following that, the city council placed limits on residential and commercial development, which affected mainly the Chinese. The Chinese, however, have not simply taken this without a fight. Chinese business owners mobilized and established an organization to oppose the English-only and antidevelopment ordinances through the electoral and judicial processes.

Some of these business owners or investors and even some professionals have chosen to return to Asia after securing the green cards, but they leave their wives and children in the United States. This transnational phenomenon typically takes place when the immigrants in question became disenchanted with the economic limits of the United States. The glass ceiling has engendered reverse migration. Rapid economic growth in Asia in the last few decades has also opened up a myriad of opportunities previously unavailable, and more immigrants are returning to their homelands to take advantage of that context. For the sake of the education of their children, however, the male head of the household usually leaves the children and the spouse behind in the United States. This practice of leaving the family behind and flying back and forth between Asia and America has become a noticeable trend. On August 22, 1993, the *San Jose Mercury News* estimated that 30 percent of the Taiwanese immigrant engineers who used to work in the Silicon Valley have returned to their homeland for better economic opportunities.[35]

WORKING-CLASS CHINESE

For ethnic entrepreneurship to be successful, business owners count on the loyalty of their co-ethnic employees and are, in turn, supposed to be concerned about the welfare of their employees. But workers in Chinese firms often find this situation difficult in spite of the intertwining of family and kinship ties with the employer-employee relationship. The rupture stems from the economic exploitation that has become part of contemporary immigrant entrepreneurship. The life of the working-class Chinese typically involves exploitation in the form of no overtime pay, no vacation or sick leave, no health or occupational safety benefits, and no job security. Working-class Chinese are also overrepresented in a few industries in the secondary sector of the economy, namely dead-end jobs that are labor intensive, sometimes seasonal in nature, and generally carry little or no social prestige.

Chinese American women, in comparison to white women, are overrepresented in low-mobility occupations. For example, Chinese women, along with Korean and Vietnamese women, are overrepresented in the garment labor force and also in services, clerical work, sales, and domestic household work. In the San Francisco Bay area, the garment industry employs over 25,000 workers of whom more than 80 percent are of Chinese ancestry and the vast majority are women. A report prepared by the International

Ladies' Garment Workers' Union (ILGWU) in the early 1980s estimated that New York City had over 400 Chinese-owned garment factories that employed more than 20,000 workers, many of which were women.[36]

This lopsided situation has been the outcome of several factors. The availability of a supply of immigrant labor has encouraged the garment industry to transform Chinatowns of New York City and San Francisco into sites specializing in garment production, particularly the volatile markets of women's wear and casual wear. Garment factory operators or their subcontractors prefer women because they consider women, in a classical case of sex typing, more suited for the detailed and routinized tasks demanded by sewing. There is also the perception that these women are working for "pin money"; they can be hired and fired in accordance with the seasonal demand for labor.

For many Chinese women, particularly the foreign born or newly arrived, the dialectic relationship between work and family remains central to their identity. Chinese women are interested in garment labor because it fits in well with their dual role as household worker and wage earner. The flexible or informal work culture of the industry allows women to supervise their children at the workplace or carry out chores at home or do both on a daily basis. Many women, often paid on a piecework basis, can do the sewing at home and still be close to their social network and ethnic amenities. Bernice Tom, fifty-six years old at the time of her interview, arrived in the United States as part of the wave of *gamsaanpo* in the 1940s and has worked in the industry since she arrived: "I liked working here because I can go home anytime. This was important when my children were small. I like being in Chinatown and I like the flexible hours, the independence. I can visit my friends and go shopping."[37]

Tom's comments indicate that, though she had gained some measure of independence, she still is responsible for the domestic realm. Like Tom, most Chinese working women see their work as a contribution to the family's income but rarely use this opportunity to transform radically the patriarchal family system. Work for them is seen as an extension of family obligations. Most of the women, however, are probably unsatisfied with their dead-end jobs; one study published in 1982 discovered that 84 percent of the 108 working women interviewed expressed little satisfaction with their current dead-end jobs.[38]

Because many of these women work for co-ethnic contractors, there is often a personal working relationship, which opens the door for more exploitation through longer working hours, subminimum wages, lack of overtime wages, the use of child labor, and hazardous job conditions. Thus the workplace in these garment sweatshops is a minefield of undesirable challenges. Paternalism and sentiments of ethnic loyalty sometimes make workers hesitate to vocalize their grievances or see the relationship as exploitative. Their participation in the labor movement is therefore marginal.

While Chinese women are overrepresented in the garment industry, Chinese men are located largely in restaurants. Because recent immigrants have yet to master English, most find themselves locked in these low-wage jobs as waiters, busboys, or cooks. Danny Lowe explained what happened to him: "Before I was a painter in Hong Kong, but I can't do it here, I got no license, no education. . . . I want a living, so it's dishwasher, janitor, or cook."[39] Family ties—some restaurant owners sponsor relatives as workers—have also forced these new immigrants to reciprocate the social debt they have incurred by continuing to work for these employers.

Apparently Chinatown workers experience a "dual form of oppression." Already blocked from entering the mainstream labor market, they are compelled to work in the ethnic-enclave economy and remain there. One sociological study revealed that "an overwhelming majority of the Chinatown immigrants who settled in San Francisco between 1962 and 1975 and who started in the ethnic labor market were confined to that market in 1980."[40] In 1980, 25 percent of the Chinatown populace in New York City lived below the poverty level, compared to 17 percent for the entire population of the city.[41]

ORGANIZING WORKERS

Chinese workers involved in ethnic immigrant enterprises have been known to resist such exploitation; however, organizing a labor movement among Chinatown workers is not an easy project. Nationwide there has a general decline in rank-and-file participation in the labor movement since the early 1980s. In the 1950s about 35 percent of all American workers held membership in a union, but by the mid-1990s that figure had dropped to 11 percent.[42] White-dominated unions also tend to be indifferent to the plight of these workers because of deep-seated stereotypes among white union leaders that the Chinese are "clannish" and are simply uninterested in being organized. Even when Chinese workers clearly belie that stereotype and succeed in drawing the support of these unions, they typically do not receive the necessary protection. For example, in 1979, New York Chinatown workers joined the American Federation of Labor and Congress of Industrial

Organizations (AFL–CIO) Hotel and Restaurant Employees and Bartenders Union, Local 69, but the union regularly refused to enforce contracts and hardly ever confronted management about violations of labor codes. Apparently Local 69 was more interested in collecting dues than in representing its Chinese members.[43]

Because of these complaints, Chinese grassroots activists formed the Chinese Staff and Workers Association (CSWA) to promote the labor movement in Chinatown. In February 1980 the association galvanized Chinese workers into action to picket against the Silver Palace, New York Chinatown's largest restaurant, when the restaurant tried to force waiters to share more of their tips with the rest of the work crew. The strike became a community-wide event, with local activists, lawyers, and other restaurant workers offering moral and material support. The strike ended when management acquiesced to the demands of the workers, who, by then, had organized their own independent restaurant union.

In the 1990s ethnic-based, grassroots organizing became the strategy for mobilizing Chinese female garment workers in New York City. The ILGWU had tried to organize the Chinese since the mid-1950s, and by 1974, nearly all Chinatown garment workers in New York City had joined. But the ILGWU, which is organized from the top down, is unable to make Chinese contractors or manufacturers comply with minimum union standards for shop floor conditions.

The incompetency of the ILGWU was evidenced in 1990 and 1991. In those years, several owners of garment factories withheld the payment of back wages. The workers, mostly Chinese women, were outraged as they expressed at one spontaneous rally: "We want justice! We are no slaves! Pay out wages now!" The workers approached the ILGWU and New York's labor department, but the investigation went nowhere. Frustrated by the impasse, they sought the assistance of the CSWA. With its bilingual skills and community ties, the CSWA is better able to deal with a fragmented industry.[44]

The CSWA, like any other community-based organization, must grapple with ethnic- and gender-specific barriers to mobilization. First, in smaller establishments like restaurants and grocery stores, Chinese employees work together with their employers who often are blood relatives, are of the same lineage, or are of the same dialect group. Such kinship or pseudo-kinship ties create a certain family-like atmosphere that inhibits the formation of class consciousness. Second, workers are afraid of losing their jobs if they take any time off for labor activities. Third, undocumented workers tend to shy away from unionism, for fear of trouble with the Immigration and Naturalization Service (INS). Fourth, women workers must contend with their lack of self-confidence. Saddled by the double burden of being unpaid household worker and wage earner, and made vulnerable by the lack of proficiency in English, these workers suffer from low self-esteem, which in turn deprives the labor movement of the sense of empowerment, the key to successful organizing.

COMMUNITY-BASED LABOR ACTIVISM

To get around some of these barriers, labor groups like the CSWA rely on consciousness-raising sessions and teach-ins and encourage the rank and file to participate actively in public education activities. Following one successful campaign in 1985 to secure job training and reemployment assistance, one local community organization based in Boston, the Chinese Progressive Association (CPA), has established a workers' mutual aid and resource center. The center provides support to unemployed garment workers fighting for back pay, unemployment insurance reform, and the upgrading of other benefits.[45]

Another community-based organization, Asian Immigrant Women Advocates (AIWA) based in San Francisco, is even more innovative in its attempt to reach out to Chinese women garment workers and other Asian women in electronics industries and the service sector. Using a multipronged approach that builds self-confidence, and is sensitive to the nuances of Asian immigrant cultures and the double burden of female labor, the AIWA has successfully empowered women to increase their accessibility to county services, to raise their awareness about occupational hazards, and to protest against specific workplace abuses.

By the mid-1990s, grassroots organizations like the AIWA were able to mobilize some support across the country for their causes because of the existence of larger umbrella organizations that brought union leaders and rank-and-file organizers of several different Asian communities together for mutual cooperation. These organizations include the Asian American Federation of Union Members (AAFUM) and the Alliance of Asian Pacific Labor (AAPL), both of which have promoted union visibility and, simultaneously, the political empowerment of Asian Americans.

Because of all this grassroots activism, institutionalized unions like the ILGWU have been forced to adapt to the changing times. Two years after that 1985 agitation in Boston, the local ILGWU began engaging in base building by offering bilingualism for public education and other services, hiring more Chinese organizers, and participating in Chinese cultural events. These activities address cultural sensitivity, communication, and access to the ethnic economy—aspects considered crucial for organizing communities of color. Yat Lee, a longtime ILGWU member, noticed a more deferential attitude from union officials toward Chinese members. "The new leadership is better than the old. When the new head [union official] comes to the factory, he always nods at us, says hello, and tries to talk to us in Chinese."[46] The ILGWU is also offering more social unionism in the form of health insurance, retirement funds, college scholarships for children of members, and an education department that offers classes in English, citizenship, and leadership training.

Like the ILGWU, the umbrella organization for the labor movement in the United States, the AFL–CIO has been forced to acknowledge the rapid increase in Chinese and other Asian workers. In recognition of the need for a formal support organization for Asian American labor activists, the AFL–CIO sponsored in 1992 the establishment of the Asian Pacific American Labor Alliance (APALA). APALA hopefully will help bridge the gap between Asian Americans and the American labor movement. These changes in established unions have, in turn, created more pro-union sentiment in the community as well, a turning point given the Chinese mistrust of these historically anti-Asian unions.[47]

UNDOCUMENTED IMMIGRANTS

Both institutionalized unions and community-based organizations, however, have yet to make significant inroads into gaining the support of undocumented aliens. The roots of this impasse lie partly in the difficulty of identifying this pool of workers whose number fluctuates and cannot be determined. These immigrants are generally reluctant to interact with the larger society.

Some Chinese undocumented immigrants are visa abusers, who arrived with nonimmigrant visas, work without acquiring working permits, and stay after their visas have expired. Most, at least initially, planned to make as much money as possible during their short stay in America and then return home. Apparently a mainland Chinese woman who works as a household servant in Southern California can earn the equivalent of almost seventeen years of the salary of a college professor in China. Given this income disparity, it is not surprising that many have chosen to lengthen their stay and eventually become illegal aliens.

Most of the Chinese undocumented workers are smuggled across the border or into U.S. harbors. This flow of illegal Chinese immigration grabbed the headlines in the mid-1990s when several ships from the PRC arrived carrying people to be smuggled into New York City.[48] According to INS estimates, from 10,000 to 15,000 PRC Chinese try to enter the United States illegally each year. In 1992 an estimated more than 3.3 million unauthorized immigrants were living in the United States.[49] The largest group—71 percent—came from Mexico, Central America, and Canada; Asia accounted for only 9 percent. Chinese undocumented immigrants overall account for only 1 percent of the illegal residents in the United States.[50]

In 1986 undocumented immigrants, mostly Mexicans, received amnesty or were legalized through the provisions of the Immigration and Reform Control Act (IRCA). This law provided for the legalization of undocumented aliens who had been residing in the United States since January 1, 1982, as well as seasonal agricultural workers who had been employed for at least ninety days during the year preceding May 1986. This same legislation, however, also sought to control future illegal immigration by requiring all employers to verify the legal status of all new employers. It also provided for sanctions against employers who knowingly hire undocumented workers. Despite this check on undocumented aliens, Chinese illegal immigrants have continued to arrive in the United States.

Since the 1960s the economic participation of Chinese Americans has seen dramatic changes. Those involved in the so-called enclave economy are no longer isolated and segregated from mainstream markets. Tied to the larger national and global restructuring, the enclave economy has offered opportunities but also has engendered class-oriented exploitation. Chinese Americans employed by or running a business linked to the larger economy also have to confront class-based barriers (and, in the case of women, also gender-based barriers) against upward mobility. Regardless of their social location or type of labor participation, most Chinese Americans have had to grapple with the politics of race, as witnessed in continuing racial (and gender) discrimination in the workplace. To overcome that, Chinese Americans since the turbulent days of the civil rights movement have turned to political empowerment and panethnic mobilization with other Asian American groups.

6

Political Mobilization and Empowerment

EMERGING PAN-ASIAN CONSCIOUSNESS

Chinese Americans today enjoy political enfranchisement, but their political participation in mainstream society has remained marginal. Certain barriers—illiteracy, lack of fluency in English, lack of understanding of the American political process, the perception that Chinese electoral power is inconsequential—have impeded the full exercise of their political rights. In the 1960s, however, the beginnings of political mobilization to circumvent those barriers were under way. That turbulent decade witnessed the emergence of the Asian American movement, a pan-Asian coalition which attempted to link all Asian ethnic groups in the struggle for racial equality and social justice. Chinese Americans participated actively in organizing a panethnic movement that would embrace a communal consciousness rooted in the commonality of historical oppression and a culturally shared sense of being Asian.

By the late 1960s, certain shifts in social and demographic factors within Asian American communities had prepared the way for the emergence of a pan-Asian consciousness. In the post–World War II years, native-born Asians who had been exposed to English and educated in American schools began to outnumber the immigrants. As language and cultural differences, which for a long time had divided Asians, began to blur, the Chinese in America began to communicate with other Asian Americans.

Equally critical to the process of developing pan-Asianism was the weakening of loyalties to the ancestral homelands. Unlike their immigrant elders,

American-born Chinese did not see the historical animosity between Chinese and Japanese Americans as pivotal to their identity. One young Chinese American explained this generational difference: "We have buried the old hatreds between Chinese and Japanese, and my friends and I must go beyond our parents' 'hang-ups.' My mother is upset because I'm engaged to a Japanese girl but she knows she can do nothing about it."[1]

Crucial to this inter-Asian interaction has been the crumbling of economic and residential barriers in the postwar period. As racial discrimination in employment and housing came under attack, Asian American residential patterns underwent a reconfiguration. Segregated ethnic enclaves declined as Asians moved out of these early immigrant neighborhoods. For example, in 1940, 50 percent of the Chinese in New York City lived in its Chinatown, but by 1960 less than one-third lived in that enclave.[2] Chinese Americans who left Chinatowns for the suburbs often ended up clustering with other Asians in certain pockets adjacent to the old ghettos. Over time Chinese Americans interacted more closely with other Asian groups and soon all realized that they shared common historical and contemporary experiences, including exploitation, oppression, and discrimination.

ASIAN AMERICAN MOVEMENT

This evolving sense of pan-Asianism was felt most keenly among young, educated Chinese and other Asian Americans. The Asian American movement emerged from the intersection of two historical phenomena: the coming of age of a generation of college-age Asian Americans and the highly volatile protest movement against the Vietnam War. By the 1960s the reunification of families, the lowering of discriminatory barriers for education, and the baby boom phenomenon had pushed the number of Asian Americans enrolled in college and universities to an all-time high.[3]

This generation of Asian students coincidentally attained youth during a traumatic period in the United States. The idealism of presidents John F. Kennedy's Great Frontier and Lyndon Johnson's Great Society—both of which, in theory, embodied a limited concept of a welfare state—was overshadowed by the failure of the civil rights movement to secure economic opportunity. Meanwhile, as the turbulent decade wore on, the U.S. military became more embroiled in the bloody Vietnam War.

Prompted by demographic changes and contemporaneous political struggles, Chinese Americans became involved in various sociopolitical movements, including the civil rights movement, women's liberation, and antiwar protests, which, in turn, sensitized them to racial issues. The civil rights and feminist movements made Chinese American women aware of their doubly impaired positions as members of a racial minority and as women. In particular, Chinese women discovered that the white, middle class–dominated feminist movement was indifferent to the unique circumstances faced by women of color in mainstream society.[4]

It was mainly the antiwar movement, however, that brought all Asian Americans, men and women, together psychologically and politically. These Asian American protesters drew the public's, and their own, attention to the racial subtext of the conflict raging in Asia and tied it to the oppression experienced in their communities. The fervent anticolonial nationalist movements in Asia stirred racial and cultural pride among Asian antiwar protesters and led them to stress the commonalities among "colonized groups," both in America and Asia, a perspective also known as the "internal colonial" model.

Soon these activists realized that the antiwar movement, which mirrored society's black-white binary understanding of race, ignored their participation and the issues they raised. Chinese Americans involved in supposedly integrationist organizations felt alienated and chose to join other Asian activists to establish their own movement for social justice and empowerment.

Part of the spark for such activism stemmed from efforts in the mid-1960s to get the San Francisco city government to rectify the socioeconomic ills in Chinatown. In San Francisco one survey completed in 1969 found that unemployment among the Chinese stood at 15 percent, a situation exacerbated by underemployment and miserly wages. Forty percent of the Chinatown residents lived below the poverty line; the average educational level was less than fifth grade; and 77 percent of the dwellings were below minimum federal standards. Most shocking of all was that the tuberculosis rate for the entire Chinese population was three times the rate of the average for the entire city. These statistics were not surprising considering the poor in Chinatown resided in squalid conditions, worked long, strenuous hours, and suffered from malnutrition.[5]

The conditions in San Francisco's Chinatown were not unique, however. In New York City's Chinatown, underemployment, crumbling tenements, a rising crime rate, and a higher-than-national average rate of tuberculosis and suicides in the early 1970s were signs of a community in crisis.[6] Health conditions among Boston Chinese in 1970 were equally poor. Infant mortality in 1966 stood at two-and-a-half times the figure for the city's general population, and new tuberculosis cases were 192 percent greater here than in the rest of the city.[7]

RADICAL ACTIVISTS AND COMMUNITY-BASED ACTIVISM

Activists in San Francisco, linked to such community-based organizations as the Chinatown Youth Council and Intercollegiate Chinese for Social Action (ICSA), organized forums and marches to draw the public's attention to conditions in the ethnic enclave and, indirectly, Chinese Americans' attention to the failure of the Chinese Consolidated Benevolent Association (CCBA) to address those ills. Another group, taking a lesson from the radical Black Panthers, organized the Chinatown Red Guards and traced the roots of these social ills to the blatant prejudice inflicted on the Chinese by the dominant society.

At this point, the plight of the underprivileged in Chinatown attracted the attention of Asian American college students in the San Francisco Bay Area, who, between 1968 and 1969, engaged in a series of so-called Third World strikes or protests on the campuses of San Francisco State College (today San Francisco State University) and the University of California at Berkeley. The protests eventually spread to other campuses such as the University of California at Los Angeles (UCLA) and the University of Washington. Initially, these student activists, who banded together with other students of color, focused on securing courses teaching the history and culture of Third World peoples. Soon the rhetoric turned to the establishment of ethnic studies programs (and later Asian American studies) in colleges and universities so that students would have access to the culturally specific knowledge they needed to solve the ills of their communities.

Members of the ICSA were particularly active in this agitation. Before the strikes many of them had already been involved in the running of a youth center in Chinatown, where English, civic education, and Chinese American history classes were offered to the community. The center also served as a drop-in center for wayward or rebellious youth.

Another group that featured Chinese American youth activists was the Asian American Political Alliance (AAPA), located at the University of California at Berkeley. Like other student organizations, Berkeley's AAPA initially focused on campus politics but soon found it less meaningful than active engagement with the ethnic community at large. To that end, they established the Asian Community Center (ACC), which was based in San Francisco's Chinatown. The ACC was dominated by Chinese Americans, mostly second-generation Chinese and later newly arrived, pro-People's Republic of Chinese (PRC) and foreign-born Chinese students. Influenced by Maoism, the ACC was committed to a leftist, revolutionary agenda that threatened to undercut the accommodationist stance of the CCBA and the Guomingdang (KMT).

Aside from showing pro-PRC propaganda films, the ACC became embroiled in the fight to save the International Hotel. The I-Hotel housed mostly elderly Filipino and Chinese bachelors, victims of antimiscegenation and anti-Asian immigration laws. When the hotel owners tried to evict the tenants in December 1968 to build a parking lot on that site, Asian American students, joined by other activists of color, mustered a campaign to halt the eviction, one that reminded Asian Americans of a racist past. The campaign, riddled by an ideological division between the left and accommodationist factions, ended in defeat and the evictions eventually did take place.

The counterpart to the ACC in the East was perhaps Asian Americans for Action or Triple A. One of the earliest pan-Asian organizations on the East Coast, Triple A began as an antiwar advocacy group. Internal divisions developed early when a Chinese American–dominated Maoist faction, which had split from the Communist party, U.S.A., infiltrated the organization. Immediately this faction's rejection of cultural nationalism (including racial pride) put it at odds with other members of this panethnic organization. Interethnic hostility and a generation gap—young Chinese American Maoists pitted against an older Japanese American leadership—deepened the rift, proving that the forging of panethnicity remained highly problematic. Alienated, the young members left and established I Wor Kuan based in New York's Chinatown.[8]

Committed to consciousness raising, I Wor Kuan, like the ACC, showed PRC films and sold publications touting Maoism. In its publication *Getting Together*, I Wor Kuan challenged the authority of the older Chinese establishment and criticized it for exploiting underprivileged co-ethnics. Its publication also showed a growing panethnic awareness because it covered issues of common interest to all Asian Americans. Beyond propaganda work, I Wor Kuan provided free medical care and legal assistance and dealt with housing complaints and workers' grievances. These efforts were designed to demonstrate to the people that the existing political structure could not ameliorate the particular plight of marginalized Chinese.

BARRIERS TO POLITICAL MOBILIZATION

Although occasionally activists were able to rally the local community to strike back at racial discrimination—most notably when Chinatown residents mobilized to protest publicly against police brutality in New York City in 1975—the process of politicization of the community faced several roadblocks. Most Chinatown residents resisted or could not relate to the activists' anti-imperialist, class-based stance. Activists generally could not ideologically transform the community. For example, radical activists in 1975 mobilized about 20,000 demonstrators in protest against police brutality, but a few months later almost the same number of Chinese participated in a rally organized by the conservative CCBA to protest against the closing of a police station in the neighborhood. This ideological barrier was shared by a number of other revolutionary groups. The Philadelphia-based Yellow Seeds, established in 1971, offered educational, recreational, and referral services, but because of ideology and limited funding, it could never muster enough community support to survive more than a few years.

The failure of the radical activists to establish a broad base of support stemmed from several factors. Their organizing efforts were stymied by a language barrier because most of the activists did not speak Cantonese. Seen as privileged "outsiders," these middle-class activists had little in common with the working-class Chinese that dominated Chinatown life. They typically were met with apprehension, if not outright hostility, from Chinatown residents. Activists who espoused a politicized Asian American identity encountered the entrenched sensibility of ethnic particularism. Most Chinese Americans remained wedded to their ethnic community, their wellspring for selfhood and cultural heritage.[9]

An example of ethnic particularism is the controversy over busing and the struggle to establish the so-called Freedom Schools. Centered in San Francisco, this issue surfaced in 1967, when a group of antibusing Euro-American mothers approached the Chinese community seeking a united front against busing children to schools in African American neighborhoods. Chinatown leaders and the media responded positively. The Chinese petitioned for an injunction against the court busing order.[10]

They were unsuccessful with the petition and soon decided to engage in a boycott. When public schools opened in mid-September 1971, Chinese students stayed away; most had joined one of the three Freedom Schools organized by Chinese mothers. But the Freedom School movement petered out when teachers and parents collided with the conservative, traditional elite, which remained staunchly pro-KMT, over the question of protesting against the admission of the PRC into the United Nations. When the traditional elite withdrew its support, the schools lost their funding, and the boycott soon collapsed.

This antibusing effort revealed several paradoxical undercurrents. While it raised Chinese Americans' sense of group identity, it also revealed that the community was still very much a divided one, polarized along the lines of generation and ideology. It demonstrated that many Chinese parents bore deep prejudices against African Americans, which, in turn, suggested that the Third World alliance forged by student activists had had little effect on the Chinese American popular consciousness.

By the mid-1970s most radical activists, in response to their persistent failure to capture community support, chose to deemphasize their radical rhetoric. Instead, they joined liberals and civil rights activists to organize moderate, community-based organizations such as the Asian American Legal Defense and Education Fund, Asian Americans for Equality (AAFE), and the Chinese Progressive Association (CPA). The objectives of such organizations zeroed in on reformist issues such as affirmative action and civil rights.

The CPA, based in San Francisco, for example, has provided support for workers' rights and initiated English and citizenship classes for new immigrants. In more recent years, it has worked closely with other community-based organizations in a broad coalition called the Northern California Coalition for Immigrant Rights against reactionary, anti-immigrant social policies such as California's 1987 Proposition 63, the "English Only" initiative. More recently it has fought against the 1994 Proposition 187, which deprived undocumented immigrants of public social services, nonemergency health care, and public education; and the 1998 Proposition 227, the Unz-Matta Initiative, which ended bilingual education in California's public schools.[11]

PROFESSIONAL REFORMERS AND THE TRADITIONAL ELITE

By the early 1970s the post-1965 influx of new Chinese immigrants had placed a heavy burden on existing social services. Traditional organizations such as the CCBA and the *huiguan* clearly could no longer meet the needs of the community. It was fortuitous that the federal government's War on Poverty—part of the Great Society program—was in full swing by then. Billions of dollars were poured into antipoverty programs. These programs engendered many of the community-based organizations that provided social, health, and legal services and offered job training and educational opportunities.

The antipoverty programs also created employment opportunities for educated, professionally trained Chinese social workers and administrators. Unlike the radical student activists, who eschewed the politics of integration, these professional reformers sought to incorporate Chinese Americans into the existing political order. Their approach to ethnic advancement collided with the separatist stance of the radical activists, who saw them as outsiders with little understanding of the authentic Chinese American experience. Because these professional reformers possessed the skills and resources to deal with government agencies and officials who allocated funding for community-based projects, they quickly undermined the credentials of these grassroots activists.

These reformers have also threatened the power of the established traditional leadership in the community. Not surprisingly, the leaders of the CCBA and traditional clan and family associations did little to assist these reformers. Since the reformers receive public funding and have a close relationship to government bodies, they are deemed to have undercut the mediatory functions of family and district associations which mainstream society used to consider as de facto representatives of the Chinese community. The control of the community was at stake, and this struggle for power was exacerbated by a division shaped by generational difference, level of Americanization, and educational background.[12]

Elites who led the traditional associations, also known as *qiao ling* (*kiu ling*), typically were born in China, were older, had little formal education, were mostly involved in business enterprises, and tended to be pro-KMT. The traditional elite have played the role of cultural conservators by organizing Chinese cultural activities such as celebrations of traditional festivals, supporting Chinese schools, maintaining clan and family associations, and serving as the conduit between the Chinese community in the United States and Taiwan.

Reformers, also known as *zhuan jia* (*chuen ka*), were born in American and often highly educated. They became involved in professional social or volunteer work out of a sense of altruism. *Zhuan jia*, unlike *qiao ling*, have focused more of their energies on the delivery of social services. To that end, they have been willing to embrace the panethnic identity, Asian American, to strengthen their movement for empowerment.

These reformers, since the late 1960s, have joined forces with other Asian ethnic agencies to establish coalitions or joint councils so that they can command attention. This has become critical in cities where Chinese Americans do not constitute a significant segment of the populace. Also, the funding structure encourages, sometimes even demands, that they operate on a pan-Asian basis. As one Chinese American director of a pan-Asian community-based agency in San Diego explains it: "It's very hard to get a grant when you are serving only one ethnic group. . . . Funding agencies prefer to support pan-Asian coalitions because it is more cost effective . . . [and] also allow funding administrators to dodge the possible political fallout from having to choose one Asian group over another."[13]

The traditional elite of the CCBA and other associations in the past firmly held ground against this expression of panethnicity or any attempt to undercut traditional authority. *Qiao ling* still considered Chinatown a self-sufficient community that could monitor and solve its own socioeconomic problems. In public it has chosen to downplay the socioeconomic ills of the community. This augmented the "model minority" image of Chinese Americans—the skewed perception that this minority group is economically (and educationally) successful.

SOCIAL-SERVICE AGENCIES

Most Chinese Americans in the late 1960s and early 1970s remained mired in poverty and privation. In short, to quote Mason Wong, then president of the ICSA, "[T]he Chinese community has the same basic problems as all other nonwhite communities."[14] In order to resolve these perplexing problems, reformers set up community-based organizations. Some of the major ones established in the 1960s in San Francisco included Self-Help for the Elderly, the Chinese Newcomers Service Center, the Chinatown Resource Center, the Chinatown Youth Center, and the Chinatown Child Development Center. These agencies have provided medical and general social services to the elderly, assistance to new immigrants, planning for low-cost housing, day-care services, and civil rights advocacy. These aside, there are two Chinatown-based organizations that have played a major role in shaping the social landscape: New York City's Chinatown Planning Council (CPC) and the San Francisco–based Chinese for Affirmative Action (CAA).

With an annual budget of about $12 million, the CPC provides job training, legal aid, mental-health services, and English-language classes. The CPC also runs day-care centers and specific facilities for young people and senior citizens. It has sponsored low-income housing projects and developed income-generating nonprofit service and rental establishments. The CPC has also expanded geographically to cover the outlying areas of New York City as the Chinese population moves into new neighborhoods.[15]

Like any other federally supported agency, the CPC has precipitated the diffusion of power within the community. This process has been encouraged by the influx of new immigrants with no ties to traditional associations, the loss of credibility of the KMT since the normalization of PRC–U.S. relations (which meant also undermining the authority of the traditional associations and the CCBA), and the emergence of a transnational ethnic economy un-connected to the concerns of the traditional elite.

However, when the CPC, composed primarily of affluent, second-generation, American-born Chinese, supported the city government's efforts in the 1980s to gentrify the core of Chinatown and encourage decentrali-zation of Chinatown through more rapid dispersal of the Chinese population and its businesses, it provoked a controversy that undermined its authority and concomitantly boosted the declining power of the CCBA and its affili-ated associations. The fact that a good number of the board members of the CPC were linked to enterprises interested in building or operating these new ventures earned the distrust of the community.

Old-time residents, benevolent associations, and activists galvanized a movement to oppose decentralization which they considered an attempt to drive small businesses and residential buildings out of the core in favor of erecting high-rise buildings to house corporate America. To block that pos-sibility, Chinatown groups mustered a united front with other Lower East Side African Americans, Puerto Ricans, and church and tenants' groups to prevent rezoning changes and the violation of tenants' rights.

The same struggle took place in San Francisco in the mid-1980s, but in this case the traditional associations were on the side of pro-growth and those who fought them were mostly community-based activists and professionals. Clearly both intracommunity conflicts were refracted by the generation gap, class interests, level of Americanization, and the politics of pro-growth versus that of pro-control.

Like the CPC, the CAA, which is based in San Francisco, relied on the community for support and sustenance. Unlike the CPC, the CAA quickly developed an Asian American perspective. Established originally to fight for fair employment practices, the CAA today also offers counseling, tutoring in English, and job-placement services. The CAA later widened its agenda to cover issues of equality and antiviolence for Asian Americans. It has worked on disseminating information about anti-Asian violence, and in the mid-1980s the CAA labored with other civil rights groups to educate Americans on the nativist subtext of the English-only movement in California and na-tionwide. Finally, it has kept vigilance on any university admission policies that discriminated against Asian Americans.[16]

GRASSROOTS RESPONSE TO ANTI-ASIAN VIOLENCE

Chinese Americans with more radical politics have tended to eschew these antipoverty or federally funded agencies because they regard them as instruments that foster the dependence of persons of color on the federal government. Chinese American radicals have banded together with other Asian Americans and established alternative grassroots organizations, which often run into the problem of securing funding and human capital from a community that often is suspicious of such organizations.

However, two alternative grassroots organizations that have remained visible, in spite of the odds, are the Asian Law Caucus, founded in 1972, and the Committee Against Anti-Asian Violence (CAAV), established in 1986. Both organizations have sought to defend the right of Chinese Americans to enjoy equal protection under the law. The Asian Law Caucus has offered legal representation to underprivileged Asian Americans. It has also educated Asians in the United States about their legal and civil rights and has participated in litigation against institutional racism. The CAAV, however, was the outgrowth of an increasing awareness among Asian Americans that equal protection under the law sometimes could be compromised by racism as expressed through physical violence.

In the early 1980s, the U.S. Civil Rights Commission and state and local civil rights bodies began highlighting the increasing number of cases of violence against persons of Asian ancestry. In fact, the commission in 1986 reported that "the issue of violence against Asian Americans is national in scope."[17] Much of the wave of violence in the early 1980s coincided with deteriorating economic conditions after 1975. In the context of high unemployment, rising inflation, and high interest rates, competition between Asians and non-Asians often escalated into intergroup conflicts. A period of economic recession in the United States in the late 1970s and early 1980s led to a downturn in major U.S. industries. American policy makers, businesspeople, labor unions, and political pundits blamed the ills of American industry on business competition with Asian countries, which simultaneously were experiencing dramatic economic growth. Anger against Asian nations, in a classic case of racial lumping, was projected onto Americans of Asian ancestry. Finally, anti-Asian sentiment was also the outgrowth of a continuing anti-immigrant mood that began in the late 1970s.

The 1986 commission report came in the wake of the brutal killing of Vincent Chin in June 1982. A twenty-seven-year-old Chinese American, Chin, mistaken for a Japanese, was bludgeoned to death in Detroit by two Euro-American auto workers, Ronald Ebens and Michael Nitz. Both Ebens and Nitz, reflecting some sentiments in that city, scapegoated Japanese Americans for the downturn in the American automobile industry, which actually was generated by Japan's aggressive marketing and sales of automobiles in the United States.[18]

Though Ebens, in a plea bargain, admitted to being guilty of manslaughter and Nitz pleaded no contest to the charge of second-degree murder, both had to serve only a three-year probation and pay a small fine. Chinese Americans were outraged by this miscarriage of justice. Lily Chin, the mother of the slain man, cried, "What kind of law is this? . . . This happened because my son is Chinese. . . . Something is wrong with this country."[19] The killing of Vincent Chin reminded many Chinese Americans of the legacy of anti-Asian sentiments. Almost a century after the passage of the Chinese Exclusion Act of 1882, Chinese Americans, still regarded as foreigners, were being blamed for the economic woes of the United States.

American Citizens for Justice (ACJ), a panethnic, grassroots group organized by concerned Chinese Americans, did succeed in getting the U.S. Justice Department to indict Ebens and Nitz for the violation of Chin's civil rights. In 1984 a jury acquitted Nitz but found Ebens guilty of having violated Chin's rights. Ebens was sentenced to twenty-five years in jail but, much to the chagrin of Asian Americans, was acquitted during the appeal and retrial.

Since Chin was killed because of his racial identity, the case reminded Chinese Americans that all Asian Americans, not just Chinese, were at risk of suffering the same fate. When a similar case, the murder of Jim Ming Hai Loo, a Chinese American mistaken for a Vietnamese, occurred in Raleigh, North Carolina, in 1989, the ethnic community quickly mobilized and formed a panethnic Asian coalition to ensure that justice would be served. As one local Chinese activist explained, "Like the Chin case, the Loo case is an Asian case. In both instances . . . the perpetrators cannot tell the difference between Asians. That's why it is an Asian problem."[20] In the end, the culprit received a stiff sentence.

All this furor over hate crimes has heightened the awareness of the need to monitor the state of anti-Asian violence. The CAAV, an organization that in 1986 brought together several advocacy groups including the Organization of Chinese Americans (OCA), is committed to public education, lobbying, and documentation of hate crimes, particularly those occurring in New York City. Since then they have also kept tabs on police brutality. The latest case took place in 1995 when an NYPD police officer confronted Yong Xin Huang, a sixteen-year-old boy who was playing with a gun, and shot him in the back of the head at point-blank range. The police claimed that Huang had turned and tried to fight and then the officer's gun had discharged accidentally. In spite of the testimony of key eyewitnesses who contradicted the claims of the police, the district attorney refused to indict the officer, claiming that Huang's death was simply an "accident." Since then the CAAV and several other advocacy groups have tried to reopen the case through public education and mass rallies but so far to no avail.[21]

ORGANIZATION OF CHINESE AMERICANS AND EQUAL RIGHTS

Perhaps of all the Chinese American advocacy groups today, the most prominent is the Organization of Chinese Americans (OCA), a national civil rights group based in Washington, D.C. Established in 1973, it has over the years sought to protect not only the interests of Chinese Americans but those of other Asian Americans as well.

The OCA has demonstrated an evolving sense of pan-Asian ethnicity. Together with other Asian American advocacy groups, it has lobbied the Bureau of the Census to have a separate count for each Asian subgroup for the censuses of 1980 and 1990. An accurate count for each Asian subgroup would allow more effective service delivery, better access to affirmative action or federal aid, and sufficient representation in the media. Recently, it has been embroiled, in conjunction with other ethnic advocacy groups, in a movement to roll back the so-called congressional welfare reforms that targeted underprivileged immigrants and new permanent residents. This 1996 Personal Responsibility and Work Opportunities Reconciliation Act dramatically altered the American welfare system in terms of limiting benefits to certain legal permanent residents who could meet stringent requirements. Otherwise, programs such as food stamps, Medicaid, and Supplementary Security Income are now beyond the reach of the vast majority of permanent residents, of which Chinese Americans constitute a substantial number.[22]

Aside from agitating for the restoration of benefits and getting states to increase their benefits to compensate for the recent federal restrictions on eligibility, the OCA has recently spoken out against legislation that could undermine Asian Americans' political rights such as the proposed 1998 Voter Eligibility Verification Act, which would allow election officials to confirm the citizenship status of registered voters and voter registration applicants by submitting names to the Immigration Naturalization Service (INS) and the Social Security Administration (SSA). This law is flawed because both the INS and SSA databases are incomplete; many Americans, including Asian Americans, could be prevented from voting through no fault of their own.[23]

In 1998 the OCA was at the forefront of opposing legislative efforts to prohibit political donations made by legal permanent residents, which would infringe upon the constitutional right to engage in free speech. Since a disproportionate number of Asian Americans are legal permanent residents, this legislation would ultimately discourage political involvement among Asian Americans.

This recent legislative effort stemmed from the spotlight on the flow of illegal foreign money from Asian governments, corporations, and individual power brokers into the U.S. political system for the 1994 and 1996 elections. Much of the furor has focused on John Huang, the former vice chairman of the Finance Committee of the Democratic National Committee (DNC), who allegedly played a role in raising illegal political campaign contributions from Asia. The DNC hired an auditing firm to investigate this controversy and soon anyone with an Asian surname became a suspect. Asian American individuals who had contributed in recent years became subjects of the investigation. Even officials of long-established Asian American organizations, such as the OCA, were subpoenaed to testify. Ethnic slurs and Yellow Peril images were bandied about. Reportedly, Senator Robert Bennett, commenting on one Asian contributor, said that these "are classic activities on the part of an Asian who comes from out of that culture." Another senator, during Senate hearings on campaign financing, used a fake Chinese accent and said, in a reference to Huang's salary arrangement with the DNC, "No raise money, no make bonus."[24]

Public figures and politicians in Congress began scapegoating Asian Americans as agents of foreign influences, which, in turn, reasserted the notion that Asian Americans are foreigners. By racializing the issue of political corruption, some quarters in Congress hoped to divert public demand for campaign finance reform. Of course, exploiting nativism and racism for political gain is nothing new; it has been in existence since the days of California's Workingmen party. (See Chapter 2.)

The OCA, in conjunction with thirteen other advocacy organizations, petitioned the U.S. Commission of Civil Rights to hold hearings in early December 1997 concerning the discriminatory ramifications of the campaign financing controversy. Asian American activists and community leaders who testified at these hearings charged that aside from the chilling effect of the proposed legislation to limit the financial contributions of permanent residents on Asian American political participation, there was also the question of the derailment of well-qualified Asian American candidates for political appointments because of the race issue.

On this question the stymied confirmation of Bill Lann Lee, the president's nominee for assistant attorney general for civil rights, comes to mind. If confirmed, Lee, the son of immigrant parents, would be one of the highest ranking Chinese American political appointees in the federal government.

Lee's nomination in late 1997, however, was deadlocked in the Senate Judiciary Committee. Republican senators in this committee opposed to the administration's support for affirmative action found Lee wanting because he was reportedly a supporter of that policy. Some critics of these Republican senators charged that this opposition was racially motivated since previous nominees for civil rights–related positions, who were Euro-American, had been confirmed with few impediments. Clearly, the campaign financing uproar had unleashed a movement to demonize Asian Americans. The end result was that, in spite of the full support of thirty-some Asian American organizations and many white and nonwhite politicians, Lee's nomination never came before the full Senate for a vote, and President Bill Clinton appointed Lee in an acting capacity for that position. In spite of the media spotlight on the Lee nomination and those well-publicized Civil Rights Commission hearings, the racialization of the campaign financing controversy did reach a new low with the passage, on March 30, 1998, of the Illegal Foreign Contributions Act which prohibited noncitizens (including permanent residents) from contributing to political campaigns.[25]

With an eye to the future, the OCA has spent its resources training the youth to carry on the civil rights struggle. Every year it sponsors an internship program that places young Asian Americans in Congress, federal agencies, and OCA chapters across the country to gain experience in public policy making and advocacy work. The OCA has also extended such leadership training to high school students.

EDUCATION: WHY CHINESE AMERICANS SUCCEED

It seems necessary for the OCA to focus some attention on the youth given the fact that mainstream society has a skewed understanding of young Chinese and other Asian Americans. The media have looked to school-age Asian Americans as the cohort that provides solid evidence that Asian Americans are the United States' model minority. For example, the media have pointed out that the 1983 first-prize winner of the Westinghouse Science Talent Search was Paul Ning, a sixteen-year-old Taiwan-born student attending Bronx High School. More significantly, of the forty finalists at the national level, no fewer than twelve were Asian Americans. Newspaper and television reports and special issues of newsmagazines in the last thirty years have applauded Asian Americans' supposed phenomenal educational achievements.

Some public commentators, even a few scholars, have attributed this success to the possession of superb genes or a certain biological inheritance.

More recently, Richard J. Herrnstein and Charles Murray's *The Bell Curve* (1994) reinvigorated the genetic debate by claiming that Asians probably have higher IQ scores than whites since they do better in "visual/spatial" than verbal skills. This factor also supposedly explains why Chinese and other Asians are overly represented in medicine, the sciences, and engineering and, conversely, underrepresented in literature, law, and politics.[26]

However, those conclusions, which ignore the impact of environmental factors, have been contested by educational researchers who have concluded that Chinese Americans and other Asian Americans simply work and study much harder than whites and blacks. To explain this difference, scholars have zeroed in on Asian cultural values which place a high priority on education, hard work, and family honor. This cultural explanation for academic success, however, slights the role of the larger social context and smacks of confirming stereotypes.

A more nuanced rationale for Asian educational achievement lies in the impact of structural forces. Without ignoring the cultural angle, scholars who subscribe to this theory, also known as relative functionalism, assert that limited opportunities, the product of discrimination, in noneducational areas, have forced Chinese Americans to pay more attention to education as an avenue for social mobility. Furthermore, the human capital—educational background, skills, and language proficiency—that new immigrants bring with them to the United States could determine the track of their educational and professional training.[27] Thus a complex combination of factors of race, class, and socio-historical context must be employed in any analysis of Chinese American academic achievement.

Notwithstanding the highly celebrated academic excellence among Chinese Americans, serious problems do exist within the student population. The most vexing is poor English proficiency. According to the 1990 U.S. Bureau of the Census, 5.8 percent of Chinese Americans between the ages of five to seven did not speak English "very well" compared to the national average of only 1.0 percent. The dilemma here most likely will be compounded by passage of the federal bill, the English Fluency Act, in Congress in September 1988. The bill, not unlike the Unz-Matta Initiative, requires the removal of limited-English proficiency (LEP) students from bilingual classrooms within two years of their entry. The law also bars funding for programs offering assistance to LEP students who have been in such programs for more than three years.[28]

Clearly this bill threatens to reduce retention and graduation rates and consequently narrow educational opportunities. It would affect the most vulnerable because LEP youngsters often come from poor socioeconomic backgrounds. Furthermore, this bill attempts to stem the progress in providing bilingual education ever since the landmark case of *Lau v. Nicholas* (1972), which had secured Chinese Americans' right to be given bilingual education so that their accessibility to equal opportunity in the classroom would not be jeopardized.[29]

BACKLASH IN HIGHER EDUCATION

At the tertiary education level, accessibility has been a recent controversial subject. Since the late 1970s, Asian American representation in higher education has increased rapidly. In 1995 Asian Americans made up less than 3 percent of the U.S. population but they constituted more than 5 percent of all college students in the United States. In some of the most elite schools of this country, the percentage of Asian Americans far exceeds the national average. At the University of California at Berkeley, Asian Americans in 1996 made up 40 percent of the undergraduates, while white students accounted for 31 percent.[30]

In spite of these impressive statistics, discrimination, not unlike what happened to Jewish Americans from the 1920s to 1950s, has reared its ugly head. Some prestigious schools, both private and public ones, including Brown, Stanford, and Berkeley, were suspected in the 1980s of having applied a quota system on students of Asian ancestry. "As soon as the percentages of Asian students began reaching double digits at some universities . . . Asian American admission rates have either stabilized or declined," stated L. Ling-Chi Wang, a professor of ethnic history at Berkeley.[31] There were numerous cases where Asian American and white applicants had the same academic qualifications, and yet the former were denied admission.

Yat-Pang Au, the son of immigrant parents from Hong Kong, was one such case. The winner of seven high school scholarships, Au graduated first in his class of 432 in his San Jose high school. He was also a school athlete, was elected to student body and club offices, and had run a Junior Achievement company that garnered him the runner-up prize for Santa Clara County's Young Businessman of the Year. In spite of these accolades, he was denied entry to the University of California at Berkeley.

Critics have charged that such institutions have manipulated admissions criteria to hold back the Asian influx. The underlying assumption held by university officials is that somehow Chinese Americans and other Asian Americans are not truly Americans, and allowing too many of them into higher education would somehow undermine the Americanism of this country's esteemed institutions.

In recent years, conservative politicians and commentators have exploited the question of admission quotas for the purpose of dismantling affirmative action in admission policies. They have chosen to explain this controversy over admission quotas as the outcome of Asian Americans being pitted against Hispanics and blacks for limited seats in leading institutions. Thus, they argue, affirmative action has discriminated against Asian Americans by setting aside the factor of merit. Ever since the *University of California Regents V. Bakke* decision (1978), which recognized the use of affirmative action in admissions as a constitutional means to advance diversity in higher education, a numerical limit on an "overrepresented minority" like Asian Americans, conservatives claim, has become necessary to promote the concept of "diversity."[32]

Asian American leaders in higher education have rejected such specious arguments. Mindful of creating any misunderstanding on the part of minority groups (such as African Americans and Latinos) targeted for affirmative action, Asian American leaders and scholars have pointed out that they are not advocating that more Asian Americans be admitted to college at the expense of less well-represented minority groups. Clearly affirmative action preferences will leave a negative impact on the admission of nontargeted groups such as Asian Americans and whites, but this negative impact, critics argue, should have an equal effect on the admission rates of all nontargeted groups, and thus cannot account for the difference in admission rates between Asians and whites. In addition, the "overrepresented minority" argument is flawed; the Asian American cohort is highly diverse in terms of race, class, and national origins. Affirmative action in admission, if employed in certain ways, can benefit the working-class Chinese who are underrepresented or could help reverse the situation of underrepresentation of Chinese Americans in the humanities.

On the whole, community leaders and scholars of education have supported the recent fight, albeit unsuccessfully, against California's Proposition 209, which prohibits the consideration of race, ethnicity, or gender in admissions of publicly funded state institutions of higher learning. A movement is also afoot to oppose a similar effort at the federal level.

PARTICIPATION IN MAINSTREAM POLITICS

Members of the mainstream society, in spite of the activism of the last thirty years, still consider Chinese Americans, as well as other Asian Americans, apolitical. In 1960 sociologist Rose Hum Lee concluded that Chinese Americans were not politically astute or active in American politics.[33] Little of this perception apparently has changed since 1960. Today the ambiguousness of the Chinese Americans' place in politics is compounded by the absence of a strong association with liberalism or conservatism.

This perception of political apathy stems from the belief that Chinese Americans possess a set of cultural values that are anathema to political participation. Supposedly a complacent and accommodating people, Chinese Americans are satisfied with their academic and economic achievements. Popular writers and scholars regard Chinese Americans as unsuited for involvement in public affairs because they consider them to be unprepared for the highly competitive, masculine-oriented American culture.[34]

Because of this widely held stereotype, political parties in the past have made little effort to cultivate ties to the Chinese American community. Of course, political parties have solicited donations from the community but with the belief that little was expected in return. Because Chinese Americans have been sidelined regularly in the political realm, many have retreated from electoral politics, which is to confirm the apolitical image of Chinese.

In the last few decades, empirical studies conducted on electoral politics among Chinese Americans seem to confirm that image. According to one 1984 study undertaken in San Francisco, the voter registration rate for the Chinese stood at 30.9 percent, far below the registration rate for the general population in California which, in 1987, was about 73 percent. Another study conducted in Los Angeles in 1986 produced similar results: the registration of Chinese stood at 35.5 percent.[35]

Such low figures, however, can be accounted for in several ways. First, the Chinese American population, as well as other Asian groups, has become more foreign than native born since World War II and thus has a high percentage of noncitizens, who are unable to register to vote. One 1989 study that took into account the factor of citizenship revealed that 77 percent of the California Asian American citizens were registered compared to 87 percent of the whites.[36] Among Asian Americans, Chinese and Japanese demonstrated the highest rates of registration; they also have the highest proportion of native-born citizens. The percentage of registered Chinese Americans who actually voted was quite similar to that for whites.[37] Other surveys in San Francisco have shown that, on certain issues, Chinese Americans actually voted as much as 5 to 10 percent above the general electorate.[38] Second, an equally important variable to consider is the existence of newly naturalized Chinese Americans who often have a lower registration rate than native-born citizens, the outcome of immigrants having to go through a long and complex process of social adaptation and learning before fully participating in their newly adopted country.[39]

One certain sign of the presence of ethnic interest in American politics is the emergence of voters associations such as the Chinese American Voters Association (CAVA) of Queens, New York. Grassroots organizations like the CAVA carry out voter-registration drives, provide information on political candidates who are running for office, and offer general political education for the community.

Studies have also shown that voter registration and voting are also contingent upon economic status and income. Areas with higher concentrations of middle, instead of lower, income dwellers have higher registration rates. In San Francisco, the Chinese registration rate in Chinatown was 23.1 percent in 1984 compared to 39.9 percent in the other important Chinese pocket, the middle-income Richmond district. However, this differentiation could also be attributed to the incidence of more foreign-born residing in the poorer parts of the city.[40]

Any consideration of the level of political apathy on the part of Chinese Americans must take into account the historical reality of the disfranchisement experienced by the community. Rejected and excluded in the past, they have retreated into their own family and community and have shunned political involvement. This legacy of political exclusion and isolation has meant that voter registration campaigns in the community have had to confront and overcome deep-seated attitudes of political alienation and mistrust of government.

Such political disengagement has been compounded by the fact that many recent Chinese immigrants face a number of structural barriers in trying to exercise their political enfranchisement. Aside from English language deficiency, an orientation toward a wider ideological spectrum in their country of birth has made it difficult for them to understand domestic issues. The situation has been exacerbated by the frequent absence of bilingual ballots and voting materials, although a new law passed in 1992 has somewhat widened accessibility to such materials. Continual loyalties to their country of origin have also dampened their interest in U.S. politics. Many underprivileged Chinese, in fact, simply do not have the time to concern themselves with political affairs; their economic survival occupies too much of their attention.

The question of Chinese American involvement in politics becomes more complex when we consider the type of political activity and political affiliation. Chinese Americans are more likely than other groups to contribute money to candidates, even though they seem less inclined than whites to work on campaigns or attend political rallies. Chinese Americans, contrary to the public perception that they have weak allegiances or none at all, actually have the same rates of party loyalty as the general populace. The Los Angeles survey conducted in 1986 revealed that of the Chinese, 41.9 percent registered as Democrats, 36.4 percent registered as Republicans, and the rest declined to choose either party. The 1984 San Francisco study showed a similar split: 48.6 percent, Democrats; 21.4 percent, Republicans. However, the continuing entry of more foreign-born who then become naturalized may change the distribution of partisan preferences in the future.[41]

The Chinese American stance toward public policies also defies simple categorization. Unlike African Americans and Latinos, but similar to whites, Chinese Americans are more likely to favor the death penalty. Similar to the other two major ethnic groups, however, most Chinese Americans favor bilingual education but parted company, as did whites, with those two groups on the question of amnesty for undocumented aliens.

Voting patterns also show no consistency. In the 1984 presidential race, Chinese and other Asian Americans, though mostly registered as Democrats, favored Ronald Reagan over Walter Mondale by 67 to 32 percent. In 1992 the vote was more evenly split: Asian Americans voted 39 percent for William Clinton, 33 percent for George Bush, and 25 percent for Ross Perot. Perhaps this inconsistency suggests that Chinese Americans are more inclined than others to cross party lines. Chinese Americans, like most Americans, have been voting on the basis of the merits of the particular candidates rather than by strict party lines.

If one were to survey the number of Chinese American public officeholders—most of whom have been Democrats—since the end of World War II, one would gain the impression that political representation has not been lacking. Chinese have run for political office at the national, state, and city levels. When Hawaii became a state in 1959, Hiram Fong, who had served in the territorial legislature, was elected U.S. Senator. The first person of Chinese descent to win state office on the mainland was Wing F. Ong. An immigrant who arrived in the United States at the age of fourteen in 1914, he went from being a houseboy to a member of Arizona's House of Representatives for two terms during the 1940s. More well known than Ong would be March Fong Eu, elected California's secretary of state in 1974 and then repeatedly reelected with wide margins until she resigned in 1994 to serve as ambassador to Micronesia. In that same year, her son Matthew Fong was elected as state treasurer. Equally significant was the successful attempt of Chinese American physicist S. B. Woo's run for the lieutenant governorship of Delaware in 1984, an office he held until 1989. Gary Locke, the newly elected governor of Washington, has the honor of being currently the top-ranking Chinese elected official in the United States. Interestingly enough,

Locke, the son of Chinese immigrants, won the governorship in a state where Asian American representation was less than 6 percent of the population. Eu, Woo, and Locke proved that a Chinese American can be elected to prominent public offices without a large Chinese or even Asian American population.

Nearly all Chinese candidates for public office, however, have had to rely on Asian American financial contributions to fund their campaigns. Chinese Americans have contributed to such campaigns disproportionately to their demographic strength; for example, in Woo's election, Chinese Americans from across the country contributed about 27 percent of the funds. Through their pocketbooks, Chinese Americans have found a way to increase their capacity to influence the political process.[42]

Chinese American visibility at the local level has been more marked than at the state or federal levels. Lily Chen became the first Chinese American woman mayor in Monterey Park, California, in 1983. Two years later, Michael Woo became the first Chinese American member of the city council of populous Los Angeles, and in 1993 he ran for mayor in that city. Woo, a liberal, lost to a conservative white but garnered almost half of the votes. Even new, well-educated Chinese immigrants, mostly in San Francisco, have run for public offices such as judgeships, school board seats, and city council positions. Successful ones include Julie Teng, Mabel Teng, Lily Sing, Wilma Chen, and Thomas Hsieh.

Some gains have also been made in the area of political appointments, although marginal political power has stymied rapid progress. In 1988 and 1989 then Mayor Art Agnos of San Francisco appointed twenty Chinese Americans, mostly immigrants, to serve on various city commissions. Chinese Americans appointed to other San Francisco city positions included Frederick Lau as the police chief, Douglas Wong as a police commissioner, and Wayne Hu as a member of the Board of Permit Appeals. Top-ranking political appointments have been few and far between, however. So far, Elaine Chao, appointed by President George Bush in 1989 to be deputy secretary of transportation, has been the highest-ranking Chinese American official in the executive branch. Of course, the recent appointment of Bill Lan Lee as acting assistant attorney general for civil rights was a milestone in Chinese American political visibility.

All of these political advancements, which have made Asian Americans a more visible electoral block, in conjunction with the widespread belief that Chinese and other Asian Americans are generous political donors, have led to heavy courting of the community by mainstream political candidates. Major political candidates, reacting to the growing demographic strength, now campaign in Chinese American communities, hoping to convince Chinese that their money, votes, and opinions do count. For example, in 1990, all three candidates for governor of California—Pete Wilson, Dianne Feinstein, and John Van de Kamp—campaigned in the Chinese American community and promised to support Chinese American political concerns ranging from quotas in higher education to more appointments in policy-making positions in the government. Similarly, presidential candidates in the last three races—1988, 1992, and 1996—have canvassed for Chinese American money and votes.

Chinese Americans, and Japanese Americans, have dominated Asian American electoral politics. A high percentage of native-born citizens, which has meant a high electoral participation rate, largely accounts for this phenomenon. But Chinese Americans have also been able to reap the political benefits in large part because they are more established and more organized than most other Asian groups. Aside from the OCA, Chinese Americans have been able to articulate their concerns through the Chinese American Citizens Alliance, the National Democratic Council of Asian and Pacific Americans, and the Pacific Leadership Council, the last two of which are considered arms of the Democratic party. The resources mustered through political advocacy bodies have allowed Chinese Americans to take advantage of the demographic shift following the arrival of the new wave of immigrants after 1965.

INTRAETHNIC CONFLICT

Any attempt on the part of Chinese Americans to play a larger political role in mainstream society is perhaps compromised by class and nativity divisions. The local political realm in Monterey Park is illustrative of the intraethnic conflict. Even though Chinese Americans on the whole were blamed in the 1980s by longtime residents of Monterey Park for the rampant development and subsequent socioeconomic problems in that city, ranging from traffic congestion to rising real estate prices, the Chinese American community was far from united in defending the pro-development agenda.[43]

Most of the native-born Chinese in Monterey Park in the late 1980s had joined a loosely organized, liberal, multiracial, multiclass coalition—composed of Asian Americans, Latinos, and progressive whites—called CHAMP (Coalition for Harmony in Monterey Park) to crusade for controlled growth and racial harmony. The native-born Chinese generally resented co-ethnic newcomers' overnight success in America without having to struggle or play by the rules of assimilation. Newcomers seemed to be taking for granted the equality and civil rights established Chinese residents had fought for in the past. However, later pro-growth elements did infiltrate the interethnic coalition, causing a rift within that group.

Foreign-born, upwardly mobile Chinese tended to support the pro-growth agenda, and a few had joined the Association for Better Cityhood (ABC), a short-lived coalition that also attracted white and Latino developers and entrepreneurs. Defending the position of Chinese entrepreneurial elites, one Chinese developer stated, "The city [Monterey Park] has become identified as a land of new opportunity. . . . It has been a success story. We [Chinese] have made Monterey Park an important cultural and economic center."[44] Most immigrant Chinese, however, were not necessarily affiliated with any formalized group; however, they voted as one voting block, which presented itself to mainstream society as allegedly nationalistic, conservative, and maybe even ethnocentric.

The division within the Chinese American community of Monterey Park, however, was not simply along the lines of foreign versus native born. Class differentiation between the foreign-born entrepreneurial elite and the native-born, social service elite (made up of American-born social service professionals) played a critical part in fostering intraethnic hostility.

In Monterey Park, there was a third, slow- or controlled-growth group called RAMP (Residents Association of Monterey Park), made up of mostly older white residents in the community and a few old-time non-Chinese minority residents who resented the ability of the newly arrived Chinese immigrants to experience economic mobility without undergoing assimilation. One faction within RAMP, however, quickly demonstrated anti-Chinese sentiments by opposing—all in the name of defending American values—Chinese language signs, supporting the English-only movement in the 1980s, and calling for the deportation of so-called illegal immigrants. The presence of this third group helped to racialize the controlled-growth movement, thus invoking in the minds of some Chinese a link among language, race, and antidevelopment.

Not surprisingly, immigrant Chinese Americans were suspicious of any multiethnic coalitions and chose to remain as one voting block. Neither did American-born Chinese necessarily remain unequivocal supporters of a liberal, multiethnic coalition against unchecked growth. When issues of culture, such as bilingualism, came under attack from white conservatives, American-born Chinese became torn between supporting ethnic solidarity against this form of nativism or looking out for individual self-interest and the larger community control.

Ethnic solidarity can triumph over class and nativity if the issue in question could have a profound impact on the fortunes of the entire ethnic community. Such was the case in Boston's Chinatown struggle of 1993 to fight against the expansion of one medical center into Chinatown. When the New England Medical Center tried to acquire a small plot of land, called Parcel C, in Chinatown to build a large parking garage, an attempt supported by the traditional Chinese elite, grassroots activists and most of the Chinese community reacted negatively. The community-wide protest took place in a context of already serious air pollution problems, chronic traffic congestion, a critical lack of open space, and a severe housing shortage in Chinatown. These environmental problems, Chinese residents reasoned, would all be exacerbated by the erection of a garage on Parcel C.[45]

A coalition was formalized which soon formed alliances with mainstream American environmental groups such as the Sierra Club and the American Lung Association, legal justice groups such as the Greater Boston Legal Services, and even one health care advocacy group, Health Care for All. With the support of these organizations, the coalition held a referendum whereby the Chinese American community overwhelmingly rejected the hospital's plan and forced the hospital to conduct an environmental review of its proposed garage. A year after the agitation had begun, the hospital was compelled to withdraw its proposal. The victory was tempered by the fact that the city turned the land over to the CCBA of Boston which, in the past, has been known to have squandered land and money given to it in trust for the community.

What happened in Monterey Park and in Boston could possibly offer clues for the future prospects of Chinese political participation in this country. Even though the Chinese American population in certain parts of cities or in some neighborhoods may have become the dominant demographic, economic, social, and cultural force, it is rarely the dominant political one. The fact that a sizable number of Chinese immigrants are noncitizens and cannot vote remains the major stumbling block to political empowerment. Furthermore, there has been much geographical mobility among the Chinese Americans, resulting in the absence of a stable population for a given area on which to build a political base. It is doubtful, with the exception of broad common issues such as bilingualism and racism, that the new Chinese entrepreneurial elite with transnational ties could dramatically influence the politics of working-class ethnics, most of whom have few or no ties to these elites. The traditional elite, as demonstrated in the case of the Boston struggle over Parcel C, could stand in the way of effective ethnic mobilization for empowerment.

INTERETHNIC ALLIANCES

Perhaps because of these barriers to political empowerment there have been cases in which educated middle-class Chinese and other Asian Americans have joined interethnic alliances designed for mutual political cooperation. One such instance in the recent past has been the political relationship established between Asian Americans (mobilized through the San Gabriel Valley Asian Pacific Americans for Fair Reapportionment) and Latinos to secure redistricting and reapportionment in the San Gabriel Valley, California, between 1990 and 1992. Both communities found common grounds on the question of increasing minority representation at the state and federal levels. Political gerrymandering in the past had fragmented each community and diluted political power. Aside from this common history, leaders of both communities in the cities of this valley had worked together previously to defeat the agenda of pro-growth. The end result of the cooperative venture in early 1990s was the creation of a new assembly district that took advantage of the concentration of Asian Americans in four cities of the valley but still gave Latinos enough of a solid block to allow the incumbent of the old district to run for reelection.[46]

Such political coalitions may not work as well in the future as more Chinese Americans and other Asians move into the valley. Once Asian Americans become a larger group than Latinos, interethnic cooperation may become elusive. The diversified composition of the Asian American population also could derail any alliances across racial lines. The multifarious nature of the Asian American populace in downtown Los Angeles, one divided along the lines of national origins, has made the process of reaching an agreement within it almost unattainable, let alone trying to forge a link to the Latino community. Finally, the highly visible presence of African Americans and the underlying tension between them and the Asian American population have thwarted efforts to create solidarity among peoples of color.

NEW DIRECTIONS

The development of the political movement since the 1960s has allowed Chinese Americans to move farther away from "the structure of dual domination," namely "freedom from racial oppression by white society and freedom from the extraterritorial rule of the Chinese government in Taiwan and its representatives in the United States."[47] An obvious turning point perhaps took place over the disputed Daoyutai Islands, which were claimed by both Japan and Taiwan.

When the United States announced it would return the islands and other U.S.–held islands to Japan in 1972, a protest movement led by foreign-born Chinese students across the United States was ignited. Beginning in 1971, students and scholars organized the Protecting Daoyutai Movement. The contested islands involved much more than just possible surrounding off-shore oil fields; reclaiming them meant preserving the sovereignty of China.[48]

When the Guomindang government failed to respond positively to this U.S.–based movement, and even called it subversive and pro-Communist, it came across as ineffectual to the Chinese intelligentsia and the Chinese community. By the late 1970s, as normalization of relations between the PRC and the United States forged ahead and the PRC's international standing began to rise, loyalty to Taiwan became less entrenched among the Chinese in the United States. The cultural exchanges made by Beijing with Chinese in North America in the 1980s and continuing to the present have helped to strengthen this evolving relationship and simultaneously to weaken loyalty to Taiwan.

Over the last several decades, the direction of the politicization of the Chinese Americans, one geared toward the integration of the community into mainstream society, has resulted in the emergence of a new identity. Conditions—geographic concentration, ethnic homogeneity, and solidarity—that used to preserve the sojourner mentality are less common these days. Instead Chinese now live and work under conditions of greater geographical dispersion, ethnic heterogeneity, and conflict, and the ethnic identity has taken on a more fluid character.

Through their involvement in political situations, Chinese Americans have not only demanded their rightful place in the United States but also have revamped the definition of their identity. This self-determining Chinese American identity—one that has confounded the zero-sum relationship between assimilation and the retention of ethnicity—has been built on shared historical experiences in the United States and on the principles of justice and equality. It is an identity that ultimately rejects chauvinistic nationalism and embraces a culturally diverse, dynamic understanding of America.

7

The Arts and Chinese Americans

EARLY CHINESE AMERICAN LITERATURE

Since the arrival of the earliest Chinese immigrants, both the the U.S. government and the mass media culture have perpetuated dehumanizing representations of the community. Whether portrayed as brute hordes, vicious villains, dragon ladies, pathetic heathens, comical servants, loyal sidekicks, oversexed Suzie Wongs, subservient Lotus Blossoms, or emasculated detectives, Chinese Americans have had to struggle against an overall perception of being unassimilable aliens. Certainly in the realm of cultural production, Chinese Americans in the past had expended efforts to elucidate the sociopolitical and economic tensions between themselves and the dominant culture, which in turn had generated those debilitating images.

Early Chinese writings on America, including student and later court official Yung Wing's *My Life in China and America* (1909) and diplomat Wu Ting Fang's *America Through the Spectacles of an Oriental Diplomat* (1914), appeared soon after the large-scale immigration of the mid-nineteenth century. These comment, albeit in a polite voice, on the social inequalities existing in American society, including those inflicted on Chinese immigrants, even they as extoll American technological and scientific achievements.

Often generated by diplomatic officials, scholars, and transitory visitors, these impressions found their way into the literature of literate Chinese sojourners, who typically harbored little desire to put down roots in the United States. Examples of these include Lee Yan Phou's *When I Was a Boy in China* (1887), Huie Kin's *Reminiscences* (1932), Chiang Yee's *A Chinese Childhood*

(1940), Adet Lin and Anor Lin's *Our Family* (1939), and Lin Yutang's manifold writings, of which *My Country and My People* (1937) is the most well known. Most of these books, also called tourist guides, provide a quaint, superficial perspective of China and its culture, including ceremonies and customs of food and dress, designed to appeal to the Western reader's craving for exoticism. More significantly, these works, written in an apologetic tone, place the blame for racial conflagrations on the failure of the predominately working-class Chinese laborers to integrate themselves into American life. Even as these authors heaped "Orientalist" praise on Chinese society and culture they disparaged the supposed "clannishness" of the Chinese working-class immigrants. These idealized, class-oriented observations, betraying the socioeconomic cleavage that existed within the turn-of-the-century Chinese community in North America, widened the rift between the community and the non-Chinese majority.

The literary voices of Chinese immigrants did not operate entirely within the abovementioned parameters, however. Notwithstanding institutionalized efforts to thwart community formation and the process of acculturation, vestiges of a Chinese American oral tradition in the form of folk rhymes— the wood-fish songs (*muyu ge*) and Gold Mountain songs (*jinshan ge*)—have been uncovered. Both genres affirm the process of cultural change that occurred after immigration to America through the use of colloquial Cantonese, Chinatown Chinese translations from English, and American-based themes. Some *muyu ge* are simply humorous and entertaining, but many are also melancholic complaints about the hardships and suffering male immigrants and the families they left behind had to endure while exclusionary practices shattered their hopes and aspirations. The thematic range of *jinshan ge* is broader. These songs also deal with the subjects of women, prostitutes, and sex, echoing the desire for female companionship among the men in predominately male Chinese America: "We're guests stranded in North America: /Must we also give up the fun in life?"[1]

Similar lamentations and longings also found their way into the poems carved by detained arrivals into the walls of the Angel Island Immigration Station. The moving, bewildered voices of these arrivals challenged the myth of America as the land of opportunity for all immigrants as suggested in these lines from a poem: "America has power, but not justice/In prison, we were victimized as if we were guilty."[2] The same counterdiscourse can be found in several novellas written in reaction to the 1905 Chinese protest boycott of American goods. Both *Kuxuesheng* (The industrious student) by Qiyouzi (pseudonym) and *Kushehui* (The bitter society) by an anonymous writer speak to the humanness of the Chinese immigrants despite their living in an overtly racist society.[3]

Writers who portrayed Chinese immigrants sympathetically include Edith Eaton, the offspring of a Caucasian-Chinese union, who had lived in Great Britain and Canada before immigrating to the United States. Considered the first Chinese American writer in English, Eaton, who used the pen name Sui Sin Far, enriched Chinese American literature through her autobiographical account "Leaves from the Mental Portfolio of an Eurasian" (1909) and her short-story collection *Mrs. Spring Fragrance* (1912). In these works, Sui Sin Far, through the use of irony and humor, exposes the wrongs done to the Chinese in America. Her writings, which consistently mirrored her developing identification with her Chinese roots, probe the duality experienced by biracial persons, the humanity of working-class women, and the bond of friendship between women against the backdrop of gender-based exclusion laws and fractured families. Sui Sin Far's legacy lies in being "a bridge between two worlds," one that nurtured the Euro-Americans' understanding of the Chinese. Her works also anticipate the post–World War II works of other Eurasian authors such as Han Suyin, perhaps most well known for her *A Many Splendoured Thing* (1952), and Diana Chang (*Frontiers of Love* [1956]) which critiques racial domination and Western imperialism and ponders on the identity dilemma experienced by biracial persons.[4]

EURO-AMERICAN WRITERS: GOOD ASIANS AND BAD ASIANS

Sui Sin Far's contributions are in stark contrast to contemporaneous works about the Chinese in fiction produced by Euro-American writers which tend to offer distorted images of the Chinese. Lingering fears of a revival of the thirteenth-century Mongol invasion of Eastern Europe perpetuated the negative image of the Chinese well before their arrival in California in the 1850s. Claiming superiority for the civilized Christian portion of humankind, Euro-Americans distinguished themselves from non-Europeans. Thus, by the early nineteenth century, contemporary relations between Euro-Americans and American Indians and Africans involving unequal power relations in the form of colonization and slavery also colored whites' perceptions of the Chinese. American traders, diplomats, and missionaries with ties to China propagated "conceptions of Chinese deceit, cunning, idolatory, despotism, xenophobia, cruelty, infanticide, and intellectual and sexual perversity."[5]

The end result, by the turn of the century, was two sets of stereotypes: the "good" Asian and the "bad" Asian. "Good" Asians are helpless heathens, loyal allies or sidekicks, and servants; "bad" Asians are sinister villains and brute hordes. According to Elaine Kim, this distorted understanding of the Asian functions as a foil to assure the Euro-American that he or she is "non-Asian." If the Asian is cruel and cunning, like Fu Manchu, the Euro-American is compassionate and honest; if the Asian is meek and subservient, the Euro-American is projected as benevolent and omnipotent. The comical and dumb-witted servant serves a savy and astute white employer; the ingenious Chinese detective—Charlie Chan—took on the cases of his morally minded white colleagues and clients. The assumption undergirding this duality of good and bad Asians is the incompatibility of the Chinese and Euro-American, one that underscores the white as superior in all respects.[6]

As bad Asians, Chinese immigrants were irredeemable. By the early decades of the twentieth century, a newly reinvigorated Yellow Peril scare, precipitated by fears of Japan's imperialistic ambitions, which did not distinguish among Asian ethnicities, engendered such negative images. Chinese women, for example, found themselves cast as promiscuous, untrustworthy, and diabolical creatures. This stock image of Chinese women, the Dragon Lady, was best projected in Sax Rohmer's *Daughter of Fu Manchu* (1931). The protagonist, Fah Lo Suee, followed the footsteps of her father, Fu Manchu, and became a champion of Asian domination over the white race.

The fiction produced by Jack London, Will Irwin, Frank Norris, and Sax Rohmer depicts the characteristics of the Chinese, whether men or women, as biologically determined. In spite of exposure to white civilization, he or she will eventually return to the "evil" ways. Even the offspring of Euro-American–Chinese unions—in spite of the presence of white blood—cannot escape the doomed fate that awaits them. Either they will die—a satisfactory fictional end to the Yellow Peril threat—or they will have to try to pass as whites.

In this imaginary Chinatown landscape, dotted with tong wars, slave girls, smoky opium dens, indescribable foodways, and rat-eating yellow men, so-called positive images equally abound. The obsequious, queer-looking Chinese servant who appears in a number of popular melodramas and stories set in the masculinized nineteenth-century American West validates the superiority of his Anglo master and his family. Ah Lam, the emotionless servant in Maud Howe's novel *The San Rosario Ranch* (1880), is typical of that image; his virtues are patronizingly described entirely in terms of servitude and obedience, and he eventually dies while trying to defend the honor of a white female visitor. The loyal servant caricature in the twentieth century took the form of the placid detective Charlie Chan, and later in television as the servant Hop Sing in *Bonanza* (1959–1973), the long-running western series.

Lotus Blossom, or China Doll, the female version of the male servant, is the opposite of the Dragon Lady; submissive and deferential, she is powerless. Lotus Blossom was the perfect foil for the virility and attractiveness of the Euro-American male. In Homer Lea's *The Vermilion Pencil* (1908), the Chinese female character will betray her husband and father, even sacrifice her life to secure the love of the white hero. In contrast, the Asian character is obsessed by his desire for the unattainable white woman, who almost always rejects him because of his race. Depicted as a sexual deviant, even a rapist, the Chinese male is as sexually undesirable as the impotent comical servant or the castrated Charlie Chan.

INTERRACIAL ROMANCES IN FILMS

The taboo subject of interracial liaisons was a common feature in early American motion pictures. Since the release of D. W. Griffith's *The Birth of a Nation* (1915), a film on racial mixing that upholds exclusionism (against African Americans) through violence, miscegenation on the silver screen has raised the specter of moral decline, echoing and reinforcing societal attitudes toward such conjugal unions. In 1919 Griffith's *Broken Blossoms* resolved the thorny subject by making the love of the Chinese, opium-smoking merchant Cheng Huan for Lucy, the abused illegitimate daughter of a brutal boxer, a platonic, unrequited relationship which ended in Cheng Huan committing suicide. Killing off the Chinese partner of an interracial liasion was a conventional device to underscore the doomed nature of miscegenation. Though scholars have applauded the humanized portrayal of Cheng Huan, it is Lucy's innocence and "whiteness" that enobles the "baseness" of Cheng Huan so much that he avenges her death at the hands of her possessive father by shooting him. Thus again, the West "saves" the inferior and offers moral salvation for the Asian "other."[7]

The fear of interracial comingling was so strong that even when interracial romances end with the union of the couple at the film's conclusion, there is often a plot twist that involves the revelation that the Chinese partner in the romance was in reality white or Eurasian. Films such as *Shanghai* (1935) and *The Lady of the Tropics* (1939) feature Eurasian characters as seducers and seductresses which enabled Hollywood to tackle forbidden sexuality without threatening the racial status quo or the film code of the times. Similarly white male actors donning "yellow faces," instead of Asian actors, were used in romantic plots. And, of course, "scotch-tape Asians" or white men and women in "yellow face" have since the early days of the motion picture industry played lead roles in Asian-themed films.

Only a few Chinese women have played romantic leads opposite white men. Chinese men, however, almost never served as equal romantic partners of white women. This double standard of miscegenation, with emphasis on the free sexual license of white men, desexualized Chinese men even as it hypersexualized Chinese women. Like their male compatriots who are asexualized, the women are depicted as sexual so as to validate the white man's superiority.

IMAGES OF WOMEN IN FILMS

Of the two images—Lotus Blossom and the Dragon Lady—the Dragon Lady has probably appeared more often on the silver screen, particularly in early escapist films. In *The Thief of Baghdad* (1924), pioneer Chinese American actress Anna May Wong played the role of a servant who used treachery to assist an unscrupulous Mongol prince to win the hand of the Princess of Baghdad.[8] Wong—whose screen appeal was due to her Caucasian-like features—played the role of a criminally complicit or sexually available Chinese woman who must die (so as to symbolically contain Asia and reinforce the idea that Asians are unassimilable) in such popular films as *The Toll of the Sea* (1922), a reworking of Puccini's opera *Madam Butterfly*; *Daughter of the Dragon* (1931), whose storyline came from the Fu Manchu books; and *Shanghai Express* (1932), opposite Marlene Dietrich.

Despite the stirrings of the second feminist movement and the post–World War II gradual liberalization of immigration laws and attitudes toward the Chinese, the filmic lot of Asian women seemed impervious to historical change. The films produced during World War II and after, reflecting the easing of tensions in Sino-American relations, offered more images of good rather than bad Asian women; however, Lotus Blossom and Dragon Lady are not necessarily opposing stereotypes. Since both stereotypes eroticize Chinese women as exotic "dolls" who are available for white male dominance, the image of women has remained static and improved little.

Perhaps the most well-known, deferential, Lotus Blossom–like Chinese female character is Suzie Wong, the "hooker with a heart of gold" in *The World of Suzie Wong* (1960). Suzie, an abused, yet alluring woman, is played by Nancy Kwan. An artist, Robert Lomax (William Holden), takes pity on her, and soon they fall in love. When Robert falls on hard times, Suzie disappears to help ease his burden. Suzie later turns up again, pleading for

Robert's help to rescue her illegitimate baby from a flood. Despite their efforts the baby dies. Though the film ends with the reunion of the couple, the cost has been high.

The influence of the Orientalist discourse in the arts after World War II— one that has emphasized the themes of death and destruction—may be ascribable to the prevalent McCarthyism in the 1950s which impugned the integration of Chinese Americans into the larger society. The terror unleashed on progressively oriented Chinese Americans suppressed the continuation of their earlier efforts to articulate racial consciousness and pride.

EXPRESSIONS OF CULTURAL NATIONALISM

In the late 1930s and 1940s the impact of the Sino-Japanese War and a revival of American liberalism and Marxism led to the development of left-wing literary groups in Chinatowns. Composed mostly of students and activists, these groups argued for a Chinatown literature independent of the literary tradition of China which would serve as a vehicle for social criticism and reform. H. T. Tsiang, a leftist writer, answered that call. One of his works, *And China Has Hands* (1936), may be the first fictional account of the bachelor society written in English by a Chinese immigrant. Contemporaries of Tsiang published prose, poetry, commentaries, and essays in Chinese-language weeklies and periodicals in New York and San Francisco. Another group of unrelated, yet still progressively minded, Chinese students at the University of Hawaii began in the 1920s to compose stories, poems, and plays about plantation life, generational conflict, and other local topics.

Perhaps the most significant literary production of this period was a body of twenty-three short stories published in 1947 and 1948 in the short-lived literary magazine *Xinmiao* (*The Bud*). Marked by an assertive pro-labor tone, openness about taboo topics, the use of Cantonese, and a wry sense of humor, these stories foreshadowed the growth of a Chinese American literary sensibility in the 1960s and 1970s. These stories, which betray the isolationist nature of the community, exhibit a strong China-centered nationalism. They clearly reflect the ambiguous identity of Chinese Americans in this transitory period between the repeal of the exclusion laws in 1943 and the later full-fledged reunification of families and restoration of citizen rights.[9]

Like other progressive writers, Chinese, American-educated, emigré authors articulated a defense of China during the war years. Women authors Helena Kuo, Adet Lin, Lin Tai-yi (Anor Lin), and Ma-Mai Sze wrote books stressing the courage and ingenuity of the Chinese people amidst the horror of war. This romanticized portrayal has become central to nostalgic novels written by such contemporary authors as Hazel Lin, Virginia Lee, and Bette Bao Lord. Lin Tai-yi's *War Tide* (1943) typifies the exuberent patriotism exhibited in these works. The plot centers on the exploits of an eighteen-year-old girl, Lo-Yin Tai, whose creativity and intelligence shelter her multi-generational family from wartime turmoil. Fueled by patriotic ardor, these women writers attempted to win Western allies for China by proving through their writings that the Chinese people deserved the assistance and respect of the international community.

SECOND-GENERATION AUTOBIOGRAPHERS

That defensive posture was shared by American-born Chinese autobiographers, including Jade Snow Wong and Padree Lowe who came of age in the 1940s. Socialized to accept the assimilationist rhetoric, these early autobiographers sought acceptance from the American society. To that end, they tried to distance themselves from their Chinese heritage; Lowe even eschewed any bicultural identity. Their writings offer a linear progression of Chinese American life from tradition to modernity, from conformity to individual freedom that accords well with the melting pot myth.[10]

Both Lowe's *Father and Glorious Descendant* (1943) and Wong's *Fifth Chinese Daughter* (1945), however, are far from being simple expositions of minorities who attained the American dream. In spite of the Chinatown "tours" of its supposed quaint customs and culture, which underscore the alienness of the Chinese and thus betray the authors' self-contempt, both works attest to the impact of racial discrimination on Chinese Americans. Lowe chose to assimilate into the dominant culture because a Chinese American identity in those days connoted an inferiority to whites on the basis of race. Wong, less alienated from the Chinese culture, could never elude the sense of being a sojourner in a foreign land in spite of her birthright and American education. To resolve this dilemma, she chose to use her Chinese background selectively—mainly her knowledge of exotic Chinese foodways—to gain the acceptance of white Americans. At the same time, she tried to elevate her female-defined status in the family and community by striving for autonomy, equal rights, and access to educational and business opportunities. But Wong, like Lowe, could find acceptance only within the white frame of reference. Like the privileged Chinese-born writers of the previous century, both downplayed racism, attributing the generational conflicts, and even failures, within family and community life to cultural propensities rather than to limitations imposed by the larger society.

SKETCHES OF CHINATOWN LIFE

This distorted perception of Chinese life in the United States received credence from the conformist nature of American society in the 1950s. Typically represented as the affluent age with heavy emphasis on consumption and leisure, the 1950s saw the reaffirmation of domesticity for women and corporatism for men. A conflict-free society supposedly prevailed. The few Chinese American sketches of Chinatown life published before the 1960s speak to that consensus. Lin Yutang's *Chinatown Family* (1948) is a maudlin story of the travails of a laundryman's family who has recently joined the father at his laundry. The characters are docile, grateful Chinese who accept prejudice and hardship cheerfully. Their eventual success in this land of plenty will come through hard work and good luck.

Similarly, *Flower Drum Song* (1957) written by Chin Yang Lee, which was adapted into a Broadway musical and popular motion picture, confirms the success narrative—the harbinger of the model minority myth—for Chinese Americans. The characters in this novel, not unlike the harmless, servile servant image, comically, and easily, solve perplexing social issues, such as a shortage of female conjugal partners and job discrimination, against a Chinatown backdrop of quaint customs and exotic foods. There is perhaps a historical parallel between these exotic guided Chinatown tours and the nineteenth-century travel books on China written by Christian missionaries and visitors. Like the earlier works, those by Wong, Lowe, Lin, and Chin offer entertaining voyeuristic insights into the adventures of the "other." Marlon K. Hom has argued that *Flower Drum Song* and other contemporaneous short stories published in the 1960s, being the products of recent immigrant writers, also poke fun at American-born Chinese who are regarded as pseudo-Americans, yet not fully Chinese.[11]

ARTICULATIONS OF A CHINESE AMERICAN SENSIBILITY

By the time the landmark *Eat a Bowl of Tea* (1961) by Louis Chu appeared, the Chinese American community was on the threshold of change. As reflected in this novel of social realism, which had its roots in the left-wing literature of the 1930s and 1940s, the community of aging bachelors was being reinvigorated in the postwar years through the reunification of families and the entry of new immigrants. Like other Chinatown bachelors, the protagonist Wah Gay is racked by guilt for abandoning his wife and family in China. To redeem himself, he arranges a marriage between his son, Ben Loy, and Chinese-born Mei Oi, the daughter of an old friend. Wah Gay decides, in a decisive move to break with the past, that Mei Oi should live in the United States and immediately start a family with Ben Loy. This plan, which allows Wah Gay to live through his son his unfulfilled responsibilities, is derailed when Ben Loy turns out to be impotent. Mei Oi has an extramarital liasion and becomes pregnant. Her affair triggers a chain of revelations: a mundane, debilitating life in Chinatown; the fallacy of patriarchal guidance; and the fragility of the sense of community. By the end of the novel, the lesson is clear: the multiple self-deceptions that pervade Chinatown can be avoided if the residents move away from constricting Chinese traditions and forge ties of affection and intimacy within the family and community.[12]

Chu's novel is a critical text in Chinese American literature because it departs from the assimilationist or Chinatown tour guide imperative found in earlier tales of Chinatown, "provides a narrative of community life at a critical historical moment, and employs 'Chinatown English' without overtones of caricature."[13] Additionally, in dramatizing the converging impact of racialized and gendered immigration laws and patriarchy on this society, as symbolically represented in Ben Loy's sexual impotence, Chu anticipated the more self-conscious articulation of such issues made by Asian Americans beginning in the late 1960s.

While *Eat a Bowl of Tea* shows the incipient development of a Chinese American sensibility, some of the later works produced during the turbulent period of the 1960s and early 1970s belie strident cultural nationalism. The Black Power and anti–Vietnam War movements gave momentum to Asian American–organized efforts to challenge racism and white cultural influence. Frank Chin's artistic contributions speak to that context. His plays *Chickencoop Chinaman* and *The Year of the Dragon*, first performed in 1972 and 1974, respectively, as well as his short stories, attempt to reclaim Chinese American manhood and provide a male-oriented Asian American heroic identity. Rejecting the stereotypes of the past, Chin offers characters who must escape the decaying, commercialized Chinatown in order to find a new identity. In both *Chickencoop Chinaman* and *Year of the Dragon*, Chin explains that this identity should not be simply "American" or "Chinese." Chin's worldview, however, is a limiting one. The criteria used to define the Chinese American identity—native birth, English speaking, and masculine ethos—ignore the changing composition and agendas of the Chinese American community. It is also one full of contradictions. Even as he rejects assimilation, he invokes icons of American popular culture (such as the Lone Ranger). Chin nevertheless also taps into the heroic exploits of Chinese classics for cultural modeling. Though the identity he seeks is supposed to be unique, his literary landscape features the tradition-bound elders such as those found in *Flower Drum Song* and Americanized individuals such as those found in *Fifth Chinese Daughter*. In short, the search for a Chinese American identity seems futile.[14]

Other works that share to some degree Chin's didacticism and pessimistic tone—one that is understandable given the temper of the times—include Jeffrey Paul Chan's short stories and, to a lesser extent, Shawn Wong's *Homebase* (1979). In Wong's *Homebase*, a lyrical paean to the Chinese American heritage, the reconciliation between father and son underscores the nexus between the past and the present and the possibility of cultural healing.

Less American-centered would be the works of Chinese-born, cosmopolitan writers who explore the diaspora of the *Huaqiao* ("overseas Chinese"). These works of the 1960s and 1970s are far less concerned with defending the Chinese culture or mediating the divide between the Chinese and Western worlds. They are focused on exploring the malleable nature of identity within the parameters of diasporic social formation. Unencumbered by nation-state boundaries, the characters and their lives in these works offer a critique of Chinese and American historical and cultural hegemony. The characters, not surprisingly, suffer from a sense of personal dislocation as revealed in Chung Hua's *Crossings* (1968) and Hualing Nieh's *Mulberry and Peach* (1981).

FEMINIST VOICES AND THE CHINESE AMERICAN IDENTITY

The theme of searching for self-definition, which has resonated since the days of the *jinshan ge*, reverberates in a revised fashion in Maxine Hong Kingston's award-winning, semiautobiographical *The Woman Warrior* (1976) and her historically grounded *China Men* (1980). Of the two, *The Woman Warrior* has received by far more attention. Because of the foregrounding of the mother-daughter relationship and the portrayal of the influence of sexism in Chinese American life, this book falls within the body of feminist scholarship. The book—a mingling of personal reminiscences, family events, folktales, and fantasies—is also, in an echo of Wong's *Fifth Chinese Daughter*, about the struggle to reconcile the tension between her Chinese ancestry and her American upbringing. Like Wong, Kingston's search for self necessarily involves a definition of "home," whether it be America or China or somewhere else. *Woman Warrior*, because of its original narrative style and exploration of gender and generational tensions, won numerous honors, culminating with the 1976 National Book Critics Circle Award for nonfiction. But Kingston's work, notwithstanding its well-deserved acclaim, was prefigured by a number of works, ranging from the Angel Island poems to the meditative prose of Shawn Wong, which also articulate protest, storytelling, nostalgia, and even experimentation.[15]

Like *Woman Warrior, China Men* addresses the intersection of racial and national identities. *China Men*, like the works of Frank Chin and others, lays claim to America for Chinese Americans. The imposed silences, such as the angry silence of the father, which parallels that of the aunt in *Woman Warrior* who cannot tell her tale, are shattered through the narrative of "talk stories." Like *Woman Warrior, China Man*, though a less personal journey, is about the reconciliation of present-day Chinese Americans and their immigrant forefathers, which is facilitated by their common roots in American soil and their shared opposition to colonialism.

Some Asian American male critics have lambasted Kingston's works. Both *Woman Warrior* and *China Men*, argue Chin and others, uphold the racist stereotypes of Chinese American men as weak-willed or brutish creatures. The male characters in these works, they allege, are also one dimensional, oppressively patriarchal, and chauvinistic, even though both texts acknowledge the interplay of structural barriers, such as racialized and gendered immigration laws, with cultural traditions and how those, in turn, established unequal gender relationships within Chinese America. Dismissing her works as the ventures of an author who has cashed in on the "feminist fad" and thus "sold out" for economic gain, Chin also alleges that Kingston has distorted Chinese traditions and language to pander to white readers' craving for Orientalism and, in that sense, is no better than those who tried to pass off Chinatown tour guides as literature.[16]

These critics have failed to note the overall vision embedded within Kingston's works: the literary creation of a unique Chinese American sensibility through a process that reconstitutes history and memory. That same innovation appears in Kingston's *Tripmaster Monkey: His Fake Book* (1989) which focuses on the antics of Wittman Ah Sing, a 1960s man of letters modeled on Frank Chin. The plot centers on Wittman who puts on a marathon show for friends and family. Along the way, Kingston manipulates Chinese literary classics and Euro-American canons and raises the question of creating a community-building Chinese American art.

Since Kingston's highly publicized success, works by Asian women writers that deal with female-centered issues include Alice Lin's autobiographical *Grandmother Had No Name* (1988); the short stories in *Home to Stay: Asian American Women's Fiction* (1990), edited by Sylvia Watanabe and Carol Bruchac; and Fae Myenne Ng's *Bone* (1993), a novel about an immigrant family with three daughters.

Amy Tan's *The Joy Luck Club* (1989), typically regarded as a thematic continuation and expansion of Kingston's *Woman Warrior*, may be the most well-known work since Kingston's works joined mainstream fiction. Tan, who is, like Kingston, a second-generation Chinese American, offers in this book interlocking stories that portray the generational and cultural differences between American-born daughters and their Chinese-born mothers. Later made into a successful Hollywood film, *Joy Luck Club* (1993), the novel like *Woman Warrior*, is an accessible work because of the apparent universality of the mother-daughter experience, particularly the struggle of daughters to free themselves from controlling mothers even as they become more aware of how their sense of self is tied inextricably to their mothers'. Unlike *Woman Warrior*, however, Tan's novel addresses the issue of race in a non-threatening way, sidelining historical legacy and containing the identity question within the convoluted dynamics of the mother-daughter relationship.[17]

Tan again examines this relationship between the two generations in her follow-up novel, *The Kitchen God's Wife* (1991), although here the focus is on exposing gender inequality in China as experienced by the mother, Winnie. Those experiences as recalled through the use of irony, humor, and allegory serve as important lessons to her daughter who, at the end of the novel, resolves to avoid her mother's fate and to fuse her husband's Western, rational humanism with her mother's ways of knowing and spiritualism. More recently Tan wrote *The Hundred Senses* (1995), which centers on the relationship between an American-born sister and her Chinese-born stepsister and how she learns from her stepsister to appreciate the mystical Chinese worldview.

STAGING THE CHINESE

Unlike their strong presence in prose fiction, Chinese Americans have been less visible on the stage. At the turn of the century, Chinese representations appeared in vaudeville, circus shows, melodramas, and even as museum displays and functioned as exotics, comic relief, or sideshow freaks. Stereotypes of the Chinese abounded in anti-Asian plays such as *Ah Sin!* (1877) and *The Chinese Must Go* (1879). Until the 1950s' staged version of *Flower Drum Song*, most Chinese characters were played by whites.

While the staging of Frank Chin's plays in the 1970s did garner some attention, the mainstream theater stage remained unreceptive to Asian American artistic expression. It took David Henry Hwang's riveting play, *M. But-*

terfly (first performed 1988; published 1989) to shatter that barrier. Set in China, *M. Butterfly* is based on the true story of a twenty-year love affair between Song Liling, a transvestive Chinese opera singer turned spy, and a French diplomat, who believed Song was a woman. The play is quite controversial. Like *Joy Luck Club*, *M. Butterfly* has been criticized for presenting stereotypes of emasculated yet conniving "Oriental" men, particularly as represented in Song Liling. On the other hand, *M. Butterfly* is also an obvious subversion of Puccini's *Madame Butterfly*, an opera that articulates the white male fantasy of dominating the submissive Asian woman. Hwang's play has received accolades because of its attempt to redefine the Chinese American identity by confronting sexism, Orientalism, and imperialism. Hwang has written other well-received plays such as *FOB* (a play about the contemporary conflict between American-born and immigrant Chinese) and *The Dance and the Railroad* (which centers on the dreams and aspirations of early Chinese railroad workers), which were first staged, respectively, in 1979 and 1981 (and collected in *Broken Promises* [1983]). But it was *M. Butterfly*, with its transgression of Puccini's opera *Madame Butterfly* and blend of naturalistic dialogue with expressionistic or fantastic sequences, that catapulated him into the national limelight, culminating in his receiving the Tony award for best American play in 1988.[18]

Few playwrights, other than Hwang and Chin, have captured national attention. Limited by budgetary restrictions, most plays have had only minimal staging and limited engagements. The few published dramas include Laurence Yep's *Pay the Chinaman* (1990), which explores hardships in the late nineteenth-century Sacramento delta, and Genny Lim's *Paper Angels* (1991), based on the experiences of Chinese detainees in the Angel Island Immigration Station.

POETIC VISIONS

Chinese American poetry, like drama, has received far less critical attention than prose fiction. Yet there is a rich body of works that reflect the growing diverse composition of Chinese America. They range from Shirley Geok-lin Lim's poems, which embody her Chinese Malaysian origins, to Wing Tek Lum's writings dealing with family and love, usually within a Chinese Hawaiian context. The themes also range from diasporic pieces from Russell Leong, a veteran of the Asian American movement, to the poetics of place of Chinese Hawaiian poet Eric Chock. Arthur Sze meditates on the power of nature, and lesbian poets Kitty Tsui, Nellie Wong, and Merle Woo have vocalized the intersection of sexuality, community, and citizenship. The work of a number of these poets can be found in *Chinese American Poetry: An Anthology* (1991), edited by L. Ling-Chi Wang and Henry Yiheng Zhao, which is the only booklength collection of such poetry.[19]

Within this multifaceted corpus, the poems of the late 1960s and early 1970s embody the spirit of an emerging ethnic consciousness against the backdrop of the Asian American movement. Since then, the demographic changes within Chinese America have problematized efforts to shape a cohesive Chinese, and Asian, American identity. Poets now focus on how history and ideology can destabilize the sense of self.

NEW TRENDS IN LITERATURE

The demographic changes have also prompted writers of all genres to respond to that reality. Gish Jen's novel *Typical American* (1992) explores the bicultural transformation that occurred when Shanghai refugees of the elite class fleeing the Communist Revolution came to America. Equally distant from the literary analysis of Cantonese male laborers is Fae Myenne Ng's *Bone* (1993), the feminist-driven, allegorical story of an immigrant family of three daughters, who, like the women in *Joy Luck Club*, struggle with the legacy of history and traditions. Writers are also in step with the phenomenon of increasing interracial unions and its impact on offspring; Sigrid Nunez's *A Feather on the Breath of God* (1995) and Gus Lee's *Honor and Duty* (1994) have deliberated on this issue. Perhaps a sign of the maturity of Chinese American literature is the emergence of the previously underexamined subject of heterosexual, erotic relations between adults as found in Shawn Wong's *American Knees* (1995), which marks a departure from the coming-of-age theme that had taken center stage in previous works.

MEDIA ARTS

Like literature, Chinese American media arts reflect the twin strands of a common experience of Western domination and the growing diversity of national origin, class background, gender, and dialect. Chinese American filmmaking during the activist era of 1960s and 1970s, given its ideological role, was irreverent, subversive, and grounded in community life. Such a vision led filmmakers to prefer the documentary format (most still do) over the feature film because the documentary allows an emphasis to be placed on self-definition and the subversions of official history. Gritty, anti-slick Chinatown documentaries that attest to that include Curtis Choy's portrayal of street culture in *Dupont Guy: The Schiz of Grant Avenue* (1975), the

Philadelphia Chinatown community's fight against redevelopment as captured in *Save Chinatown* (1973), and *From Spikes to Spindles* (1976), which outlines the convergence of Third World political culture in New York City's lower eastside. Perhaps the most well-known movement-oriented documentary is *The Fall of the I-Hotel* (1983), which documents a powerful, collective resistance against the city's real estate interests bent on evicting the aging Asian residents of that hotel.[20]

By the 1980s Asian American filmmakers were gaining access to funding and mainstream venues. Simultaneously the movement became more institutionalized as arts centers, legal aid, public health centers, and advocacy groups secured offices and professional staffs. Similarly, the disparate media arts centers (including New York Chinatown–based Asian Cinevision), which mushroomed in the 1970s to support media activity in production, exhibition, distribution, and advocacy, pooled their resources in 1980 and organized the National Asian American Telecommunications Association (NAATA) to end stereotyped depictions of Asian Americans in the media arts and increase the visibility of Asian Americans in public broadcasting.

As Asian American cinema became more market driven, and greater attention was given to art and professionalism over politics, filmmakers began branching out into documentaries for public television, low-budget feature films with limited theatrical release, and, for a few, film school product. Of the three genres, documentaries have stood out in quality and quantity. Apparently, investors are reluctant to invest in Asian American feature films for commercial release given their supposed lack of mass market appeal, and experimental films made by film school students vary in quality.

INNOVATIVE DOCUMENTARIES

Noteworthy documentaries for the Public Broadcasting Service (PBS)— most of which traverse at least one of the terrains of racism, identity formation, and community—have, like works in literature, typically covered turning points in Chinese American history. Outstanding documentaries include Christina Choy and Renee Tajima's *Who Killed Vincent Chin?* (1989), an exploration of the traumatic outcome of a mistaken identity in Detroit in 1981. Arthur Dong's colorful *Forbidden City* (1989) explodes the myth of the Chinese as "bowlegged" performers by depicting the exuberent lives of Chinatown cabaret artists who offered American-style shows for predominately white audiences in the 1930s and 1940s. Deborah Gee's provocative *Slaying the Dragon* (1990) outlines Hollywood's recycling of skewed images of Asian American women over the past sixty years; *Slaying the Dragon* demonstrates that these images are deeply embedded within the American popular consciousness. No less important is *Carved in Silence* (1988) by Felicia Lowe, which reveals the arbitrariness of the immigration clearance process that played out on Angel Island before World War II. Earlier Lowe made a personal diary film, *China: Land of My Father* (1979), a chronicle of her moving return to her family village in Canton. Like *China*, Lisa Hsia's *Made in China* (1986) speaks to the deep, enduring ties between American-born Chinese and China.

Perhaps the most well-known PBS, and now independent, filmmaker and producer is Loni Ding, whose *Bean Sprouts*, which began airing in 1981, was the first national children's television series to portray the lives of Chinese American children with a multicultural approach. She went on to make the critically acclaimed *Nisei Soldier: Standard Bearer for an Exiled People* (1984) and *The Color of Honor* (1987), both of which recounted the heroic deeds of Japanese American soldiers, and the stylized *Island of Secret Memories* (1987), a program about Chinese detention on Angel Island. Ding also contributed to *With Silk Wings, Asian American Women at Work* (1990), a series of four short documentaries. Notwithstanding the title, *With Silk Wings* examines, aside from work, the immigration process, personal aspirations, and daily challenges of these women.[21]

FEATURE FILMS AND MAINSTREAMING

Like the documentary genre, Chinese American feature films raise questions about cultural and personal identity. Such questions, like the similar ones asked in literature, are deliberated within the conflicts that ensue when the traditions of two societies affect an individual's life. In Wayne Wang's *Dim Sum* (1985), these conflicts are put in the context of a traditionally minded Chinese mother who wants her American-born daughter to marry before the mother passes away. Wang also made the film version of Louis Chu's novel *Eat a Bowl of Tea* in 1988. Wang, a Hong Kong–born immigrant, is probably best known for his critically acclaimed 1981 film, *Chan Is Missing*. The plot centers on the efforts of a middle-aged Chinese man and his nephew to solve a mystery, but the parade of a diverse set of characters undermines the stereotype that all Chinese are alike.

Even as Chinese independent filmmakers receive more attention, Chinese American actors, directors, writers, and producers, like their Asian-descent counterparts, are experiencing the stirrings of mainstreaming. Joan Chen is perhaps one of the most recognized Chinese actresses in Hollywood with major roles in such blockbusters as *The Last Emperor* (1987) and *Heaven and*

Earth (1993). Jason Scott Lee has been dubbed the first Chinese American actor cast as a romantic lead with broad market appeal with roles in *Map of the Human Heart* (1992), *Dragon: The Bruce Lee Story* (1993), and *Jungle Book* (1994). Director Wang's big break came with his involvement in the film version of *The Joy Luck Club* (1993). Taiwan-born Ang Lee, who directed the Academy Award nominee, *The Wedding Banquet* (1993), a touching farce with a comical gay theme about family, marriage, and commitment, went on to work behind the camera on *Sense and Sensibility* (1995), based on the Jane Austen's novel. Finally, action-film director John Woo, born and raised in Hong Kong, has directed two box-office hits, *Broken Arrow* (1996) and *Face Off* (1997).

Asian American artists still have to contend with serious barriers. Chinese Americans involved in mainstream media arts face the risk of the culture, history, and experiences being commodified for the consuming pleasure of mass audiences. Since the mainstream industry panders to nostalgic sentimentality and avoids controversial topics, artists may have to compromise their integrity and vision.

Artists must also contend with racist depictions of Asians and Asian Americans. Michael Camino's film *Year of the Dragon* (1984), as well as *China Girl* (1987) and *Casualties of War* (1989), all of which feature stereotypes and violence, raised objections from Asian American activist groups. *Year of the Dragon*, for example, features Hollywood actor Mickey Rourke in the role of a straight-laced lawman, Stanley White, who receives the assignment of cleaning up the corrupted New York's Chinatown as embodied in the Chinese villain, Joey Tai (John Lone). The romance subplot also misrepresents Chinese Americans; Tracy Tzu (Ariane), who plays the China Doll role, submits to White's advances. On the other hand, the martial-arts exponent Bruce Lee, in his films, such as the blockbuster *Enter the Dragon* (1972), is portrayed as lacking sexual interest or even a social life. In more recent years, popular action-thrillers like *The Shadow* (1994) and *The Phantom* (1996) have also revived Fu Manchu–like Asian characters.[22]

TELEVISION

Chinese Americans on television have fared no better than their co-ethnic peers in films. Like the movies, network television has portrayed Chinese Americans in a distorted manner. Chinese American men, until recently, were cast as helpful domestic servants to whites. In the series *Bachelor Father* (1957–1960), *Have Gun Will Travel* (1957–1960), *Bonanza* (1959–1973), *The Green Hornet* (1966–1967), and *Falcon Crest* (1981–1990), Chinese male actors functioned as submissive foils for heroic, overly masculine masters or employers. Another race-typed role for Chinese American men is the loyal sidekick police detective to strong-willed white superiors—a role that revives the Charlie Chan persona. In the long-running *Hawaii-Five-O* (1968–1980), actors Kam Fong and others, without any questions, carried out the orders of the white men in charge. Similarly, in the series *Midnight Caller* (1988–1991), actor Dennis Dun played the role of an able assistant to Jack Killian (Gary Cole), a radio talk show host who solved crimes in his spare time. Like the Chinese American male characters in literature and films, those on television are asexual or bereft of romantic inclinations. One example of this is Hop Sing (Victor Sen Yung) in *Bonanza* who, throughout the long run of this series, seemed content to be a womanless bachelor.[23]

The female counterparts of these sexless male characters, like those in literature and films, embody sexual prowess and are naturally drawn to white males. The theme of Asian female sexual possession by white men has appeared in a number of television Western series, including *Bonanza* and *How the West Was Won* (1978–1979), and more recently in the PBS rendition of Ruthanne Lum McCunn's semibiographical novel of the life of a woman sold into prostitution, *Thousand Pieces of Gold* (1992). The well-known actress Joan Chen has played roles akin to Anna May Wong's; for example, in the miniseries *Tai-Pan*, she is the China-Doll harlot of a rugged British sea merchant. Chen was cast in a similar role in a 1989 episode from the series, *Wiseguy* (1987–1990), where she turns from a committed labor organizer into a kinky sexpot while seducing the lead character, an FBI agent.

In more recent years, the general voyeuristic interest in Asian American gangs has led to a revival of the stock theme of the omnipotent role of tongs in the life of the Chinese American community. In an episode of *Gideon Oliver* (1989), the presence of such Chinese secret societies is seen as endemic to this community. Such a perception has been reinforced by numerous segments on television magazine shows and television specials that ignore the structural barriers—alienation, racism, parental problems, and limited job opportunities—which have led to such antisocial behavior in favor of sensationalistic, Yellow Peril coverage. In television series that have featured gang-themed episodes, such as the action-packed *MacGyver* (1985–1992), Chinatown is riddled with gratuitous violence that gangs perpetrate for the sake of profits and power. Like the nineteenth-century progenitors portrayed in literature, the contemporary Chinese American criminal exploits his country people, keeps women in sexual bondage, and seeks to undermine the moral fabric of this Christian country.

Clearly, since the beginning of the television industry, the representation of Chinese Americans has always been skewed to reinforce existing power relations; however, there are hopeful signs of a change for the better. The standard portrayal of the Chinese American male as a nonheroic victim or evil villain was first altered a little with the appearance of the program *Kung Fu* (1972–1975). Featuring the character of a Shaolin martial arts expert, this series broke new grounds because Kwai Chang Caine, the lead, never ran away from his attackers or allowed himself to be bullied. Unfortunately, Kwai, the offspring of an interracial union, was played by a white character, David Carradine. *Kung Fu* was also controversial because Bruce Lee was originally considered for the leading role, but the racist perception that an Asian man could never come across on the tube as heroic cost him the role, No Chinese American, male or female, would ever star in a role until the syndicated miniseries *Vanishing Son* (1994–1995) came along. *Vanishing Son* featured Russell Wong as Jian-Wa Chang, a fugitive from the law who is framed for two murders. Unlike Carradine's Kwai, Chang is as virile and sexual as he is fearless. Though it turned into a weekly series in 1995, declining ratings eventually killed the show.[22]

VISUAL ARTS AND MUSIC

Chinese American contributions to the arts have included other less highly visible means of expression. In the visual arts, Hung Liu's 1991 San Francisco exhibit of paintings of young Chinese prostitutes from the early decades of this century is noteworthy because it documents the forgotten lives of these women and interplays illusions and gazes. In her 1994 installation at the San Francisco DeYoung Museum entitled *Jiu Jin Shan* (On Gold Mountain), Liu has turned her attention to the barren promise of America. The main elements of the installation are asymptotic railroad tracks covered by a mountain of fortune cookies. The lesson is clear: the early Chinese railroad laborers, like Kingston's grandfather in *China Men*, never found gold or riches as suggested by the fortune cookies, which contain no fortune and are not even Chinese.[25]

In the visual arts, particularly in public architecture, no one has rivaled the career of Maya Lin. The daughter of educated refugees who fled Communist rule on mainland China, Lin's Vietnam Veterans Memorial, dedicated in 1982, captured the imagination of the American public but raised a firestorm of controversy. The memorial is a simple, but meaningful, structure: two black granite walls in the shape of a chevron, which meet at a 125-degree angle. Created to evoke "personal reflection and private reckoning" on the meaning of death and loss, to quote Lin herself, the design of the memorial in the minds of some veterans, political commentators, and politicians was antiheroic and made a mockery of the courage and sacrifice of the Vietnam veterans. The passage of time, however, has proven that Lin's Asian-influenced artistic vision was on the mark; the memorial has become a place of reconciliation and healing.[26]

The participation of Chinese Americans in the arts has come of age. Perhaps no other cultural expression captures this artistic maturity as clearly as the development of Chinese American jazz and creative music, which blends different musical styles, including African American jazz, Asian folk rhythms, Arabic modes, reggae beats, and uses Korean and Chinese instruments as well as Western ones. Characterized often by changing meters and moods, this music, as reflected in the works of Fred Wei-han Ho and Jon Jang, speaks to the rising Chinese American national consciousness, one that articulates *xungen wenzu* (searching for one's roots and ancestors) within a diasporic framework.[27]

Innovative, energetic, and breaking the boundaries of time, space, and culture, the arts as shaped by Chinese American writers, artists, and performers will continue to challenge both neoassimilationism—the argument that nonwhite minorities will and must conform to the dominant American culture and institutions—and liberal pluralism, that is, the assumption that members of diverse cultures can develop their own culture in the confines of the larger, common culture. The process of forging a Chinese American sensibility in this changing republic will be ongoing, multifaceted, and even subversive.

Chinese American Families and Identities

THE MODEL MINORITY

The Chinese American family, which before the 1960s suffered harsh immigration laws and other structural barriers, has since then undergone a transformation. No longer a fractured or split-household unit, the family is now a highly complex one. Furthermore, because of the changing composition of new arrivals since the end of World War II and the pervasive presence of acculturative forces, the nature of Chinese American families is ever fluid.

Research into Chinese American family life is still in its infancy. The literature on the family is limited primarily because some social scientists did not consider this "model minority" as being beset with social and economic problems. Also, until recently, Asian Americans were underrepresented among social scientists so that few insiders were available to conduct community-oriented research. Finally, the small number of Chinese Americans and their geographical concentration in just a few states have made them seem invisible and sociologically unimportant.

Much of the existing literature to date argues that Chinese American success in educational and economic advancement stems from deeply held values embedded in the Chinese culture, particularly Confucianism. Strong familial ties, close control of children, traditional family values, and collective solidarity over individual interest supposedly explain why Chinese Americans have overcome racism and poverty to attain educational and income levels that exceed even those of Euro-Americans. The low rates of divorce, illegitimacy, adolescent rebellion, and delinquency are also attributed to the co-hesiveness of Chinese culture. Any change over time, such as the decline in female subordination, is regarded as the product of assimilation; any cultural continuity, such as economic self-sufficiency, attests to the strength of the Chinese ethos.[1]

Since the mid-1960s that overall portrait has contributed to the emergence of the model-minority myth. In a reversal of negative Orientalism, Chinese (along with other Asian Americans) have received high commendation from the media and politicians for their good social behavior and economic success. Such celebrations of Asian American achievements have, however, exagger-ated this success and created a damaging new myth. Comparisons of incomes between Chinese and whites fail to take into account that the Chinese are concentrated in states with higher costs of living which negate the higher incomes of this group. Pundits and politicians also herald the fact that Chi-nese Americans enjoy a higher average family income than whites, which in 1990 ranged from $4,000 to $5,000 higher than that of white families. What is typically ignored, however, is that Chinese American families have more persons working per family than the white family; in 1980, white nuclear families in California had 1.6 workers per family compared to 2.0 for im-migrant Chinese.[2] Hence the higher family incomes of Chinese Americans are the product of having more workers in each family, rather than higher income per person. That approximately 11 percent of all Chinese American families in 1990 live in poverty, compared to 7 percent of all white families, is a piece of information that is rarely discussed in the popular media.[3]

The model-minority image is harmful to Chinese Americans in several ways. It is framed within the assimilationist paradigm, which homogenizes Chinese American families and ignores the diversity in classes and subgroups. Clearly, the myth diverts needed attention from segments of the population that are still grappling with socioeconomic barriers. This static understanding also dismisses structural forces such as immigration laws, labor market con-ditions, and the lack of political rights that have forced families and individ-uals to reshape culture constantly for survival. The myth also downplays the level of racial discrimination Chinese Americans encounter in their lives. Asian American youth face undue tension because the myth places pressure on them to succeed in school. Finally, the myth can fuel competition and resentment between Asian Americans and other racial minorities. The first media article printed, in 1966, on the Chinese American success story, states, "At a time when . . . hundreds of billions be spent to uplift Negroes and other minorities, the nation's 300,000 Chinese-Americans are moving ahead on their own, with no help from anyone else."[4] In contrasting the supposed self-sufficiency of Chinese Americans to African American demands for government support for community social services, pundits and politicians are in effect arguing that welfare and affirmative action are obsolete since all racial minorities can emulate Asian Americans if they just work hard, remain politically quiet, and assimilate into the dominant American culture.

CONTEXT OF FAMILY FORMATION

Changing historical and contemporary circumstances explain why Chinese American families seem to be cohesive and achievement oriented. Before World War II, the sojourning status of most immigrants meant that they were motivated to defer gratification to maximize future mobility. Then the almost complete halt of Asian immigration for several decades in the twentieth century probably reduced economic pressures on the Chinese American community and allowed for more social investment in the small second generation.

The perceived stability of Chinese families is an illusion. Before the 1960s, spouses in Chinese families rarely divorced because of the lack of alternative options outside of the ghettoized family-oriented businesses. Women seldom sought divorce because the Chinese community deemed that measure distasteful. Some women resorted to the more desperate measure of suicide. A low delinquency rate before World War II stemmed from the shortage of adolescents in the population. Few Chinese in that period turned to welfare because of the "paper son" and "paper daughter" status of many immigrants. Their lack of knowledge of American institutions and their general distrust of officials also explain why Chinese are reluctant to approach social service agencies.[5]

Legal obstacles in immigration to the United States account for the prolonged existence of extended (and pseudo-) kinship ties within the Chinese American community. Without these ties Chinese would not have found their way to America via chain migration and fraudulent entries. Kinship-like institutions, such as benevolent associations, ameliorate economic and political discrimination. By the same extension, family cohesiveness reflects the historical exigency for all members of the family to work together as part of the adaptation to American life.[6]

The lingering legacy of anti-Asian sentiments, as reflected in the anti-immigration climate of the 1980s and 1990s; the entrenched existence of a split-labor market that relegates racial minorities to low-paying dead-end jobs; the revival of the enclave economy that embraces small-producer enterprises; and the continuing entry of new Chinese immigrants (as many as two-thirds of the Chinese in 1990 were foreign-born) who are unattuned to the American culture have all perpetuated these so-called cultural dynamics. Kinship ties, benevolent associations, Chinese schools, family cohesion, and the informal transmission of Chinese heritage are still necessary for survival.

CHARACTERISTICS OF CHINESE AMERICAN FAMILIES

Since the liberalization of immigration laws in the mid-1960s, heterogeneity among Chinese American families along the lines of nativity, class, and generation has been a salient characteristic. Among recent immigrant families, large and extended households are fairly typical. The 1990 census shows that a greater proportion of Chinese, compared to white, households had three, four, five, six, seven, or more persons. In contrast, the majority of white households—59 percent—consisted of one or two persons.[7] The disparity between Chinese and whites can be accounted for in several ways. First, Chinese adult children tend to live at home while completing their education. In fact, some married offspring and their own families still reside in their parents' homes. Furthermore, more elderly relatives live with their families. The size of these households has been augmented by newly arrived immigrant relatives. These circumstances explain why a smaller proportion of members in Chinese households were nonfamily members compared to white households.[8]

Nuclear family units, which are more akin to Euro-American families, can be found among professional suburban families. Even among these professional families, however, some chain migration has increased the size of the households. Some recent immigrants from Taiwan and Hong Kong, whether of the professional or self-employed cohort, have set up one-person households in America, leaving their wives and children behind at least until they are ready to send for them through this relay immigration process.

The Bureau of Census statistics that show 81.6 percent of the Chinese in 1990 under the age of eighteen lived in two-parent households do not necessarily indicate family stability. The low rate of divorce (2.0 percent in 1990) and the high marriage rate, which in turn produced the preponderance of two-parent household units, in fact stemmed from the rising number of reconstituted families that were separated before the 1960s.[9] Furthermore, a number of the post–World War II conjugal unions possibly included hasty marriages, in which Chinese women entered into relationships with Chinese American men to circumvent existing restrictive laws through war bride and other subsequent legislation. Thus there is some doubt that these matrimonial ties involve strong emotional bonds and cohesive households.

Contrary to popular perception, some contemporary Chinese American families are headed by females. The 1990 Bureau of Census statistics reveal that 7.8 percent of all Chinese households are headed by females, and, of that figure, 28.3 percent live below the poverty line.[10] Such households reflect in part the unremitting entry of displaced persons from parts of Asia suffering from economic dislocation. This figure has also been shaped by return migration of Chinese males, particularly those of the professional and self-employed groups. These men return to Asia to seek better fortunes leaving their wives to shoulder the burden of child rearing and share in the responsibility of economic support.

WORKING-CLASS IMMIGRANT FAMILIES

Most working-class immigrant parents today have had to forsake parental supervision as a result of their labor-intensive jobs in the secondary labor market or enclave economy. Unlike those involved in family enterprises or self-employment, husbands and wives in these dual-worker families experience a complete segregation of work and family life. In one study published in 1987, conducted among Chinese immigrants in New York City, 82 percent of the children lived with both mother and father, but 32 percent did not see their fathers from one day to the next and 21 percent never even caught a glimpse of their mothers. The parents' fatigue, lack of common experience, and endless hours of separation hinder communication between parents and their children. In most families, parental authority is often exercised by the mothers, who, compared to the fathers, spend more time with their children because of their domestic responsibilities.[11]

As a result of that mother-child dynamic, immigrant working-class fathers seemingly have suffered a loss of status whereas the mothers enjoy an elevation of status. The situation has been compounded by the downward occupational mobility fathers typically suffer following their immigration to America. Mothers face different fortunes; most, who rarely were wage earners in Asia, now hold low-skilled jobs that provide some measure of economic freedom. It is likely that this reversal of gender roles has put a strain on conjugal relationships at the importune time of adjustment to life in the United States.

Some of these immigrant conjugal unions also suffer from tensions resulting from spousal incompatibility. Many new and old Chinese male immigrants are still returning to Asia to marry, a process that has received a boost following the Chinese government's 1979 rectification of its policy toward overseas Chinese. This rectification in essence has meant that the political rights and interests of the overseas Chinese and their relatives in China are once again under legal protection.[12]

Encouraged by this climate, overseas Chinese, including Chinese Americans, are now returning to China for a range of social and economic activities, including finding prospective conjugal partners. Consequently, the number of "out-of-town" or trans-Pacific marriages involving U.S. citizens, mostly in the mid to late twenties, and women from China, Hong Kong, and Taiwan have increased in the late 1970s and 1980s; about 5,000 brides arrived in America in the late 1980s.[13] According to one study of 307 males involved in such unions, most were of working-class backgrounds with low incomes.[14]

Perhaps not surprisingly, another study has found that the women they married, like the brides of the reunited broken families, suffer from shock and a sense of betrayal when they arrive in America.[15] Led to believe that their *gam saan* husbands are prosperous, they are unprepared for the harsh reality of grinding poverty and economic disempowerment. One interviewed woman remembered that "when he [her husband] was courting me, he said he was a restaurant owner and he owned a house and a car. That made me all the more excited about the marriage."[16] When she found out that the couple's apartment was tiny and poorly furnished, she complained about the deceit and he physically abused her, which apparently is a common plight suffered by these out-of-town brides.

MIDDLE-CLASS PROFESSIONAL FAMILIES

Aside from the working-class or dual-worker family, there is also the middle-class, white-collar or professional family. Some of these families are quite different from the Cantonese-dominated split-household families of the past; these families, hailing from Hong Kong, Taiwan, and even Southeast Asia, are of different linguistic and regional backgrounds. These immigrant, and the native-born middle-class families, are often more cosmopolitan and Westernized than the working-class families, and they seem to lead American-like suburban lifestyles. According to one study, a high percentage of the professional immigrants in California had been exposed to Western education and languages while still living in their country of birth, which accounts for their seemingly easy adjustment to American society.[17] Although their work and neighborhood contacts are primarily white, they may socialize with other Chinese of similar class and educational backgrounds. For example, those of the business and professional groups tend to join ethnic-oriented alumni, commercial, and political organizations, which working-class Chinese, due to their lack of time, rarely join. Both groups, according to one New York study, however, celebrate both Chinese festival days and American holidays.[18]

Generally, the professional families exhibit more egalitarianism in gender roles than working-class families. The family income is derived from the earning capacity of both husband and wife. When both are professionals, there is a sense of economic partnership and therefore some measure of equality. One extensive study made of San Francisco's Chinatown in the early 1980s reported that 51 percent of the women surveyed were "pretty satisfied" and another 21 percent were "very satisifed" with their marriages, which the researchers attribute in part to spousal relations being less patriarchally oppressive today.[19] In such relationships, women, like their working-class peers, still carried out most of the household labor, even though these families have moved toward less sex-role-segregated arrangements. Unlike the situation in working-class families, professional parents, because of the relative affluence and availability of time to spend with their offspring, are able to offer the resources for and participate actively in their children's educational success.

It is imperative to avoid the impression that there are only two types of family life in contemporary Chinese America. Aside from the working-class and professional families, there is the revived small-producer family involved in ethnic enterprises in Chinatowns or in surrounding multiracial neighborhoods. Usually wives and children are unpaid workers in these self-exploitative ventures. Women generally perform both production and reproduction in the same site. Finally, according to the 1990 census statistics, nearly a third of the Chinese labor force was involved in technical occupations which suggests the possible emergence of a type of family that has yet to be documented.[20]

The interpersonal dynamics within Chinese American families are certainly changing and evolving as the families adapt to the challenges of life in American society. Preliminary evidence shows that, as acculturation works its way into Chinese America, these families will begin to replace familial supervision—considered traditionally as a way to show love—with more demonstrations of affection and Euro-American forms of nurturance. Instead of restrained verbal communication and the discouragement of emotional expression—the by-products of a culture that emphasizes nonverbal communication, anticipation of the needs of others, and well-defined social behavior and roles—members of the family may become more individually assertive and less situation centered or socially dependent on each other.

IDENTITY DILEMMA

Meanwhile, the progeny of these families have to grapple with the psychological and social dilemma of the identity crisis. Many Chinese American youth feel torn between being Chinese and American, a predicament shaped by their Chinese upbringing and American education and socialization. As a result of this process, certain personality types have begun to emerge, ranging from the "banana," or so-called modernist who rejects or denies everything Chinese in order to appear completely Euro-American, to the "radical" Chinese, who adheres to the panethnic Asian identity and rejects traditional Euro-American and Chinese values.[21]

The development of an Americanized identity is countered by the concomitant pull of the ethnic identity. The ethnic identity is, in turn, determined by the harsh reality of racism which may lead one to reject or enhance his or her ethnic identity. Nativity and generational differences must also be taken into account in any analysis of ethnic identity; presumably, the progeny of the first generation, compared to their parents, would become much more assimilated into the dominant society and thus have less ethnic identification. However, the consciousness, adoption, and application of ethnic identity will ebb and flow within an individual's lifetime depending on the environment encountered. A person may choose to adopt only certain aspects of ethnicity or to invoke the identity only in certain settings such as at home but not at work or school. Furthermore, a person who lives in a predominately ethnic neigborhood would most likely invoke his identity more often than one who lives in a white-dominated area.[22]

The conflict between assimilation and ethnicity, exacerbated by the shifting nature of the family, has been partly responsible for the rise in Chinese American juvenile delinquency. During the exclusion era, a low level of delinquency was ascribed to the small youth population and perhaps to the close integration of the family. The social problem of juvenile delinquency began to surface in the 1960s. New York City police sources in 1965 estimated that about 3 percent of the Chinese community's teenagers were known to be juvenile delinquents, although that was still the lowest rate of any racial group.[23] Against the backdrop of the sociopolitical discontentment of that decade, frustrated youths organized themselves into juvenile gangs. Supposedly such activities served to fill status and identity needs for those whose lives had not yet been incorporated into the larger society.

The continuing rise in juvenile delinquency in the 1970s and 1980s can be ascribed to several factors. Aside from the increase in the juvenile population, the increase in youth crime is due to several interrelated changes: the language and socializing adjustment they face in school, the shortage of job opportunities especially for recent low-skilled immigrants, the lack of parental supervision, and the overall breakdown of community controls as Chinatowns become less insulated and more exposed to dominant capitalism. Additionally, most of today's immigrant youngsters hail from urbanized, Westernized settings. Already influenced by the dominant youth culture, they are less willing to put up with traditional cultural expectations.[24]

The tension engendered by the constant roving between two worlds has resulted in attitudinal changes among both Chinese American men and women. According to one study, the Asian-born Chinese American women sampled through a mailed questionnaire are more conservative about certain social aspects. For example, they expect special courtesies from men and consider drinking, swearing, and telling jokes bad manners. On the other hand, these same women, reflecting the impact of acculturation, give high priority to achievements in educational and intellectual areas and are not willing to be subservient in their marital relationships.[25]

In the realm of sexual permissiveness, Chinese American male and female youth, notwithstanding their exposure to American life, seem more conservative than their white counterparts. According to one study of 114 Chinese male and female college students, most of the Chinese respondents, in spite of the fact that more than three-quarters of them had grown up in non-Chinese neighborhoods, had yet to engage in premarital intercourse. Most of those who had had delayed their first incident of sexual intimacy until late adolescence or early youth. The reasons for this lower level of sexual permissiveness include (1) the need to be certain of an emotional commitment, (2) the absence of social acculturation, especially on the part of men who are saddled with the burden of attaining economic and educational success and therefore have less time for socialization, (3) the negative body image instilled in Chinese through history and popular media, which causes some to feel sexually modest, and (4) the traditional Chinese culture's emphasis on modesty.[26]

Young Chinese women, compared to their male peers, probably encounter more pressure in their attempt to negotiate between the boundaries of family life and selfhood. Though still expected by their parents to fulfill the role of obedient daughters, enter into matrimony, and perform the cycle of domestic responsibilities, these women aspire to explore new ideas and cultures. Jennifer Ng, who emigrated from Hong Kong as a child and grew up in Manhattan, recalled that during her college days her attempts to shape her own selfhood were constantly thwarted by her working-class parents' insistence that she live near Chinatown while in college, suppress her personal ambition to be an investment consultant, and marry as soon as possible. Ng was able to board at her school rather than commute from her parents' home in Chinatown, but she had to return every weekend to work in a garment factory alongside her mother.[27] Scholars argue that Chinese American women brought up in middle-class surroundings probably have more access to education and freedom than those of working-class backgrounds. The process of staking out a self-defined identity becomes less encumbered by parental opposition as the offspring come of age.

DOMESTIC VIOLENCE

The contemporary familial challenge for Chinese women also includes the issue of domestic violence. Such violence may stem from a value conflict between the traditional patriarchal values of husbands and the modern gender equality sought by wives; the suspicion of infidelity; an inequality in marital power; and an overwhelming sense of hopelessness due to grinding poverty and blocked economic mobility. Some of the husbands of these battered women take advantage of their immigrant wives' immigration status before they receive permanent residency. Even though a wife can petition for permanent resident status without her spouse's signature, the high standard of proof required to demonstrate family violence has probably deterred many female victims from seeking help.

Abused Chinese women face other barriers in resisting domestic violence. They have to grapple with widely shared assumptions that Asian cultures accept gender violence. That, in turn, has enabled Chinese men and the larger society to resort to "cultural defenses" of Chinese men who abuse, assault, or even murder their wives or partners. This scenario played out in the case of Dong Lu Chen, a Chinese man in New York City who killed his wife in 1987 by pounding her skull with a hammer. During the trial, Chen's attorney claimed that in China if a man believes that his wife has been involved in an extramarital relationship, he will threaten to kill her; otherwise, Chinese society would consider him emasculated and morally weak. In sentencing Chen to five years on probation, the lightest sentence possible, the judge commented that Chen "was driven to violence by traditional values about adultery and loss of manhood." Violence against Chinese women was thus rationalized as the product of cultural proclivities.[28]

Chinese women who are willing to fight back in spite of that public perception run up against other roadblocks. These women in general are discouraged, even perhaps intimidated, from speaking up about domestic violence. The subject matter is rarely discussed within the ethnic community because it is considered a private or personal crime that happens randomly to individuals and is not a social problem of major proportions. Furthermore, women often have no idea where or to whom to turn for help. Unattuned to the American social welfare system, and unable to cope with their problems, women who live in Chinatown are reported to have a high rate of depression and in some cases commit suicide.

GAY MEN AND LESBIANS

Like Chinese American women, Chinese American gay men and lesbians must contend with traditions while striving to define their identity within the community and in the society at large. The Chinese, as do Asian Americans generally, consider homosexuality a Western phenomenon, a myth well corroborated by the media, which rarely feature or portray gay men and lesbians of color. Chinese Americans who profess this sexual orientation are seen as having rejected the importance of Asian family and culture and having become totally assimilated into mainstream American life. Worse still, they have betrayed the ethnic group and besmirched the family honor. Some parents of Chinese American queers* reject homosexuality because they associate this with gender role reversals. The men are feminine and the women look like males; gay men and lesbians, in their minds, simply undermine the natural boundaries of biological sex. Parents typically express disbelief, shock, and denial of their offspring's sexual orientation as expressed in Liz Lee's recollections when she discovered her daughter's sexual identity: "I didn't accept [it] for a long time. I didn't think she would come out in the open like this. I thought she would just keep it and later on get married."[29]

Rejected by their own ethnic community, Chinese American gay men and lesbians find that their participation in the mainstream queer community is a qualified one. Many feel stereotyped or unacknowledged by the queer community. Chinese American gays and lesbians complain that white gay men and lesbians consider them "exotic" and rarely admit the existence of any racism or race-related issues in the queer community. For example, the queer community supports domestic partnership legislation that would extend employee benefits to life partners, but such legislation could create complications for Asian gays and lesbians. Until a recent 1990 congressional amendment, immigration laws considered "sexual deviants" part of the undesirable list. Asian arrivals who were gay or lesbian could have been denied entry or

*The term "queers" is used in the positive sense and encompasses gay men, lesbians, bisexuals, and transgendereds.

turned down for permanent residency or naturalization. Thus Asian partners who register their gay relationships under the requirements of domestic partnership legislation could have suffered from legal complications. The mainstream queer community kept silent on this matter. More recently the lack of vocal support for the fight against California's Proposition 187 (which passed in 1994), which denies education, health care, and social services to individuals suspected of being undocumented immigrants, has added to the impression that the mainstream queer community ignores racial difference in favor of a homogenized matrix of sexual politics.[30]

The invisibility of Asian gays and lesbians in the queer community is compounded by the politics of tokenism and exotification. They are enlisted to participate in mainstream queer politics only for the sake of maintaining balance in racial representation. Additionally, like heterosexual Chinese women and men, Chinese American gay men and lesbians are often victimized by the existing gender and racial power relations in U.S. society. Seen as exotic, submissive "Orientals," Chinese gay men and lesbians are considered desirable by white queers but not as the social equals of their potential white partners.

Because of the silences imposed by both the ethnic and queer communities, Chinese gays and lesbians, the bearers of a double minority status, have had to experience the worlds of Chinese America and gay America as separate places. The "domain of the Asian American 'home' is usually kept separate from the desire of the sexual and emotional 'body,' " according to poet and editor Russell Leong.[31] Chinese and other Asian American queers take great care to keep these worlds distant from each other. For most Chinese American gay men and lesbians, their self-identity is situationally determined and fluid; they may be gay in a gay leather bar but become Asian when paying their respect to their ancestors at the temple. To cope with this double consciousness, Chinese Americans have since the 1980s joined other Asian American queers forming Asian American lesbian and gay organizations in major U.S. cities for political activism and social support. These include the Boston Gay Males and Lesbians (1979), the Asian Pacific Lesbians and Gays (Los Angeles, 1980), the Association of Lesbians and Gay Asians (San Francisco, 1981), the Asian Lesbians of the East Coast (New York, 1983), the Asian Pacifica Sisters (San Francisco, 1989), and the Gay Asian Pacific Islander Men of New York (1990).

MENTAL HEALTH

Chinese Americans, along with other racial minorities, suffer from certain pressures that can generate mental problems. Racism and its attending badge of inferiority can be so virulent that some Chinese Americans have internalized the negative "Oriental" images. The end result is self-hatred that has led some to reject ethnic identification and to prefer to be Euro-American rather than Chinese American. In addition, some Chinese Americans experience cultural and generational conflicts when their adoption of American values clashes with the customs adhered to within the family.

In spite of these problems, Chinese and other Asian Americans have consistently underutilized mental health services. In one San Francisco Chinatown study conducted in the late 1970s and early 1980s, only 5 percent of the respondents sought mental health services—one-fourth of the proportion of Americans who sought the same services in 1976.[32] The figure for the Chinese is disturbing because almost half of the respondents admitted to suffering from emotional tension or depression. The underutilization of such services is also ironic given the fact that as early as the 1950s the suicide rate for Chinese Americans was two and one-half times more than the national rate and has remained critical as evidenced in one 1986 study that shows the suicide rate for elderly Chinese immigrants is almost three times higher than the rate for U.S.-born older Chinese Americans.[33]

Several reasons can be used to explain why Chinese rarely use mental health services. Perhaps one of the most important is the lack of knowledge of available services, particularly among new working-class immigrants. Another reason is that some ascribe to the cultural belief that mental disorders cannot be prevented. Some Chinese believe that mental illness is caused by spiritual unrest, hereditary weakness, or metaphysical factors such as fate or weakness of character, which means that the remedies cannot be found within the realm of science or psychology. Others are reluctant to admit to psychological symptoms because of the cultural stigma attached to such admissions and the use of mental health services. Those who seek professional counseling are regarded by co-ethnics as weak, immature, and lacking in self-discipline. Not surprisingly some Chinese have chosen to ignore or downplay their problems. Finally, a few who do not trust or are suspicious of Euro-American mental health professionals may choose alternative forms of treatment ranging from herbalists to visits to the Chinese temple.

Chinese Americans who do desire such services find that there is a shortage of ethnic minority and bilingual professionals in the mental health field. Existing trained professionals generally have had little or no preparation in understanding the sociocultural determinants of mental illness. Bereft of such knowledge, such therapists rarely take the following factors into consideration when prescribing treatment: the circumstances of immigration, generation and age, degree of assimilation, educational level, socioeconomic status, occupational skills, religious beliefs, and support system.

Potential Chinese patients also face certain ingrained myths held by the dominant society about the ethnic community. Some mental health professionals believe that Chinese do not require mental health therapy because they are family centered and help one another. Another myth is that the Chinese culture is so shame based that Chinese are reluctant to seek help from such professionals for fear of losing face. In fact, there is no empirical evidence to substantiate this belief. Awareness and use of mental health services will increase over time because acculturated Chinese Americans have shown a proclivity for such services.

INTERRACIAL MARRIAGE

Acculturated Chinese Americans have demonstrated a propensity to enter into interracial marriages. Before World War II miscegenation laws and the negative body image of Asian men depressed the rate of white-Chinese unions. In the immediate postwar years, though most of the interracial marriages involved American servicemen stationed in Asia and their Japanese, Filipino, or Korean "war brides," about 6,000 of these involved Chinese women. After the liberalization of the immigration laws, the dramatic influx of new immigrants probably played a role in suppressing any increase in Chinese interracial marriage, at least for the foreign born.

In the late 1970s some studies show that Chinese were engaging in outmarriage (marriage between two persons from a different race or from a different ethnic group) in a disproportionate rate. One study, centered in Los Angeles County, found that 41.2 percent of the Chinese Americans who registered to marry in 1979 married non-Chinese (which includes other Asians and non-Asians); 30.2 percent of those surveyed entered into interracial marriages, presumably with whites.[34] These findings were confirmed by two separate studies that used the 1980 census. About 31.5 percent of all Chinese marriages, according to the compiled statistics, involved non-Chinese, and 22 percent of all Chinese marriages involved white partners.[35] An overwhelming number of the outmarriages were interracial unions. The Chinese, among Asian ethnic groups, however, have the lowest level of intermarriage; Japanese Americans have the highest outmarriage level.[36]

The increase in outmarriages, particularly interracial ones, can be ascribed to a number of factors, some of which seem to validate an assimilationist interpretation. The march of the civil rights movement and the attending affirmative action laws, along with declining racial prejudice, have enabled Chinese, particularly those of the professional and managerial occupations, to increase their social contacts with whites which, in turn, may have led to greater acceptance of Chinese as potential marriage partners. Residence and geographical mobility are contributing factors to the opportunities conducive to intermarriage. Chinese who move out of Chinatowns and Chinese neighborhoods and into areas with low concentrations of co-ethnics expose themselves possibly to more socialization with members of the dominant group and thus increase their pool of potential marriage partners. Concomitantly, this change of residence reduces the opportunity for ingroup marriages as the pool of potential Chinese partners is reduced.

The level of acculturation can be positively correlated with the prevalence of intermarriage. Those who have more facility with the English language and are familiar with dominant values are often more likely to consider intermarriage. Not surprisingly, interracial marriage occurs most frequently among second-generation Chinese Americans. Second-generation or native-born Chinese Americans have the necessary skills to engage in outgroup contact, and their prolonged exposure to American values encourages them to cast aside traditional attitudes and expectations along with familial control over marital practices. Unlike members of the second generation or the native born, foreign-born immigrants, already handicapped by language and cultural barriers, are less likely to marry out of the ethnic group; they may, in fact, already have married before moving to the United States.

Since those who intermarry seemingly must already be engaged in frequent outgroup contact and possess language and social skills, it is perhaps to be expected that most of them are also in the professional and managerial occupations rather than in manual labor or the service sector, both of which offer limited opportunities for socialization in the dominant culture. In a study published in 1987, sociologist Betty Lee Sung concluded that those who intermarried were disproportionately involved in high status-oriented professional and technical occupations and consequently enjoyed a higher average family income than their ingroup married peers.[37]

In the same study, Sung found that the non-Chinese husbands of the Chinese women were highly concentrated in the professional and technical occupations; very few were at the lower end of the job scale.[38] Other studies have shown that outgroup married Chinese women, who are mostly concentrated in highly skilled occupations, tend to marry up. Perhaps this offers a clue to our understanding of why Chinese women intermarry.[39] According to the hypergamy theory, individuals, males or females, sometimes choose to maximize their status in a racially stratified society through outmarriage. If this is true, then highly accomplished Chinese American women can maximize their status by intermarrying with the most advantaged individuals with the highest racial position, namely, Caucasian men of the professional and managerial class. Chinese men can also maximize their status by marrying white women who are occupationally and educationally in a lower level but who, by virtue of the color of their skin, are in a higher racial position in society.[40]

Though some Chinese women and men may enter into interracial marriages because they are a means of gaining upward mobility, other factors may be involved in the decision to pursue these relationships. Some marry non-Chinese because it is a personal choice; they happen to meet a person of another race, fall in love, and get married. For both men and women, intermarriage is undoubtedly facilitated by the lowering of racial barriers and the assimilation process, but it is also tied to racial and gender power relations in today's society.

Specifically, interviewed Chinese American women and men cited aversion to Asian patriarchal family structure—such as overbearing or manipulative parents, strict discipline, or spousal domination or abuse—and the concomitant media promotion of white beauty and power as important variables in their decision to avoid intraethnic marriages. Nellie Tsui, who emigrated from Hong Kong, remembered that in college she found Chinese American men unattractive whereas the Jewish colleague whom she married "was very feminine, very caring, and very verbal . . . he's always done the dishes no matter who cooks. . . . There's no way my father would do that. You know, its too demeaning."[41] Chinese American women and men who have intermarried consider co-ethnics as simply too wedded to patriarchal or old-fashioned values and disinterested or ignorant of the existing popular youth culture. While Chinese men and women were conservative, boring, and unattractive, Caucasian men and women were extroverted, sexually appealing, and offered racial empowerment.[42]

Since both women and men find other co-ethnics unappealing, the question of why more Chinese women than men outmarry is a salient one. In just about all existing studies, Chinese American women far outnumber men in their involvement in this type of union. In some studies, women were twice as likely as Chinese males to intermarry. Perhaps this differentiation stems from the interplay of American racial and gender hierarchy and stereotypes. Asian American women are portrayed in the media as petite, submissive, and sexually desirable, which fits in with the general definition of an attractive, feminine woman. This image may make Chinese women attractive in the eyes of some white men. Concomitantly, white men may be drawn to Chinese women because they consider Caucasian American women too liberated, demanding, and career oriented. Meanwhile, the popular culture regards Asian American men as desexualized, even nerdy, which goes against what constitutes an attractive masculine man. These prevailing images probably account for why white and Chinese American women would not be attracted to Chinese men. Finally, Chinese American women choose intermarriage because they want equal partners in marriage, which they do not think they will find with Asian American men.

MULTIRACIAL CHINESE AMERICANS

The phenomenon of interracial unions has led to the emergence of a cohort of mixed-race people within the Chinese American population. Such multiracial individuals are marginal persons in both the Chinese American community and the larger American society. During the exclusion era, the specter of miscegenation and general anti-Asian sentiments caused white Americans not only to shun interracial couples but also their racially mixed children. White America considered Chinese Caucasians, the products of miscegenation, physically, morally, and mentally weak; racial mixing only lowers the biologically superior race. Unmixed Chinese Americans also harbored deep ambivalence about part-Chinese persons. The biracial writer Sui Sin Far, writing at the dawn of the twentieth century, remembered that the Chinese were "a little doubtful as to whether one [a Chinese man] could be persuaded to care for me, full-blooded Chinese people having a prejudice against the half-white."[43] The sense of isolation that multiracial Chinese experienced, however, has ebbed to some degree following the rise of the civil rights movement, the repeal of antimiscegenation laws, the integration of neighborhoods, and the general decline in white and Chinese resistance to interracial marriages.[44]

Part-Chinese persons still face certain barriers. First, these people are confronted with rigid racial categories that deny their existence. The Bureau of Census, for example, has no separate category for them, which has forced some to choose one of the existing racial classifications or simply ignore the question; either way, their self-identity is compromised. Second, multiracial Chinese Americans find that they are generally treated with suspicion and are less likely to be included in Chinese America or even in larger society. Any level of acceptance often comes with the condition that they renounce their non-Asian background, in the case of their interaction with the Chinese community, or pass as white when interacting in the larger society. An exception to this overall pattern exists in Hawaii, where the long existence of intermarriage among this polyglot of ethnicities and the visible presence of *hapas* (people of mixed ancestry) have fostered tolerance and even acceptance of multiracial Chinese Americans. Aside from this unique case, many Chinese of mixed ancestry adopt "situational identity": they feel and act mainly white, black, or Latino, depending on their mix, when among whites, blacks, or Latinos, and act mainly Chinese when among Chinese.

In recent decades, marriage patterns among Chinese Americans are characterized not only by a rising number of interracial marriages but also by an increasing rate of interethnic marriages (i.e., Asian Americans marrying other Asian Americans). This new phenomenon stems from the increasing sense of racial consciousness and unity which has been forged through the bridging of cultural and language differences by a common marginalized experience in the United States. Equally crucial in forging this trend is the growing homogenizing of the Asian American population in terms of socioeconomic attainment and middle-class status. If this trend persists, the development of the Asian American identity would receive further encouragement.[45]

CONCLUSION

Since the immigration of Chinese to the United States seems set to continue unabated into the next century, it is likely that this ethnic community will face challenges similar to those it is encountering today and perhaps others yet to be determined. Occupational downgrading, the glass ceiling, self-exploitation in economic life, and marginalization in mainstream politics, just to name a few, may remain critical issues, as long as new immigrants, who often find adjustment to American society problematic, continue to enter the republic. Exacerbating these problems is the persisting perception that Chinese, along with other Asian Americans, are neither white nor black. Caught in this binary understanding of race in America, Chinese Americans have been portrayed in the past either as the quintessence of the Yellow Peril or members of the model minority. The end result of such representation in the past has been their subordination to white domination and sometimes their placement in a circumscribed role in this racially based society.

Since the first few came ashore on the eastern seaboard in the 1780s, Chinese Americans, across time and space, have demonstrated resilience to refashion their self-identities and cultural expressions. Though divided along the lines of class, gender, generation, language, time of arrival and place of origin, and sexual orientation, Chinese immigrants and their native-born progeny have striven to break free from the weight of historical and societal injunctions. For most, the choice between Asia and America, between the East and the West, has been a false one. Rather, Chinese Americans have labored to project a fluid identity shaped by the interconnections of Asia and America. More specifically, their identity, against a backdrop of structural barriers, ultimately belies a synthesis of selective Chinese cultural values with adherence to the republic's creed of democracy and equality. Chinese Americans, like so many other racial minorities, have played their share in redefining the American peoplehood.

Appendix: Noted Chinese Americans

Kenneth R. Spurgeon

Chan, June (1956–   ): Chan was born in lower Manhattan and was educated in New York City's public school system. She attended graduate school at the State University of New York at Buffalo, earning a master's degree in biology. Along with Katherine Hall, in 1983, Chan formed Asian Lesbians of the East Coast (ALOEC) and established herself early as a self-identified Asian American lesbian. In addition to providing support and education for the Asian American lesbian community, ALOEC focuses on racism, homophobia in the Asian women's community, and sexism. Chan also works as a laboratory technician at Cornell Medical College in Manhattan where she conducts research in neurobiology.

Chen, William Shao Chang (1939–   ): Chen was born in Shanghai, China. On the eve of the Chinese Communist victory in 1949, Chen's family fled the raging civil war and came to America. Chen earned a bachelor's degree in engineering mathematics in 1960 and a master's degree in aeronautical and astronautical engineering in 1961. Upon graduation, he was offered a regular army commission as a first lieutenant. Imbued by patriotism and with the model of his father's service to the U.S. Army Air Corps, Chen joined the military. In his more than thirty years of service, he focused on project management of weapons systems. Chen, the first Chinese American major general in the U.S. armed forces, served as the commanding general of the U.S. Army Missile Command.

Chew, Ng Poon (1866–1931): Chew was born in Guangdong province, China, and arrived in America in 1881 at the age of 15. A progressive journalist, he established the *Chung Sai Yat Bo* (literally Chinese American daily newspaper) in 1900. An ordained Presbyterian minister, Chew led his church in speaking out against the exclusion laws and in bridging the gap between Chinese Americans and non–Chinese Americans. He endured ridicule from Chinese Americans for his attempts to be more like Euro-Americans. Conversely, he was discriminated against by many Euro-Americans for being Chinese. Chew viewed Christianity and modernization as forms of salvation for Chinese Americans and as a way to end discrimination. He served as a vice-consul for China, a lecturer on the Chautauqua circuit, and a general public speaker.

Eu, March Fong (1922–   ): Eu was born in the small farming community of Oakdale, California, in the back room of a hand laundry. She received her B.S. degree from the University of California at Berkeley, her master's degree in education from Mills College, and her Ph.D. in education from Stanford University. She was elected to the California State Assembly in 1966 and made history by being the first Asian American assemblywoman. In 1974 Eu became California's first female secretary of state and was reelected to that position five times. In 1994 Eu was appointed ambassador to Micronesia by President William Clinton. She is well known as an outspoken advocate of all citizens.

Fugh, Major General John Liu (1934–   ): Born in Beijing, China, Fugh immigrated to the United States with his family in the midst of the Chinese civil war. Fugh served in the U.S. Army for more than thirty years. He was the first Chinese American to attain general officer status in the military, and he served as judge advocate general from 1991 to 1993. Fugh received his B.S. degree from Georgetown University's School of Foreign Service in international relations and graduated from the George Washington University School of Law. He went on to graduate from the Army Command and General Staff College, the Army War College, and the Kennedy School of Government at Harvard University. Fugh has garnered numerous awards including the Distinguished Service Medal, the Legion of Merit (with Oak Leaf Cluster), the Meritorious Service Medal (with Oak Leaf Cluster), and the Army Commendation Medal (with Oak Leaf Cluster).

Kingston, Maxine Hong (1940–   ): Born in Stockton, California, Kingston, through her well-crafted, riveting works, has played an instrumental role in introducing Asian American literature to the American public. Both of Kingston's parents were first-generation immigrants from China. She received her B.A. degree from the University of California at Berkeley in 1962. From 1965 to 1977, Kingston taught high school in California and Hawaii. After the success of her first book, *The Woman Warrior: Memoirs of a Girlhood Among Ghosts* (1976), Kingston was invited by the University of Hawaii in Honolulu to teach English and writing as a visiting associate professor. She later began teaching at the University of California at Berkeley. Other works by Kingston include *China Men* (1980) and *Tripmaster Monkey* (1989). Both *China Men* and *Woman Warrior* won the National Book Critics Circle Award.

Lee, Ang (1954–): Lee, the son of a high school principal, was born in Taiwan. After Lee failed the college entrance examinations in Taiwan, he moved in 1978 to the United States. He attended the University of Illinois's theater arts program and later earned a master's degree in cinema from New York University. *Fine Line*, his 1984 award-winning thesis film, garnered Lee some acclaim and an offer of representation from the William Morris agency. Although some potential projects fell through, Lee finally received considerable success with his family-centered trilogy of films *Pushing Hands* (1992), *The Wedding Banquet* (1993), and *Eat, Drink, Man, Woman* (1995), all of which explore the unspoken tensions and conflicts with traditions that separate generations moving rapidly from one world to the next. Lee has also displayed his abilities in films with non-Asian themes, such as the adaptation of Jane Austen's *Sense and Sensibility* (1996), *The Ice Storm* (1997), a tale of American suburban sexuality in the 1970, and the adventurous Civil War movie, *To Live On*, currently in production.

Lee, Tsung-Dao (1926–): The son of a businessman, Lee was born in Shanghai. Lee is best known for his work with Dr. Chen Ning Yang on parity laws in physics. After receiving his bachelor's degree, Lee came to America on a government scholarship to study physics at the University of Chicago, where he obtained his doctorate in 1950. In 1951 Lee worked at the Institute for Advanced Study at Princeton University. While there, Lee was reunited with Yang, a fellow student from his undergraduate days in China. Lee and Yang solved a puzzling deadlock in elementary particle physics which other scientists validated through experimentation. For their work, they were awarded the Nobel Prize in physics. Lee has received awards and honors in other areas and has undertaken substantial theoretical work in statistical mechanics, astrophysics, hydrodynamics, and turbulence.

Lee, Yuan T. (1936–   ): Born in Taiwan, Lee's education was interrupted by World War II when the Japanese took control of the island. In 1959 he continued his graduate studies at the University of California at Berkeley and received his Ph.D. in 1965. Lee became a professor and the principal investigator at the University of California's Lawrence Berkeley laboratory in 1974. He has won several prestigious awards and honors. While at Berkeley, he worked with Dudley R. Herschbach and John C. Polany, with whom he shared the 1986 Nobel Prize in chemistry. Lee also developed the first successful universal crossed-molecular beam device.

Lin, Maya (1959–   ): Lin was born in Athens, Ohio, into an academic and artistic family. For her senior thesis project at Yale University in 1981, Lin submitted a design to a national contest for the Vietnam Veterans Memorial. Her design was selected from a competition that attracted 1,421 entries. The design called for two highly polished walls of black granite, set in a "V," to be inscribed with the names of the almost 58,000 dead or missing veterans of the Vietnam War. One arm of the 594–foot work points to the Washington Monument; the other arm, to the Lincoln Memorial. Lin's success is evidenced by the thousands who have been deeply moved by her design which evokes reconciliation even as it memorializes losses. In 1986 Yale conferred upon her an honorary doctorate degree of fine arts. Lin has designed other memorials including the Civil Rights Memorial in Montgomery, Alabama.

Locke, Gary (1950–   ): Locke was born in one of the poorest neighborhoods in Seattle, Washington. He studied political science at Yale University and graduated in 1972. After obtaining a law degree from Boston University in 1975, he returned to Seattle and took a job as a King County deputy prosecutor. Following a 1981 staff job with the state senate's higher education committee, Locke won election to the state house of representatives in 1982. In 1994 he won the King County executive post, becoming the first Chinese American to head a county government in North America. In 1996 Locke established another first when he was elected the governor of Washington, which is particularly noteworthy because Washington has only a small Asian American population.

Ma, Yo-yo (1955–   ): An extraordinary cellist, born in Paris, France, Ma gave his first public recital at the age of five at the University of Paris. He made his debut in Carnegie Hall at the age of nine. Raised in a highly musical family, he studied at the Julliard School and later attended Harvard University. Internationally known for his recordings and the winner of several Grammy awards, Ma is consistently developing his sizable repertoire.

Pei, I. M. (1917–   ): The son of a prominent banker and economist, Pei was born in Guangzhou (Canton), China, and earned his master's degree from Harvard University. In 1948, Pei became the director of architecture for Webb & Knapp, Inc. In 1955 he formed the partnership of I. M. Pei and Associates. Pei gained recognition for his abstract designs of the East Building of the National Gallery of Art in Washington, D.C., and the John F. Kennedy Library in Boston. He has designed many other equally striking monumental minimalist buildings including the Bank of China in Hong Kong, one of Asia's tallest buildings. Pei holds a number of honorary degrees, and many of his projects have won major awards.

Wong, Anna May (1907–1961): Born in Los Angeles, California, Wong made her debut as an actress at the age of twelve in *The Red Lantern* (1919). Despite her father's objections, Wong began making the rounds of the casting offices, aspiring to become a movie actress such as Theda Bara or Gloria Swanson. She became the first well-known Chinese American actor and played in more than a hundred films in her forty-year career. Always typecast as the evil, untrustworthy or seductive "Oriental" character, Wong never came across on the silver screen as a complex character with positive redeeming qualities. Although she performed alongside such well-known actors as Douglas Fairbanks, Laurence Olivier, and Lana Turner, Wong's full potential was never realized because of racial discrimination.

Wong, B. D. (1962–   ): Born in San Francisco, California, Wong attended San Francisco State University for a year, where he spent most of his time in the drama department. While touring with the musical, *La Cage aux Folles*, he auditioned for *M. Butterfly* written by David Henry Hwang. He won the part, and his performance secured the theater's highest accolade: a Tony award as best featured actor. Wong has acted in many other productions on stage and screen including such mainstream productions as *Mystery Date* (1991), *Father of the Bride* (1991), *And the Band Played On* (1993), and *Jurassic Park* (1993). He has campaigned vigorously for racial equality, particularly in the area of representations of Asian Americans in the performing arts.

Notes

CHAPTER 1

1. Tin-Yuke Char, *The Sandalwood Mountains: Readings and Stories of the Early Chinese Immigrants in Hawaii* (Honolulu: University of Hawaii Press, 1975), 54–57; Thomas W. Chinn, Him Mark Lai, and Philip P. Choy, eds., *A History of the Chinese in California: A Syllabus* (San Francisco: Chinese Historical Society of America, 1969), 7–8, 22.

2. Herbert Passin, quoted in Tu Wei-ming, "Cultural China: The Periphery as the Center," in *The Living Tree: The Changing Meaning of Being Chinese Today*, ed. Tu Wei-ming (Stanford, Calif.: Stanford University Press, 1994), 1.

3. The information contained in this and the next three paragraphs comes from Him Mark Lai, "The Guangdong Historical Background, with Emphasis on the Development of the Pearl River Delta Region," in *Chinese America: History and Perspectives 1991* (San Francisco: Chinese Historical Society of America, 1991), 75–81, 88.

4. L. Ling-chi Wang, "Roots and the Changing Identity of the Chinese in the United States," in *The Living Tree: The Changing Meaning of Being Chinese Today*, ed. Tu Wei-ming (Stanford, Calif.: Stanford University Press, 1994), 186–87.

5. Lai, "Guangdong Historical Background," 76, 87.

6. Molly Joel Coye and Jon Livingston, *China: Yesterday and Today*, 2d ed. (New York: Bantam Books, 1979), 13.

7. Lai, "Guangdong Historical Background," 76–77.

8. Yu-Kuang Chu, "The Chinese Language," in *An Introduction to Chinese Civilization*, ed. John Meskill (New York: Columbia University Press, 1973), 590–91.

9. John King Fairbank, *The United States and China*, 4th ed. (Cambridge, Mass.: Harvard University Press, 1979), 43.

10. The information in this and the next four paragraphs comes from Immanuel C. Y. Hsu, *The Rise of Modern China*, 4th ed. (New York: Oxford University Press, 1990), 47, 70–80; Jonathan D. Spence, *The Search for Modern China* (New York: W. W. Norton, 1990), 46.

11. For peasant life in southern China in the late Qing dynasty, see Philip C. C. Huang, *The Peasant Family and Rural Development in the Yangzi Delta, 1350–1988* (Stanford, Calif.: Stanford University Press, 1990).

12. The information in this and the next three paragraphs comes from Lloyd E. Eastman, *Family, Fields and Ancestors: Constancy and Change in China's Social and Economic History, 1550–1949* (New York: Oxford University Press, 1988), 75–76, 87–88.

13. Fairbank, *United States and China*, 47–49.

14. The information in this and the next paragraph comes from David Johnson, "Communication, Class, and Consciousness in Late Imperial China," in *Popular Culture in Late Imperial China*, ed. David Johnson et al. (Berkeley: University of California Press, 1985), 34–72.

15. The information in this and the next six paragraphs comes from James Legge, ed., *The Chinese Classics*, 5 vol. (Oxford: Clarendon Press, 1893–1895), 1:264–65, 309, 2:370; C. K. Yang, "The Role of Religion in Chinese Society," in *An Introduction to Chinese Civilization*, ed. John Meskill (New York: Columbia University Press, 1973), 644–45, 661–64; Eastman, *Family, Fields, and Ancestors*, 42.

16. The information in this and the next three paragraphs comes from Maurice Freedman, "Ritual Aspects of Chinese Kinship and Marriage," in *Family and Kinship in Chinese Society*, ed. Maurice Freedman (Stanford, Calif.: Stanford University Press, 1970), 165–79; Yang, "Role of Religion," 649–50, 664; Richard J. Smith, *China's Cultural Heritage: The Qing Dynasty, 1644–1912*, 2d ed. (Boulder, Colo.: Westview Press, 1994), 167–68.

17. The information in this and the next two paragraphs comes from John K. Fairbank, Edwin O. Reischauer, and Albert M. Craig, "Taoism and Buddhism," in *China: Yesterday and Today*, 2d ed., ed. Molly Joel Coye and Jon Livingston (New York: Bantam Books, 1979), 48; Kenneth Chen, *Buddhism in China* (Princeton, N.J.: Princeton University Press, 1964), 436–39.

18. David Yoo, "For Those Who Have Eyes to See: Religious Sightings in Asian America," *Amerasia Journal* 22, no. 1 (1996): xvi. See also Stephan Feuchtwang, *The Imperial Metaphor: Popular Religion in China* (London: Routledge, 1992).

19. The information in this and the next two paragraphs comes from Thomas W. Chinn, *Bridging the Pacific: San Francisco Chinatown and Its People* (San Francisco: Chinese Historical Society of America, 1989), 10–12.

20. Hsu, *Rise of Modern China*, 19.

21. Ibid., 121.

22. Eastman, *Family, Fields, and Ancestors*, 4–5.

23. Yen-p'ing Hao, *The Commercial Revolution in Ninteenth-Century China: The*

Rise of Sino-Western Mercantile Capitalism (Berkeley: University of California Press, 1986), 1, 4.

CHAPTER 2

1. Ho Ping-ti, *Studies on the Population of China, 1368–1953* (Cambridge, Mass.: Harvard University Press, 1959), 281–83.

2. Sucheng Chan, "European and Asian Immigration into the United States in Comparative Perspectives, 1820s to 1920s," in *Immigration Reconsidered: History, Sociology, and Politics,* ed. Virginia Yans-McLaughlin (New York: Oxford University Press, 1990), 37–75.

3. June Mei, "Socioeconomic Origins of Emigration: Guangdong to California, 1550–1882," in *Labor Immigration under Capitalism: Asian Workers in the United States Before World War II,* ed. Lucie Cheng and Edna Bonacich (Berkeley: University of California Press, 1984), 232.

4. Chinn, Lai, and Choy, *History of the Chinese in California,* 20; "The Celestials at Home and Abroad," *Littell's Living Age,* 14 August 1852, 294.

5. The information in this and the next four paragraphs comes from Yong Chen, "Internal Origins to Chinese Immigration Reconsidered," *Western Historical Quarterly* 25 (Winter 1997): 538–41, 545–46.

6. For return migration, see Franklin Ng, "The Sojourner, Return Migration, and Immigration History," in *Chinese America: History and Perspectives 1987* (San Francisco: Chinese Historical Society of America, 1987), 53–71.

7. The information in this and the next two paragraphs comes from Ronald Takaki, *Pau Hana: Plantation Life and Labor in Hawaii* (Honolulu: University of Hawaii Press, 1983), 32, 76–77, 121.

8. The information in this and the next three paragraphs comes from Judy Yung, *Unbound Feet: A Social History of Chinese Women in San Francisco* (Berkeley: University of California Press, 1995), 6, 19, 293; Ronald Takaki, "They Also Came: The Migration of Chinese and Japanese Women to Hawaii and the Continental United States," in *Chinese America: History and Perspectives 1990* (San Francisco: Chinese Historical Society of America, 1990), 4.

9. Lai Chun-Chuen, *Remarks of the Chinese Merchants of San Francisco upon Governor Bigler's Message* (San Francisco: Whitton, Towne, 1855), 3.

10. For Chinese prostitution in America, see Benson Tong, *Unsubmissive Women: Chinese Prostitutes in Nineteenth-Century San Francisco* (Norman: University of Oklahoma Press, 1994).

11. The information in this and the next paragraph comes from Takaki, "They Also Came," 4, 7–9.

12. *Littell's Living Age,* 3 July 1852, 33.

13. George Anthony Peffer, "Forbidden Families: Emigration Experiences of Chinese Women Under the Page Law, 1875–1882," *Journal of American Ethnic History* 6 (Fall 1986): 31.

14. The information in this and the next paragraph comes from Robert J. Schwendinger, *Ocean of Bitter Dreams: Maritime Relations Between China and the United States, 1850–1915* (Tucson, Ariz.: Westernlore Press, 1988), 66–76, 121.

15. Marlon K. Hom, *Songs of Gold Mountain: Cantonese Rhymes from San Francisco Chinatown* (Berkeley: University of California Press, 1987), 161.

16. Huie Kin, *Reminiscences* (Peiping: San Yu Press, 1909), 24.

17. Him Mark Lai, Genny Lim, and Judy Yung, *Island: Poetry and History of Chinese Immigrants on Angel Island. 1910–1940* (San Francisco: Hoc Doi, 1986), 13.

18. The information in this and the next paragraph comes from Madeline Hsu, "Gold Mountain Dreams and Paper Son Schemes: Chinese Immigration under Exclusion," in *Chinese America: History and Perspectives 1997* (San Francisco: Chinese Historical Society of America, 1997): 46–47, 51, 56–58.

19. Chinn, Lai, and Choy, *History of the Chinese in California: A Syllabus*, 18.

20. Randall E. Rohe, "After the Gold Rush: Chinese Mining in the Far West, 1850–1890," *Montana: The Magazine of Western History* 32 (Autumn 1980): 2–19.

21. Chinn, Lai, and Choy, *History of the Chinese in California*, 36–41.

22. For Chinese contributions to California's agriculture, see Sucheng Chan, *This Bittersweet Soil: The Chinese in California Agriculture, 1860–1910* (Berkeley: University of California Press, 1986).

23. For a history of the Chinese in the salmon-canning industry, see Chris Friday, *Organizing Asian American Labor: The Pacific Coast Canned-Salmon Industry, 1870–1942* (Philadelphia: Temple University Press, 1994); for Chinese in the South, see Lucy M. Cohen, *Chinese in the Post–Civil War South: A People Without a History* (Baton Rouge: Louisiana State University Press, 1984) and George E. Pozzetta, "The Chinese Encounter with Florida, 1865–1920," in *Chinese America: History and Perspectives 1989* (San Francisco: Chinese Historical Society of America, 1989): 43–57.

24. Frederick Rudolph, "Chinamen in Yankeedom: Anti-Unionism in Massachusetts in 1870," *American Historical Review* 53 (October 1947): 4, 8, 9; John Kuo Wei Tchen, "New York Chinese: The Nineteenth-Century Pre-Chinatown Settlement," in *Chinese America: History and Perspectives 1990* (San Francisco: Chinese Historical Society of America, 1990), 160–63, 168–73; K. Scott Wong, " 'The Eagle Seeks a Helpless Quarry': Chinatown, the Police, and the Press—The 1903 Boston Chinatown Raid Revisited," *Amerasia Journal* 22, no. 3 (1996): 90.

25. Ronald Takaki, *Strangers from a Different Shore: A History of Asian Americans* (Boston: Penguin Books, 1989), 87, 239; Robert S. Greenwood, *Down by the Station: Los Angeles Chinatown, 1880–1933* (Los Angeles: University of California, 1996), 12.

26. Paul M. Ong, "Chinese Labor in Early San Francisco: Racial Segmentation and Industrial Expansion," *Amerasia Journal* 8, no. 1 (1981): 69–92.

27. Yung, *Unbound Feet*, 295.

28. The information in this and the next three paragraphs comes from Yung, *Unbound Feet*, 26, 83; Huping Ling, *Surviving on the Gold Mountain: A History of*

Chinese American Women and Their Lives (Albany: State University of New York Press, 1998), 52–61, 70–72; Yen Le Espiritu, *Asian American Women and Men: Labor, Laws, and Love* (Thousand Oaks, Calif.: Sage Publications, 1997), 34–37.

29. The information in this and the next three paragraphs comes from Sucheng Chan, "The Exclusion of Chinese Women, 1870–1943," in *Entry Denied: Exclusion and the Chinese Community in America, 1882–1943*, ed. Sucheng Chan (Philadelphia: Temple University Press, 1991), 98–99; Lucy E. Salyer, *Laws Harsh as Tigers: Chinese Immigrants and the Shaping of Modern Immigration Law* (Chapel Hill: University of North Carolina Press, 1995), 13; Charles J. McClain and Laurence Wu McClain, "The Chinese Contribution to the Development of American Law," in *Entry Denied: Exclusion and the Chinese Community in America, 1882–1943*, ed. Sucheng Chan (Philadelphia: Temple University Press, 1991), 8–13; Greenwood, *Down by the Station*, 11.

30. McClain and McClain, "The Chinese," 92.

31. For education see Victor Low, *The Unimpressible Race: A Century of Educational Struggle by the Chinese in San Francisco* (San Francisco: East/West Publishing, 1982), 10–73, 92–132.

32. The information in this and the next two paragraphs comes from Alexander Saxton, *The Indispensable Enemy: Labor and the Anti-Chinese Movement in California* (Berkeley: University of California Press, 1971), 113–37, 261–65; Xinyang Wang, "Economic Opportunity, Artisan Leadership, and Immigrant Workers' Labor Militancy: Italian and Chinese Workers in New York City, 1890–1970," *Labor History* 37 (Fall 1996): 486; William Wei, "The Anti-Chinese Movement in Colorado: Interethnic Competition and Conflict on the Eve of Exclusion," in *Chinese America: History and Perspectives 1995* (San Francisco: Chinese Historical Society of America, 1995), 184–86.

33. For information on Chinese in Idaho, see Liping Zhu, *A Chinaman's Chance: The Chinese on the Rocky Mountain Mining Frontier* (Niwot: University Press of Colorado, 1997), 133–40.

34. Charles J. McClain, *In Search of Equality: The Chinese Struggle Against Discrimination in Nineteenth-Century America* (Berkeley: University of California Press, 1994), 70–73.

35. Shih-shan Henry Tsai, *China and the Overseas Chinese in the United States, 1868–1911* (Fayetteville: University of Arkansas Press, 1983), 53–59.

36. Linda Pomerantz, "The Chinese Bourgeoisie and the Anti-Chinese Movement in the United States, 1850–1905," *Amerasia Journal* 11, no. 1 (1984): 13.

37. The information from this and the next three paragraphs comes from Christian G. Fritz, "Due Process, Treaty Rights, and Chinese Exclusion, 1882–1891," in *Entry Denied: Exclusion and the Chinese Community in America, 1882–1943*, ed. Sucheng Chan (Philadelphia: Temple University Press, 1991), 26–40, 46–48.

38. Salyer, *Laws Harsh as Tigers*, 46.

39. The information in this and the next three paragraphs comes from Salyer,

Laws Harsh as Tigers, 28, 46; McClain and McClain, "Chinese Contribution," 18; Fritz, "Due Process," 46, 49.

40. Yung, *Unbound Feet*, 293.

CHAPTER 3

1. The information in this and the next paragraph comes from L. Eve Armentrout-Ma, *Revolutionaries, Monarchists, and Chinatowns: Chinese Politics in the Americas and the 1911 Revolution* (Honolulu: University of Hawaii Press, 1990), 1–40, 100–113, 139–40.

2. The information in this and the next four paragraphs comes from Him Mark Lai, "Historical Development of the Chinese Consolidated Benevolent Association/*Huiguan* System," in *Chinese America: History and Perspectives 1987* (San Francisco: Chinese Historical Society of America, 1987), 16–31; L. Eve Armentrout-Ma, "Chinatown Organizations and the Anti-Chinese Movement, 1882–1914," in *Entry Denied: Exclusion and the Chinese Community in America, 1882–1943*, ed. Sucheng Chan (Philadelphia: Temple University Press, 1991), 148–50, 154–55.

3. The information in this and the next five paragraphs comes from Renqui Yu, *To Save China. To Save Ourselves: The Chinese Hand Laundry Alliance of New York* (Philadelphia: Temple University Press, 1992), 12–15, 30; Shih-shan Henry Tsai, *The Chinese Experience in America* (Bloomington: Indiana University Press, 1986), 53–54; Armentrout-Ma, *Revolutionaries, Monarchists, and Chinatowns*, 23–24.

4. For information on Chinese Christians, see Wesley Woo, "Chinese Protestants in the San Francisco Bay Area," in *Entry Denied: Exclusion and the Chinese Community in America, 1882–1943*, ed. Sucheng Chan (Philadelphia: Temple University Press, 1991), 213–45; Timothy Tseng, "Chinese Protestant Nationalism in the United States, 1880–1927," *Amerasia Journal* 22, no. 1 (1996): 31–56.

5. The information in this and the next two paragraphs comes from Delber L. McKee, "The Chinese Boycott of 1905–1906 Reconsidered: The Role of Chinese Americans," *Pacific Historical Review* 55 (May 1986): 168–89; Tsai, *China and the Overseas Chinese*, 105, 108.

6. The information in this and the next eight paragraphs comes from Sue Fawn Chung, "Fighting for Their American Rights: A History of the Chinese American Citizens Alliance," in *Claiming America: Constructing Chinese American Identities During the Exclusion Era*, ed. K. Scott Wong and Sucheng Chan (Philadelphia: Temple University Press, 1998), 95–116; Qingsong Zhang, "The Origins of the Chinese Americanization Movement: Wong Chin Foo and the Chinese Equal Rights League," in *Claiming America: Constructing Chinese American Identities During the Exclusion Era*, ed. K. Scott Wong and Sucheng Chan (Philadelphia: Temple University Press, 1998), 41–54; Yung, *Unbound Feet*, 157, 168.

7. Chung, "Fighting for Their American Rights," p. 115.

8. Armentrout-Ma, "Chinatown Organizations," 159–60.

9. Arthur Bonner, *Alas! What Brought Thee Hither? The Chinese in New York. 1800–1950* (Cranbury, N.J.: Associated University Presses, 1997), 97–112; Lorraine Dong, "The Forbidden City Legacy and Its Chinese American Women," in *Chinese America: History and Perspectives 1992* (San Francisco: Chinese Historical Society of America, 1992), 125–48.

10. Diane Mei Lin Mark and Ginger Chih, *A Place Called Chinese America* (San Francisco: Organization of Chinese Americans, 1982), 51.

11. Takaki, *Strangers from a Different Shore*, 239.

12. Kit King Louis, "A Study of American-born and American-reared Chinese in Los Angeles" (Master's thesis, University of Southern California, 1931), 109.

13. Betty Lee Sung, *Mountain of Gold: The Story of the Chinese in America* (New York: Macmillan, 1967), 143–44.

14. Ching Chao Wu, "Chinatowns: A Study of Symbiosis and Assimilation" (Ph.D. diss., University of Chicago, 1928), 86–93.

15. Takaki, *Strangers from a Different Shore*, 252–53.

16. Peter Kwong, *Chinatown, New York: Labor and Politics, 1930–1950* (New York: Monthly Review Press, 1979), 61; Yu, *To Save China, To Save Ourselves*, 8.

17. Sin Jang Leung, "A Laundryman Sings the Blues," trans. Marlon K. Hom, in *Chinese America: History and Perspectives 1991* (San Francisco: Chinese Historical Society of America, 1991), 13, 15.

18. The information in this and the next five paragraphs comes from Kwong, *Chinatown, New York*, 62–66, 121–24; Him Mark Lai, "To Bring Forth a New China, to Build a Better America: The Chinese Marxist Left in America to the 1960s," in *Chinese America: History and Perspectives 1992* (San Francisco: Chinese Historical Society of America, 1992), 20–26.

19. Him Mark Lai, "The Kuomintang in Chinese American Communities Before World War II," in *Entry Denied: Exclusion and the Chinese Community in America, 1882–1943*, ed. Sucheng Chan (Philadelphia: Temple University Press, 1991), 191, 195–96; Kwong, *Chinatown, New York*, 122–23.

20. Yung, *Unbound Feet*, 229–45.

21. Eiichiro Azuma, "Interethnic Conflict under Racial Subordination: Japanese Immigrants and Their Asian Neighbors in Walnut Grove, California, 1908–1941," *Amerasia Journal* 20, no. 2 (1994): 27–56.

22. William F. Wu, *The Yellow Peril: Chinese Americans in American Fiction, 1850–1940* (Hamden, Conn.: Archon Books, 1982), 164–74; Julie Shuk-yee Lam, "The Chinese Digest, 1935–1940," in *Chinese America: History and Perspectives 1989* (San Francisco: Chinese Historical Society of America, 1989), 119–37; Editorial, *Chinese Digest*, November 15, 1935, 8.

23. *Chinese Digest*, November 15, 1935, 8.

24. William Hoy, "Reviews and Comments," *Chinese Digest*, June 26, 1936, 10.

25. Gary Y. Okihiro, *Margins and Mainstreams: Asians in American History and Culture* (Seattle: University of Washington Press, 1994), 143–44.

26. Gloria H. Chun, " 'Go West . . . to China': Chinese American Identity in

the 1930s," in *Claiming America: Constructing Chinese American Identities During the Exclusion Era*, ed. K. Scott Wong and Sucheng Chan (Philadelphia: Temple University Press, 1998), 169–70.

27. Yung, *Unbound Feet*, 226.

28. Sucheng Chan, "Race, Ethnic Culture, and Gender in the Construction of Identities among Second-Generation Chinese Americans," in *Claiming America: Constructing Chinese American Identities During the Exclusion Era*, ed. K. Scott Wong and Sucheng Chan (Philadelphia: Temple University Press, 1998), 131–33.

29. Joel S. Franks, "Chinese Americans and American Sports, 1880–1940," in *Chinese America: History and Perspectives 1996* (San Francisco: Chinese Historical Society of America, 1996), 133, 144.

30. Flora Belle Jan, "Interview with Flora Belle Jan, Daughter of Proprietor of the 'Yet Far Low' Chop Suey Restaurant, Tulare St. and Ching Alley, Fresno." Survey of Race Relations Collection, Hoover Institution on War, Revolution, and Peace, Stanford University, n.d.

31. Dong, "Forbidden City Legacy," 125–48.

32. Victoria Wong, "Square and Circle Club: Women in the Public Sphere," in *Chinese America: History and Perspectives 1994* (San Francisco: Chinese Historical Society of America, 1994), 127–53.

33. Chun, " 'Go West . . . to China,' " 167, 173.

34. Mark and Chih, *A Place Called Chinese America*, 88–89.

35. Chan, "Race, Ethnic Culture, and Gender," 155.

36. The information in this and the next paragraph comes from Chun, " 'Go West . . . to China,' " 172, 174–76.

37. W.E.B. Du Bois, *The Souls of Black Folk* (New York: Fawcett Publications, 1961), 15.

38. "How to Tell Your Friends from the Japs," *Time*, December 22, 1941, 33.

39. Yung, *Unbound Feet*, 253.

40. Espiritu, *Asian American Women and Men*, 51–52; Victor G. Nee and Brett de Bary Nee, *Longtime Californ': A Documentary Study of an American Chinatown* (New York: Pantheon Books, 1973), 154.

41. John Hayakawa Torok, " 'Interest Convergence' and the Liberalization of Discriminatory Immigration and Naturalization Laws Affecting Asians, 1943–1965," in *Chinese America: History and Perspectives 1995* (San Francisco: Chinese Historical Society of America, 1995), 8–9.

CHAPTER 4

1. Mely Giok-lan Tan, *The Chinese in the United States: Social Mobility and Assimilation* (Taipei, Taiwan: Orient Cultural Service, 1973), 40.

2. Sung, *Mountain of Gold*, 241.

3. Sucheng Chan, *Asian Americans: An Interpretive History* (Boston: Twayne Publishers, 1991), 121.

4. Ibid., 122; Esther Ngan-ling Chow, "Family, Economy, and the State: A Legacy of Struggle for Chinese American Women," in *Origins and Destinies: Immigration, Race, and Ethnicity in America,* ed. Silvia Pedraza and Rubén G. Rumbaut (Belmont, Calif.: Wadsworth Publishing, 1996), 119.

5. The information in this and the next two paragraphs comes from Rose Hum Lee, *The Chinese in the United States of America* (Hong Kong: Hong Kong University Press, 1960), 65–68, 262–66.

6. Roger Daniels, *Asian America: Chinese and Japanese in the United States Since 1850* (Seattle: University of Washington Press, 1988), 315.

7. Bill Ong Hing, *Making and Remaking Asian America Through Immigration Policy, 1850–1990* (Stanford, Calif.: Stanford University Press, 1993), 36–37.

8. The information in this and the next paragraph comes from Judy Yung, *Chinese Women of America: A Pictorial History* (Seattle: University of Washington Press, 1986), 80–81; Lee, *Chinese in the United States,* 23–25.

9. Daniels, *Asian America,* 190–91; Tan, *Chinese in the United States,* 43.

10. The information in this and the next five paragraphs comes from Hing, *Making and Remaking Asian America,* 37–38; Roger Daniels, "United States Policy Towards Asian Immigrants: Contemporary Developments in Historical Perspective," in *New American Destinies: A Reader in Contemporary Asian and Latino Immigration,* ed. Darrell Y. Hamamoto and Rodolfo D. Torres (New York: Routledge, 1997), 78; Kwong, *Chinatown, New York,* 144.

11. Kwong, *Chinatown, New York,* 144.

12. Daniels, "United States Policy," 78; Hing, *Making*

13. Hing, *Making and Remaking Asian America,* 37–38.

14. Min Zhou, *Chinatown: The Socioeconomic Potential of an Urban Enclave* (Philadelphia: Temple University Press, 1992), 64–65; Jeff Gillenkirk and James Motlow, *Bitter Melon: Stories from the Last Rural Chinese Town in America* (Seattle: University of Washington Press, 1987), 43, 49.

15. The information in this and the next three paragraphs comes from Chinn, Lai, and Choy, *History of the Chinese in California,* 29; Daniels, "United States Policy Towards Asian Immigrants," 79–80; Daniels, *Asian America,* 306; Tan, *Chinese in the United States,* 42–58.

16. Tan, *Chinese in the United States,* 83.

17. Ibid.; Sung, *Mountain of Gold,* 252.

18. See Peter Kwong, *The New Chinatown, New York* rev. ed. (New York: Hill and Wang, 1996).

19. Chalsa M. Loo, *Chinatown: Most Time, Hard Time* (New York: Praeger, 1991), 49–50; Sam Sue, "Growing Up in Mississippi," in *Asian Americans: Oral Histories of First to Fourth Generation Americans from China, the Philippines, Japan, India, the Pacific Islands, Vietnam and Cambodia,* ed. Joann-Faung Jean Lee (New York: New Press, 1992), 7.

20. J. E. Conant, "The Other Face of Chinatown," *San Francisco Examiner,* August 14, 1967, 1.

21. Yung, *Chinese Women of America*, 81.

22. Espiritu, *Asian-American Women and Men*, 57, 58.

23. The information in this and the next two paragraphs comes from Espiritu, *Asian American Women and Men*, 57–58; Rose Hum Lee, "The Recent Immigrant Chinese Families of the San Francisco–Oakland Area," *Marriage and Family Living* 18 (February 1956): 23; Stanford Lyman, *Chinese Americans* (New York: Random House, 1974), 123.

24. The information in this and the next paragraph comes from Low, *Unimpressible Race*, 134–35, 142–44.

25. Betty Ann Bruno, "Never Rebecca of Sunnybrook Farm," in *Asian Americans: Oral Histories of First to Fourth Generation Americans from China, the Philippines, Japan, India, the Pacific Islands, Vietnam, and Cambodia*, ed. Joann Faung Jean Lee (New York: New Press, 1992), 208–15.

26. Ben Fong-Torres, *The Rice Room: Growing Up Chinese-American—From Number Two Son to Rock'n'Roll* (New York: Hyperion, 1994), 75.

27. Bruno, "Never Rebecca of Sunnybrook Farm," 212.

28. Fong-Torres, *Rice Room*, 6.

29. Charles Choy Wong and Kenneth Klein, "False Papers, Lost Lives," in *Origins and Destinations: 41 Essays on Chinese America*, ed. Chinese Historical Society of Southern California and UCLA Asian American Studies Center (Los Angeles: Chinese Historical Society of Southern California and UCLA Asian American Studies Center, 1994), 355–74.

30. For details on the confession program, see Daniels, *Asian America*, 307–9; Jack Chen, *The Chinese of America* (San Francisco: Harper & Row, 1980), 215.

31. The information in this and the next five paragraphs comes from Lai, "To Bring Forth a New China," 43–52; Kwong, *Chinatown, New York*, 141–42; Chen, *Chinese of America*, 214.

32. Yung, *Chinese Women of America*, 83.

33. The information in this and the next paragraph comes from Wing Chung Ng, "Scholarship on Post–World War II Chinese Societies in North America: A Thematic Discussion," in *Chinese America: History and Perspectives 1992* (San Francisco: Chinese Historical Society of America, 1992), 198–99.

34. The information in this and the next two paragraphs comes from Him Mark Lai, "Chinese Organizations in America Based on Locality or Origin and/or Dialect-Group Affiliation, 1940s–1990." in *Chinese America: History and Perspectives 1996* (San Francisco: Chinese Historical Society of America, 1996), 25–26, 54–56.

35. The information in this and the next six paragraphs comes from Ong, *Making and Remaking Asian America*, 39–41; Rubén G. Rumbaut, "Origins and Destinies: Immigration to the United States Since World War II," in *New American Destinies: A Reader in Contemporary Asian and Latino Immigration*, ed. Darrell Y. Hamamoto and Rodolfo D. Torres (New York: Routledge, 1997), 19–21; Daniels, "United States Policy Towards Asian Immigrants," 74, 80–84.

36. Hing, *Making and Remaking Asian America*, 40.

37. Daniels, *Asian America*, 312–313.

CHAPTER 5

1. Larry Hajime Shinagawa, "The Impact of Immigration on the Demography of Asian Pacific Americans," in *The State of Asian Pacific America: Reframing the Immigration Debate*, ed. Bill Ong Hing and Ronald Lee (Los Angeles: LEAP Asian Pacific American Public Policy Institute and UCLA Asian American Studies Center, 1996), 66.

2. Zhou, *Chinatown*, 65.

3. Ong, *Making and Remaking Asian America*, 82; Zhou, *Chinatown*, 56–57.

4. Paul Ong, Edna Bonacich, and Lucie Cheng, "The Political Economy of Capitalist Restructuring and the New Asian Immigration," in *The New Asian Immigration in Los Angeles and Global Restructuring*, ed. Paul Ong, Edna Bonacich, and Lucie Cheng (Philadelphia: Temple University Press, 1994), 3–35.

5. Ong, *Making and Remaking Asian America*, 115–16.

6. Shinagawa, "Impact of Immigration," 69.

7. Don Mar and Marlene Kim, "Historical Trends," in *The State of Asian Pacific America: Economic Diversity, Issues, & Policies*, ed. Paul Ong (Los Angeles: LEAP Asian Pacific American Public Policy Institute and UCLA Asian American Studies Center, 1994), 13–30.

8. Ibid.

9. The information in this and the next two paragraphs comes from Paul Ong and Suzanne J. Hee, "The Growth of Asian Pacific America Population: Twenty Million in 2020," *The State of Asian Pacific America: Policy Issues to the Year 2020* (Los Angeles: LEAP Asian Pacific American Public Policy Institute and UCLA Asian American Studies Center, 1993), 13; Shinagawa, "Impact of Immigration," 69, 90.

10. Timothy P. Fong, *The First Suburban Chinatown: The Remaking of Monterey Park, California* (Philadelphia: Temple University Press, 1994), 26, 29–31.

11. Wing-Cheung Ng, "An Evaluation of the Labor Market Status of Chinese Americans," *Amerasia Journal* 4, no. 2 (1977): 107–10; Morrison G. Wong, "Chinese Americans," in *Asian Americans: Contemporary Trends and Issues*, ed. Pyong Gap Min (Thousand Oaks, Calif.: Sage Publications, 1995), 77.

12. The third and sixth preferences became a part of a larger employment-based immigration scheme in 1990.

13. The information in this and the next paragraph comes from Bill Ong Hing, "Immigration Policy: Making and Remaking Asian Pacific America," in *New American Destinies: A Reader in Contemporary Asian and Latino Immigration*, ed. Darrell Y. Hamamoto and Rodolfo D. Torres (New York: Routledge, 1997), 317–18; Paul Ong and Evelyn Blumenberg, "Scientists and Engineers," in *New American Destinies: A Reader in Contemporary Asian and Latino Immigration*, ed. Darrell Y. Hamamoto and Rodolfo D. Torres (New York: Routledge, 1997), 167–70.

14. Hing, "Immigration Policy," 318.

15. Ong and Blumenberg, "Scientists and Engineers," 170.

16. The information in this and the next two paragraphs comes from Hsiang-shui Chen, *Chinatown No More: Taiwan Immigrants in Contemporary New York* (Ithaca, N.Y.: Cornell University Press, 1992), 66–68; Zhou, *Chinatown*, 72.

17. Zhou, *Chinatown*, 72.   '

18. Takaki, *Strangers from a Different Shore*, 429–30.

19. Tom Abate, "Heavy Load for Silicon Valley Workers," *San Francisco Examiner*, May 23, 1993.

20. Elisa Lee, "Silicon Valley Study Finds Asian Americans Hitting the Glass Ceiling," *Asian Week*, October 8, 1993.

21. Amado Cabezas, et al., "Empirical Study of Barriers to Upward Mobility for Asian Americans in the San Francisco Bay Area," *Frontiers of Asian American Studies*, ed. Gail Nomura, et al. (Pullman: Washington State University Press, 1989), 87.

22. The information in this and the next two paragraphs comes from U.S. Commission on Civil Rights, *Civil Rights Issues Facing Asian Americans in the 1990s* (Washington, D.C.: U.S. Government Printing Office, 1992), 135–44.

23. Paul Ong and Suzanne J. Hee, "Economic Diversity," in *The State of Asian Pacific America: Economic Diversity, Issues, and Policies*, ed. Paul Ong (Los Angeles: LEAP Asian Pacific American Public Policy Institute and UCLA Asian American Studies Center, 1994), 40–41.

24. Chow, "Family, Economy, and the State," 120.

25. Cabezas, "Barriers to Upward Mobility," 88.

26. Bernard P. Wong, *Ethnicity and Entrepreneurship: The New Chinese Immigrants in the San Francisco Bay Area* (Boston: Allyn and Bacon, 1998), 41.

27. U.S. Bureau of the Census, *Survey of Minority-Owned Business Enterprises: Asian Americans, American Indians, and Others* (Washington, D.C.: Department of Commerce, 1987).

28. Kwong, *New Chinatown*, 26.

29. Chen, *Chinatown No More*, 65.

30. For a discussion of the enclave economy, see Don Mar, "Another Look at the Enclave Economy Thesis: Chinese Immigrants in the Ethnic Labor Market," *Amerasia Journal* 17, no. 3 (1991): 5–21.

31. The information in this and the next three paragraphs comes from Yen-fen Tseng, "Suburban Ethnic Economy: Chinese Business Communities in Los Angeles" (Ph.D. diss., University of California at Los Angeles, 1994), 60–67.

32. Tseng, "Suburban Ethnic Economy," 63–64.

33. Ibid., 60.

34. John Horton, *The Politics of Diversity: Immigration, Resistance, and Change in Monterey Park, California* (Philadelphia: Temple University Press, 1995), 20–21.

35. The information in this and the next paragraph comes from Wong, *Ethnicity and Entrepreneurship*, 74, 86–89.

36. The information in this and the next paragraph comes from Miriam Ching

Louie, "Immigrant Asian Women in Bay Area Garment Shops: 'After Sewing, Laundry, Cleaning and Cooking, I Have No Breath Left to Sing,' " *Amerasia Journal* 18, no. 1 (1992): 2–6; International Ladies Garment Workers' Union and the New York Skirt and Sportswear Association (hereafter ILGWU and NYSSA), *The Chinatown Garment Industry Study* (New York: Abeles, Schwartz, Haeckel and Silverblatt, 1983), 41, 59.

37. Diane Yen-Mei Wong with Dennis Hayashi, "Behind Unmarked Doors: Developments in the Garment Industry," in *Making Waves: An Anthology of Writings by and about Asian American Women*, ed. Asian Women United of California (Boston: Beacon Press, 1989), 161–62.

38. Chalsa Loo and Paul Ong, "Slaying Demons with a Sewing Needle: Feminist Issues for Chinatown's Women," *Berkeley Journal of Sociology* 27 (1982): 82–83.

39. Nee and Nee, *Longtime Californ'*, 285.

40. Paul Ong, "Chinatown Unemployment and the Ethnic Labor Market," *Amerasia Journal*, vol. 11, no. 1 (1984): 45.

41. Kwong, *New Chinatown*, 58; Peter Kwong, *Forbidden Workers: Illegal Chinese Immigrants and American Labor* (New York: New Press, 1997), 185, 193–98.

42. Kwong, *Forbidden Workers*, 193.

43. Peter Kwong, "Chinese Staff and Workers' Association: A Model for Organizing in the Changing Economy?," in *New American Destinies: A Reader in Contemporary Asian and Latino Immigration*, ed. Darrell Y. Hamamoto and Rodolfo D. Torres (New York: Routledge, 1997), 183–86.

44. Ibid., 183.

45. Lydia Lowe, "Chinese Immigrant Workers and Community-based Labor Organizing in Boston: Paving the Way," *Amerasia Journal* 18, no. 1 (1992): 39–48.

46. Ibid., 43.

47. Alex Hing, "Organizing Asian Pacific American Workers in the AFL–CIO: New Opportunities," *Amerasia Journal* 18, no. 1 (1992): 141–54.

48. Elliott Robert Barkan, *And Still They Came: Immigrants and American Society, 1920s to the 1990s* (Wheeling, Ill.: Harlan Davidson, 1996), 127.

49. Tseng, "Suburban Economy," 33.

50. Horton, *Politics of Diversity*, 18.

CHAPTER 6

1. Melford S. Weiss, *Valley City: A Chinese Community in America* (Cambridge, Mass.: Schenkman, 1974), 234–35.

2. D. Y. Yuan, "Chinatown and Beyond: The Chinese Population in Metropolitan New York," *Phylon* 27, no. 4 (1966): 331.

3. Unless otherwise noted, the discussion on the Asian American movement comes from William Wei, *The Asian American Movement* (Philadelphia: Temple University Press, 1993), 1–42.

4. Esther Ngan-ling Chow, "The Feminist Movement: Where Are All the Asian

American Women?," in *Making Waves: An Anthology of Writings by and about Asian American Women,* ed. Asian Women United of California (Boston: Beacon Press, 1989), 363–64.

5. *Report of the San Francisco Chinese Community Citizens' Survey and Fact Finding Committee* (San Francisco: H. J. Carle & Sons, 1969), 55, 60–61, 91, 93, 154–55.

6. Rocky Chin, "New York Chinatown Today: Community in Crisis," *Amerasia Journal* 6, no. 1 (March 1971): 1–23.

7. Tsai, *Chinese Experience in America,* 167.

8. The information in this and the next paragraph comes from Chin, "New York Chinatown Today," 7–13; Lyman, *Chinese Americans,* 167.

9. Chia-ling Kuo, *Social and Political Change in New York's Chinatown: The Role of Voluntary Associations* (New York: Praeger, 1977), 107.

10. The information in this and the next two paragraphs comes from Philip A. Lum, "The Creation and Demise of San Francisco Chinatown Freedom Schools: One Response to Desegregation," *Amerasia Journal* 5, no. 1 (1978): 57–73.

11. Eric Mar, "Celebrate the Chinese Progressive Association's 25th Anniversary" [electronic bulletin board] (cited February 12, 1998); available from owner— aaascommunity@listlink.berkeley.edu.

12. The information in this and the next two paragraphs comes from Bernard P. Wong, *Patronage, Brokerage, Entrepreneurship and the Chinese Community of New York* (New York: AMS Press, 1988), 61–62, 178–82.

13. Yen Le Espiritu, *Asian American Panethnicity: Bridging Institutions and Identities* (Philadelphia: Temple University Press, 1992), 92–93.

14. Wei, *Asian American Movement,* 174.

15. The information in this and the next three paragraphs comes from Kuo, *Social and Political Change,* 54–56; Kwong, *New Chinatown,* 107–8, 132–33; Loo, *Chinatown,* 75–76.

16. Kathy Fong, "A Chinaman's Chance Revisited," *Bridge* 2 (August 1973): 19–22.

17. U.S. Commission on Civil Rights, *Recent Activities against Citizens and Residents of Asian Descent* (Washington, D.C.: Clearinghouse Publication no. 88, 1986), 56.

18. For the Vincent Chin case, see Espiritu, *Asian American Panethnicity,* 137–43.

19. Ronald Takaki, "Who Really Killed Vincent Chin?," *San Francisco Examiner,* September 21, 1983.

20. Espiritu, *Asian American Panethnicity,* 157–59.

21. Alexander Suh, "Yong Xin Huang Memorial" [electronic bulletin board] (cited March 2, 1998); available from owner—aaascommunity@listlink.berkeley.edu; Tomio Geron, "APA Activism, New York Style," *Asian Week,* April 15, 1996.

22. Espiritu, *Asian American Panethnicity,* 126; Organization of Chinese Americans (OCA), "Welfare Reform Recap" [electronic bulletin board] (cited October 15,

1997); available from owner—aaascommunity@listlink.berkeley.edu; OCA, "APA LPRs and Food Stamp Fixes" [electronic bulletin board] (cited April 14, 1998); available from owner—aaascommunity@listlink.berkeley.edu.

23. OCA, "Action Alert on Anti-Asian . . ." [electronic bulletin board] (cited June 2, 1998); available from owner—aaascommunity@listlink.berkeley.edu.

24. Bert Eljera, "DNC Investigates APA Contributors," *Asian Week*, January 29, 1997; "Asian Americans Charge Fund-Raising Scandal Biases Civil Rights," *Los Angeles Times*, September 12, 1997.

25. OCA, "Bill Lee: Sign On" [electronic bulletin board] (cited November 14, 1997); available from owner—aaascommunity@listlink.berkeley.edu; OCA, "Press Release" [electronic bulletin board] (cited March 31, 1998); available from owner—aaascommunity@listlink.berkeley.edu.

26. See Richard J. Herrnstein and Charles Murray, *The Bell Curve: Intelligence and Class Structure in American Life* (New York: Free Press, 1994).

27. Stanley Sue and Sumie Okazaki, "Asian-American Educational Achievements: A Phenomenon in Search of an Explanation," *American Psychologist* 46, no. 8 (1990): 913–20.

28. Wong, "Chinese Americans," 80–81; OCA, "Bilingual Educational Program Under . . ." [electronic bulletin board] (cited June 9, 1998); available from owner—aaascommunity@listlink.berkeley.edu; Eric Mar, "Northern California Regional Meeting to . . ." [electronic bulletin board] (cited February 28, 1998); available from owner—aaascommunity@listlink.berkeley.edu.

29. L. Ling-chi Wang, "Lau v. Nichols: History of a Struggle for Equal and Quality Education," *Amerasia Journal* 2, no. 2 (1974): 16–45.

30. Timothy P. Fong, *The Contemporary Asian American Experience: Beyond the Model Minority* (Upper Saddle River, N.J.: Prentice Hall, 1998), 95.

31. The information in this and the next paragraph comes from Linda Mathews, "When Being Best Isn't Good Enough: Why Yat-pang Au Won't Be Going to Berkeley," *Los Angeles Times Magazine*, July 19, 1987, 22–28.

32. The information in this and the next paragraph comes from Jeffrey K. D. Au, "Asian American College Admissions—Legal, Empirical, and Philosophical Questions for the 1980s and Beyond," in *Reflections on Shattered Windows: Promises and Prospects for Asian American Studies*, ed. Gary Y. Okihiro et al. (Pullman: Washington State University Press, 1988), 51–56.

33. Lee *Chinese in the United States*, 178.

34. Ibid., 140.

35. Fong, *Contemporary Asian American Experience*, 250.

36. Hing, *Making and Remaking Asian America*, 157.

37. Espiritu, *Asian American Panethnicity*, 75–77.

38. Hing, *Making and Remaking Asian America*, 157. On barriers to political participation, see Paul Ong and Don Nakanishi, "Becoming Citizens, Becoming Voters: The Naturalization and Political Participation of Asian Pacific Immigrants," in *The State of Asian Pacific America: Reframing the Immigration Debate*, ed. Bill Ong

Hing and Ronald Lee (Los Angeles: LEAP Asian Pacific American Policy Institute and UCLA Asian American Studies Center, 1996), 287, 289.

39. Espiritu, *Asian American Panethnicity*, 57–58.

40. Hing, *Making and Remaking Asian America*, 157.

41. The information in this and the next two paragraphs comes from ibid., 159–61.

42. For the Chinese financial contribution to political campaigns, see Espiritu, *Asian American Panethnicity*, 61–64.

43. For intraethnic conflict in Monterey Park, see Horton, *Politics of Diversity*; Fong, *First Suburban Chinatown*.

44. Horton, *Politics of Diversity*, 36.

45. Andrew Leong, "The Struggle over Parcel C: How Boston's Chinatown Won a Victory in the Fight Against Institutional Expansion and Environmental Racism," *Amerasia Journal* 21, no. 3 (Winter 1995/1996): 99–103.

46. Leland T. Saito, "Asian Americans and Latinos in San Gabriel Valley, California: Ethnic Political Cooperation and Redistricting 1990–92," *Amerasia Journal* 19, no. 2 (1993): 55–68.

47. Wang, "Roots and the Changing Identity of the Chinese," 207.

48. For information on the Protecting Daoyutai Movement, see Tsai, *Chinese Experience in America*, 172–73.

CHAPTER 7

1. Marlon Hom, "Chinatown High Life: A Literary Pride," in *Chinese America: History and Perspectives 1988* (San Francisco: Chinese Historical Society of America, 1988), 127.

2. Lai, Lim, and Yung, *Island*, 58.

3. June Mei and Jean Pang Yip with Russell Leong, "The Bitter Society: *Ku Shehui*. A Translation, Chapters 37–46," *Amerasia Journal* 8, no. 1 (1981): 33–67.

4. Amy Ling, *Between Worlds: Women Writers of Chinese Ancestry* (New York: Pergamon Press, 1990), 49, 118–19, 170, 173.

5. Stuart Creighton Miller, *The Unwelcome Immigrant: The American Image of the Chinese, 1785–1882* (Berkeley: University of California Press, 1969), 201.

6. The information in this and the next two paragraphs comes from Elaine H. Kim, *Asian American Literature: An Introduction to the Writings and Their Social Context* (Philadelphia: Temple University Press, 1982), 5, 9. For a review of literature until the mid-1970s, see Frank Chin, Jeffrey Paul Chan, Lawson Fusao Inada, and Shawn Hsu Wong, *Aiiieeeee!: An Anthology of Asian-American Writers* (Washington, D.C.: Howard University Press, 1974).

7. The information in this and the next paragraph comes from Gina Marchetti, *Romance and the "Yellow Peril": Race, Sex, and Discursive Strategies in Hollywood*

Fiction (Berkeley: University of California Press, 1993), 32–45, 68–71; Eugene Franklin Wong, *On Visual Media Racism: Asians in the American Motion Pictures* (New York: Arno Press, 1978), 44–45.

8. Renee E. Tajima, "Lotus Blossoms Don't Bleed: Images of Asian Women," in *Making Waves: An Anthology of Writings by and about Asian American Women*, ed. Asian Women United of California (Boston: Beacon Press, 1989), 309.

9. See Wenquan, "Chinatown Literature During the Last Ten Years (1939–1949)," trans. Marlon K. Hom, *Amerasia Journal* 9, no. 1 (1982): 75–100; Kim, *Asian American Literature*, 109; Sau-Ling C. Wong, "Tales of Postwar Chinatown: Short Stories of *The Bud*, 1947–1948," *Amerasia Journal* 14, no. 2 (1988): 61–79.

10. The information in this and the next two paragraphs comes from Kim, *Asian American Literature*, 58–72; Ling, *Between Worlds*, 120–21.

11. Marlon K. Hom, "A Case of Mutual Exclusion: Portrayals by Immigrant and American-born Chinese of Each Other in Literature," *Amerasia Journal* 11, no. 2 (1984): 31–34.

12. Jinqi Ling, *Narrating Nationalisms: Ideology and Form in Asian American Literature* (New York: Oxford University Press, 1998), 54, 60–61, 74.

13. Sau-ling Cynthia Wong, "Chinese American Literature," in *An Interethnic Companion to Asian American Literature*, ed. King-kok Cheung (New York: Cambridge University Press, 1997), 48.

14. Jinqi Ling, "Identity Crisis and Gender Politics: Reappropriating Asian American Masculinity," in *An Interethnic Companion to Asian American Literature*, ed. King-kok Cheung (New York: Cambridge University Press, 1997), 319.

15. The information in this and the next three paragraphs comes from Ling, *Between Worlds*, 142, 145; Ling, *Narrating Nationalism*, 133; Sau-ling Cynthia Wong, "Autobiography as Guided Chinatown Tour? Maxine Hong Kingston's *The Woman Warrior* and the Chinese-American Autobiographical Controversy," in *Multicultural Autobiography: American Lives*, ed. James Robert Payne (Knoxville: University of Tennessee Press, 1992), 248–71.

16. Frank Chin, "This Is Not an Autobiography," *Genre* 18 (Summer 1985): 110, 130.

17. Leslie Bow, "Cultural Conflict/Feminist Resolution in Amy Tan's *The Joy Luck Club*," in *New Visions in Asian American Studies: Diversity, Community, Power*, ed. Franklin Ng et al. (Pullman: Washington State University, 1994), 245–46.

18. James S. Moy, *Marginal Sights: Staging the Chinese in America* (Iowa City: University of Iowa Press, 1993), 7–47, 115–119, 123, 126.

19. For Hawaiian Chinese poets, see Gayle K. Fujita Sato, "The Island Influence on Chinese American Writers: Wing Tek Lum, Darrell H. Y. Lum, and Eric Chock," *Amerasia Journal* 16, no. 2 (1990): 17–33.

20. Renee Tajima, "Moving the Image: Asian American Independent Filmmaking 1970–1990," in *Moving the Image: Independent Asian American Media Arts*, ed. Russell Leong (Los Angeles: UCLA Asian American Studies Center and Visual Communications, Southern California Asian American Studies Central, 1991), 12–21.

21. Loni Ding, "Strategies of an Asian American Filmmaker," in *Moving the Image: Independent Asian American Media Arts*, ed. Russell Leong (Los Angeles: UCLA Asian American Studies Center and Visual Communications, Southern California Asian American Studies Central, 1991), 54, 59.

22. See Elaine Kim, "Asian Americans and American Popular Culture," in *Dictionary of Asian American History*, ed. Kim Hyung-Chan (Chicago: University of Chicago Press, 1986), 106–7.

23. The information in this and the next two paragraphs comes from Darrell Y. Hamamoto, *Monitored Peril: Asian Americans and the Politics of TV Representation* (Minneapolis: University of Minnesota Press, 1994), 7–9, 18, 33–37, 181–93.

24. Jeff Yip, "A Heroic Leading Role for One Asian 'Son'," *Los Angeles Times*, March 25, 1995.

25. Elaine H. Kim, " 'Bad Women': Asian American Visual Artists Hanh Thi Pham, Hung Liu, and Yong Soon Min," in *Making More Waves: New Writing by Asian American Women*, ed. Elaine H. Kim, Lilia V. Villaneuva, and Asian Women United of California (Boston: Beacon Press, 1997), 188–90.

26. Franklin Ng, "Maya Lin and the Vietnam Veterans Memorial," in *Chinese America: History and Perspectives 1994* (San Francisco: Chinese Historical Society of America, 1994), 212.

27. See Wei-hua Zhang, "Fred Ho and Jon Jang: Profiles of Two Chinese American Jazz Musicians," in *Chinese America: History and Perspectives 1994* (San Francisco: Chinese Historical Society of America, 1994), 175–99.

CHAPTER 8

1. An early example of this argument is found in Norman S. Haynor and Charles N. Reynolds, "Chinese American Family Life in America," *American Sociological Review* 2 (1937): 630–37; a more recent example is found in Tsai, *Chinese Experience in America*, 162.

2. Morrison G. Wong, "The Chinese-American Family," in *Ethnic Families in America: Patterns and Variations*, 4th ed., ed. Charles H. Mindel, Robert W. Habenstein, and Roosevelt Wright, Jr. (Upper Saddle River, N.J.: Prentice Hall, 1998), 300. For early model-minority coverage, see "Success Story of One Minority Group in the U.S.," *U.S. News and World Report*, December 26, 1966, 73–78; "Asian-Americans: A Model Minority," *Newsweek*, December 6, 1982, 39–51.

3. Takaki, *Strangers from a Different Shore*, 475.

4. "Success Story of One Minority Group in the U.S.," 73.

5. Evelyn Nakano Glenn and Stacey G. H. Yap, "Chinese American Families," in *Minority Families in the United States: A Multicultural Perspective*, ed. Ronald L. Taylor (Englewood Cliffs, N.J.: Prentice Hall, 1994), 119, 125.

6. Peter S. Li, "Fictive Kinship, Conjugal Tie and Kinship Chain among Chinese Immigrants in the United States," *Journal of Comparative Family Studies* 8 (Spring 1977): 61.

7. Wong, "Chinese Americans," 71–72.

8. The information in this and the next three paragraphs comes from Fong, *Contemporary Asian American Experience,* 206–7.

9. Fong, *Contemporary Asian American Experience,* 206.

10. Ibid., 210.

11. The information in this and the next paragraph comes from Betty Lee Sung, *The Adjustment Experience of Chinese Immigrant Children in New York City* (New York: Center for Migration Studies, 1987), 182–87.

12. The information in this and the next two paragraphs comes from Wu Xingci and Li Zhen, "*Gum San Haak* in the 1980s: A Study on Chinese Emigrants Who Return to Taishan County for Marriage," *Amerasia Journal* 14, no. 2 (1988): 23–24.

13. Ko-lin Chin, "Out-of-Town Brides: International Marriage and Wife Abuse among Chinese Immigrants," *Journal of Comparative Family Studies* 25 (Spring 1994): 54.

14. Wu and Zhen, *Gum San Haak,* 26.

15. Chin, "Out-of-Town Brides," 56.

16. Ibid., 60.

17. See Edwin G. Clausen and Jack Bermingham, *Chinese and African Professionals in California: A Case Study of Equality and Opportunity in the United States* (Washington, D.C.: University Press of America, 1982), 801–87.

18. Chen, *Chinatown No More,* 80–81.

19. Loo, *Chinatown,* 199.

20. Wong, *Chinese American Family,* 297.

21. For personality types, see Stanley Sue and Derald W. Sue, "Chinese American Personality and Mental Health," in *Roots: An Asian-American Reader,* ed. Amy Tachiki et al. (Los Angeles: Continental Graphics, 1971), 72–81.

22. Laura Uba, *Asian Americans: Personality Patterns, Identity, and Mental Health* (New York: Guilford Press, 1994), 89–118.

23. Lucy Jen Huang, "The Chinese American Family," in *Ethnic Families in America: Patterns and Variations,* ed. Charles H. Mindel and Robert W. Habenstein (New York: Elsevier, 1976), 143–44.

24. Stanford Lyman, *The Asian in the West* (Reno: Desert Research Institute, 1970), 103; Glenn and Yap, "Chinese American Families," 137.

25. Jean S. Braun and Hilda M. Chao, "Attitudes Toward Women: A Comparison of Asian-Born Chinese and American Caucasians." *Psychology of Women Quarterly* 2 (Spring 1978): 200.

26. Karen Huang and Laura Uba, "Premarital Sexual Behavior among Chinese College Students in the United States," *Archives of Sexual Behavior* 21, no. 3 (1992): 227–40.

27. "Asian-American Women Struggling to Move Past Cultural Expectations," *New York Times,* January 23, 1994, 14.

28. Helen Zia, "Violence in Our Communities: Where Are the Asian Women?,"

in *Making More Waves: New Writing by Asian American Women*, ed. Elaine H. Kim, Lilia V. Villaneuva, and Asian Women United of California (Boston: Beacon Press, 1997), 212.

29. Alice Y. Hom, "Stories from the Homefront: Perspectives of Asian American Parents With Lesbian Daughters and Gay Sons," *Amerasia Journal* 20, no. 1 (1994): 21, 23.

30. Connie S. Chan, "Issues of Identity Development Among Asian-American Lesbians and Gay Men," *Journal of Counseling and Development* 68 (September/October 1989): 17, 19; Ignatius Bau, "Queer Asian American Immigrants: Opening Borders and Closets," in *Q & A: Queer in Asian America*, ed. David L. Eng and Alice Y. Hom (Philadelphia: Temple University Press, 1998), 57, 60–61.

31. Russell Leong, "Home Bodies and the Body Politic," in *Asian American Sexualities: Dimensions of the Gay and Lesbian Experience*, ed. Russell Leong (New York: Routledge, 1996), 5.

32. Loo, *Chinatown*, 171.

33. Marshall Jung, *Chinese American Family Therapy: A New Model for Clinicians* (San Francisco: Jossey-Bass Publishers, 1998), 45–47.

34. Harry L. Kitano, Wai-Tsang Yeung, Lynn Chai, and Herbert Hatanaka, "Asian-American Interracial Marriage," *Journal of Marriage and the Family* 46 (February 1984): 179–90.

35. Morrison G. Wong, "A Look at Intermarriage Among the Chinese in the United States in 1980," *Sociological Perspectives* 32, no. 1 (1989): 87–107.

36. Sharon M. Lee and Keiko Yamanaka, "Patterns of Asian American Intermarriage and Marital Assimilation," *Journal of Comparative Family Studies* 21 (Summer 1990): 287–305.

37. Betty Lee Sung, "Intermarriage among the Chinese in New York City," in *Chinese America: History and Perspectives 1987* (San Francisco: Chinese Historical Society of America, 1987), 111–12.

38. Ibid.

39. Larry Hajime Shinagawa and Gin Yong Pang, "Marriage Patterns of Asian Americans in California, 1980," *Mellen Studies in Sociology* 3 (1990): 261–62.

40. Ibid., 261–62, 270.

41. Colleen Fong and Judy Yung, "In Search of the Right Spouse: Interracial Marriage among Chinese and Japanese Americans," *Amerasia Journal* 21 (Winter 1995/1996): 85.

42. Ibid., 78, 84, 90–93.

43. Paul R. Spickard, "What Must I Be? Asian Americans and the Question of Multiethnic Identity," *Amerasia Journal* 23, no. 1 (1997): 49.

44. Maria P. Root, "Multiracial Asians: Models of Ethnic Identity," *Amerasia Journal* 23, no. 1 (1997): 32.

45. Larry H. Shinagawa and Gin Yong Pang, "Asian American Pan-Ethnicity and Intermarriage," *Amerasia Journal* 22, no. 2 (1996): 143.

Selected Bibliography

Abate, Tom. "Heavy Load for Silicon Valley Workers." *San Francisco Examiner*, May 23, 1993.

Armentrout-Ma, L. Eve. "Chinatown Organizations and the Anti-Chinese Movement, 1882–1914." In *Entry Denied: Exclusion and the Chinese Community in America, 1882–1943*, ed. Sucheng Chan, 147–169. Philadelphia; Temple University Press, 1994.

Armentrout-Ma, Eve L. *Revolutionaries, Monarchists, and Chinatowns: Chinese Politics in the Americas and the 1911 Revolution.* Honolulu: University of Hawaii Press, 1990.

"Asian Americans: A Model Minority." *Newsweek*, December 6, 1982, 39–51.

"Asian Americans Charge Fund-Raising Scandal Biases Civil Rights." *Los Angeles Times*, September 12, 1997.

Asian Women United of California, ed. *Making Waves: An Anthology of Writings by and about Asian American Women.* Boston: Beacon Press, 1989.

Au, Jeffrey K. D. "Asian American College Admissions—Legal, Empirical, and Philosophical Questions for the 1980s and Beyond." In *Reflections on Shattered Windows: Promises and Prospects for Asian American Studies*, ed. Gary Y. Okihiro, et al., 51–58. Pullman: Washington State University Press, 1988.

Azuma, Eiichiro. "Interethnic Conflict under Racial Subordination: Japanese Immigrants and Their Asian Neighbors in Walnut Grove, California, 1908–1941." *Amerasia Journal* 20, no. 2 (1994): 27–56.

Barkan, Elliott Robert. *And Still They Came: Immigrants and American Society, 1920s to the 1990s.* Wheeling, Ill.: Harlan Davidson, 1996.

Barth, Gunther. *Bitter Strength: A History of the Chinese in the United States, 1850–1870.* Cambridge, Mass.: Harvard University Press, 1964.

Bau, Ignatius. "Queer Asian American Immigrants: Opening Borders and Closets." In *Q & A: Queer in Asian America*, edited by David L. Eng and Alice Y. Hom, 57–64. Philadelphia: Temple University Press, 1998.

Bonner, Arthur. *Alas! What Brought These Hither? The Chinese in New York. 1800–1950*. Cranbury, N.J.: Associated University Presses, 1997.

Bow, Leslie. "Cultural Conflict/Feminist Resolution in Amy Tan's *The Joy Luck Club*." In *New Visions* in *Asian American Studies: Diversity, Community, Power*, ed. Franklin Ng et al., 235–47. Pullman: Washington State University, 1994.

Braun, Jean S. and Hilda M. Choo. "Attitudes Toward Women: A Comparison of Asian-Born Chinese and American Caucasians," *Psychology of Women Quarterly* 2 (Spring 1978): 195–201.

Bruno, Betty Ann. "Never Rebecca of Sunnybrook Farm." In *Asian Americans: Oral Histories of First to Fourth Generation Americans from China, the Philippines, Japan, India, the Pacific Islands, Vietnam, and Cambodia*, ed. Joann Foung Jean Lee, 208–15. New York: New Press, 1992.

Cabezas, Amado, et al. "Empirical Study of Barriers to Upward Mobility for Asian Americans in the San Francisco Bay Area." In *Frontiers of Asian American Studies*, ed. Gail Nomura, et al., 85–97. Pullman: Washington State University Press, 1989.

"The Celestials at Home and Abroad." *Littell's Living Age*, 14 August, 1852, 289–98.

Chan, Connie S. "Issues of Identity Development among Asian-American Lesbians and Gay Men." *Journal of Counseling and Development* 68 (September/October 1989): 16–20.

Chan, Sucheng. *Asian Americans: An Interpretive History*. Boston: Twayne Publishers, 1991.

———. "European and Asian Immigration into the United States in Comparative Perspectives, 1820s to 1920s." In *Immigration Reconsidered: History, Sociology, and Politics*, edited by Virginia Yans-McLaughlin, 37–78. New York: Oxford University Press, 1990.

———. "The Exclusion of Chinese Women, 1870–1943." In *Entry Denied: Exclusion and the Chinese Community in America 1882–1943*, edited by Sucheng Chan, 94–146. Philadelphia: Temple University Press, 1991.

———. "Race, Ethnic Culture, and Gender in the Construction of Identities among Second-Generation Chinese Americans." In *Claiming America: Constructing Chinese American Identities During the Exclusion Era*, edited by K. Scott Wong and Sucheng Chan, 127–64. Philadelphia: Temple University Press, 1998.

———. *This Bittersweet Soil: The Chinese in California Agriculture, 1860–1910*. Berkeley: University of California Press, 1986.

Char, Tin-Yuke. *The Sandalwood Mountains: Readings and Stories of the Early Chinese Immigrants in Hawaii*. Honolulu: University of Hawaii Press, 1975.

Chen, Hsiang-shui. *Chinatown No More: Taiwan Immigrants in Contemporary New York.* Ithaca, N.Y.: Cornell University Press, 1992.

Chen, Jack. *The Chinese of America.* San Francisco: Harper & Row, 1980.

Chen, Kenneth. *Buddhism in China.* Princeton, N.J.: Princeton University Press, 1964.

Chen, Yong. "Internal Origins to Chinese Immigration Reconsidered." *Western Historical Quarterly* 25 (Winter 1997): 521–46.

Chew, Ron. *Reflections on Seattle's Chinese Americans: The First 100 Years.* Seattle: Wing Luke Asian Museum, 1994.

Chin, Frank. *The Chickencoop Chinaman and the Year of the Dragon.* Seattle: University of Washington Press, 1981.

———. "This Is Not an Autobiography," *Genre* 18 (Summer 1985): 109–30.

Chin, Frank, Jeffrey Paul Chan, Lawson Fusao Inada, and Wong Shawn Hsu, eds. *Aiiieeeee! An Anthology of Asian-American Writers.* Washington, D.C.: Howard University Press, 1974.

Chin, Ko-lin. "Out-of-Town Brides: International Marriage and Wife Abuse among Chinese Immigrants." *Journal of Comparative Family Studies* 25 (Spring 1994): 53–69.

Chin, Rocky. "New York Chinatown Today: Community in Crisis." *Amerasia Journal* 6, no. 1 (March 1971): 1–23.

Chinese Historical Society of Southern California and UCLA Asian American Studies Center, eds. *Origins and Destinations: 41 Essays on Chinese America.* Los Angeles: Chinese Historical Society of Southern California and UCLA Asian American Studies Center, 1994.

Chinn, Thomas W. *Bridging the Pacific: San Francisco Chinatown and Its People.* San Francisco: Chinese Historical Society of America, 1989.

Chinn, Thomas W., Him Mark Lai, and Philip P. Choy, eds. *A History of the Chinese in California: A Syllabus.* San Francisco: Chinese Historical Society of America, 1969.

Chow, Esther Ngan-ling. "Family, Economy, and the State: A Legacy of Struggle for Chinese American Women." In *Origins and Destinies: Immigration, Race, and Ethnicity in America,* edited by Silvia Pedraza and Rubén G. Rumbaut, 110–24. Belmont, Calif.: Wadsworth Publishing, 1996.

———. "The Feminist Movement: Where Are All the Asian American Women?" In *Making Waves: An Anthology of Writings by and about Asian American Women,* edited by Asian Women United of California, 362–76. Boston: Beacon Press, 1989.

Chu, Louis. *Eat a Bowl of Tea.* New York: Lyle Stuart, 1961.

Chu, Yu-Kuang, "The Chinese Language." In *An Introduction to Chinese Civilization,* ed. John Meskill, 587–615. New York: Columbia University Press, 1973.

Chun, Gloria H. " 'Go West . . . to China': Chinese American Identity in the 1930s." In *Claiming America: Constructing Chinese American Identities Dur-*

ing the Exclusion Era, edited by K. Scott Wong and Sucheng Chan, 165–90. Philadelphia: Temple University Press, 1998.

Chung, Christy, et al. "In Our Own Way: A Roundtable Discussion." *Amerasia Journal* 20, no. 1 (1994): 137–47.

Chung, Sue Fawn. "Fighting for Their American Rights: A History of the Chinese American Citizens Alliance." In *Claiming America: Constructing Chinese American Identities During the Exclusion Era*, edited by K. Scott Wong and Sucheng Chan, 95–126. Philadelphia: Temple University Press, 1998.

Clousen, Edwin G., and Jack Bermingham, *Chinese and African Professionals in California: A Case Study of Equality and Opportunity in the United States.* Washington, D.C.: University Press of America, 1982.

Cohen, Lucy M. *Chinese in the Post–Civil War South: A People Without a History.* Baton Rouge: Louisiana State University Press, 1984.

Conant, J. E. "The Other Face of Chinatown." *San Francisco Examiner*, August 14, 1967, 1.

Coolidge, Mary Roberts. *Chinese Immigration.* New York: Henry Holt, 1909.

Coye, Molly Joel, and Jon Livingston. *China: Yesterday and Today.* 2d ed. New York: Bantam Books, 1979.

Daniels, Roger. *Asian America: Chinese and Japanese in the United States Since 1850.* Seattle: University of Washington Press, 1988.

———. "United States Policy Towards Asian Immigrants: Contemporary Developments in Historical Perspectives." In *New American Destinies: A Reader in Contemporary Asian and Latino Immigration*, edited by Darrell Y. Hamamoto and Rodolfo D. Torres, 73–89. New York: Routledge, 1997.

Ding, Loni. "Strategies of an Asian American Filmmaker." In *Moving the Image: Independent Asian American Media Arts*, ed. Russell Leong, 46–59. Los Angeles: University of California, at Los Angeles Asian American Studies Center and Visual Communications, Southern California Asian American Studies Central, 1991.

Dong, Lorraine. "The Forbidden City Legacy and Its Chinese American Women." In *Chinese America: History and Perspectives 1992*, 125–48. San Francisco: Chinese Historical Society of America, 1992.

Dubois, W.E.B. *The Souls of Black Folk.* New York: Fawcett Publications, 1961.

Eastman, Lloyd E. *Family, Fields, and Ancestors: Constancy and Change in China's Social and Economic History, 1550–1949.* New York: Oxford University Press, 1988.

"Editorial." *Chinese Digest*, November 15, 1935, 8.

Eng, David L., and Alice Y. Hom, eds. *Q & A: Queer in Asian America.* Philadelphia: Temple University Press, 1998.

Espiritu, Yen Le. *Asian American Panethnicity: Bridging Institutions and Identities.* Philadelphia: Temple University Press, 1992.

———. *Asian American Women and Men: Labor, Laws, and Love.* Thousand Oaks, Calif.: Sage Publications, 1997.

Fairbank, John King. *The United States and China.* 4th ed. Cambridge, Mass.: Harvard University Press, 1979.

Fairbank, John K., Edwin O. Reischauer, and Albert M. Craig. "Taoism and Buddhism." In *China: Yesterday and Today,* 2nd ed., ed. Molly Joel Coye and Jon Livingston, 48–50. New York: Bantam Books, 1979.

Feuchtwang, Stephen. *The Imperial Metaphor: Popular Religion in China.* London: Routledge, 1992.

Fong, Colleen, and Judy Yung. "In Search of the Right Spouse: Interracial Marriage among Chinese and Japanese Americans." *Amerasia Journal* 21 (Winter 1995/1996): 77–97.

Fong, Kathy, "A Chinaman's Chance Revisited." *Bridge* 2 (August 1973): 19–22.

Fong, Timothy P. *The Contemporary Asian American Experience: Beyond the Model Minority.* Upper Saddle River, N.J.: Prentice Hall, 1998.

———. *The First Suburban Chinatown: The Remaking of Monterey Park, California.* Philadelphia: Temple University Press, 1994.

Fong-Torres, Ben. *The Rice Room: Growing Up Chinese-American—From Number Two Son to Rock 'n' Roll.* New York: Hyperion, 1994.

Franks, Joel S. "Chinese Americans and American Sports, 1880–1940." In *Chinese American: History and Perspectives 1996,* 133–48. San Francisco: Chinese Historical Society of America, 1996.

Freedman, Maurice. "Ritual Aspects of Chinese Kinship and Marriage." In *Family and Kinship in Chinese Society,* ed. Maurice Freedman, 165–79. Stanford: Stanford University Press, 1970.

Friday, Chris. *Organizing Asian American Labor: The Pacific Coast Canned-Salmon Industry, 1870–1942.* Philadelphia: Temple University Press, 1994.

Fritz, Christian G. "Due Process, Treaty Rights, and Chinese Exclusion, 1882–1891." In *Entry Denied: Exclusion and the Chinese Community in America, 1882–1943,* edited by Sucheng Chan, 25–56. Philadelphia: Temple University Press, 1991.

Gee, Emma, ed. *Counterpoint: Perspectives on Asian America.* Los Angeles: University of California, Asian American Studies Center, 1976.

Geron, Tomio. "APA Activism, New York Style," *Asian Week,* April 15, 1996.

Gillenkirk, Jeff, and James Motlow. *Bitter Melon: Stories from the Last Rural Chinese Town in America.* Seattle: University of Washington Press, 1987.

Glenn, Evelyn Nakano, and Stacey G. H. Yap. "Chinese American Families." In *Minority Families in the United States: A Multicultural Perspective,* edited by Ronald L. Taylor, 115–46. Englewood Cliffs, N.J.: Prentice Hall, 1994.

Glick, Clarence Elmer. *Sojourners and Settlers: Chinese Migrants in Hawaii.* Honolulu: University Press of Hawaii, 1980.

Greenwood, Robert S. *Down by the Station: Los Angeles Chinatown, 1880–1933.* Los Angeles: University of California, 1996.

Hamamoto, Darrell Y. *Monitored Peril: Asian Americans and the Politics of TV Representation.* Minneapolis: University of Minnesota Press, 1994.

Hao Yen-p'ing. *The Commercial Revolution in Nineteenth Century China: The Rise of Sino-Western Mercantile Capitalism.* Berkeley: University of California Press, 1986.

Haynor, Norman S, and Charles N. Reynolds. "Chinese American Family Life in America." *American Sociological Review* 2 (1937): 630–37.

Herrnstein, Richard J., and Charles Murray. *The Bell Curve: Intelligence and Class Structure in American Life.* New York: Free Press, 1994.

Hing, Alex. "Organizing Asian Pacific American Workers in the AFL–CIO: New Opportunities." *Amerasia Journal* 18, no. 1 (1992): 141–54.

Hing, Bill Ong. "Immigration Policy: Making and Remaking Asian Pacific America." In *New American Destinies: A Reader in Contemporary Asian and Latino Immigration,* ed. Darrell Y. Hamamoto and Rodolfo D. Torres, 316–23. New York: Routledge, 1997.

———. *Making and Remaking Asian America Through Immigration Policy, 1850–1990.* Stanford, Calif.: Stanford University Press, 1993.

Hing, Bill Ong, and Ronald Lee, eds. *The State of Asian Pacific America: Reframing the Immigration Debate.* Los Angeles: LEAP Asian Pacific American Public Policy Institute and UCLA Asian American Studies Center, 1996.

Hirschman, Charles, and Morrison G. Wong. "Trends in Socioeconomic Achievement among Immigrant and Native-born Asian-Americans, 1960–1976." *Sociological Quarterly* 22 (Autumn 1981): 495–513.

Ho Ping-Ti. *Studies on the Population of China, 1368–1953.* Cambridge, Mass.: Harvard University Press, 1959.

Hom, Alice Y. "Stories from the Homefront: Perspectives of Asian American Parents with Lesbian Daughters and Gay Sons." *Amerasia Journal* 20, no. 1 (1994): 19–32.

Hom, Marlon K. "A Case of Mutual Exclusion: Portrayals by Immigrant and American-born Chinese of Each Other in Literature." *Amerasia Journal* 11, no. 2 (1984): 29–45.

———. "Chinatown High Life: A Literary Pride." In *Chinese America: History and Perspectives 1988,* 103–30. San Francisco: Chinese Historical Society of America, 1988.

———. *Songs of Gold Mountain: Cantonese Rhymes from San Francisco Chinatown.* Berkeley: University of California Press, 1987.

Horton, John. *The Politics of Diversity: Immigration, Resistance, and Change in Monterey Park, California.* Philadelphia: Temple University Press, 1995.

"How To Tell Your Friends from the Japs." *Time,* December 22, 1941, 33.

Hoy, William. "Reviews and Comments." *Chinese Digest,* June 26, 1936, 10.

Hsu, Immanuel C. Y. *The Rise of Modern China.* 4th ed. New York: Oxford University Press, 1990.

Hsu, Madeline. "Gold Mountain Dreams and Paper Son Schemes: Chinese Immigration under Exclusion." In *Chinese America: History and Perspectives 1997,* 46–60. San Francisco: Chinese Historical Society of America, 1997.

Huang, Karen, and Laura Uba. "Premarital Sexual Behavior among Chinese College

Students in the United States." *Archives of Sexual Behavior* 21, no. 3 (1992): 227–40.

Huang, Lucy Jen. "The Chinese American Family." In *Ethnic Families in America: Patterns and Variations*, ed. Charles H. Mindel and Robert W. Habenstine, 124–47. New York: Elsevier 1976.

Huang, Philip C. C. *The Peasant Family and Rural Development in the Yangzi Delta, 1350–1988*. Stanford Calif.: Stanford University Press, 1990.

International Ladies Garment Workers' Union and the New York Skirt and Sportswear Association. *The Chinatown Garment Industry Study*. New York: Abeles, Schwartz, Haeckel, and Silverblatt, 1983.

Jan, Flora Belle. "Interview with Flora Belle Jan Daughter of Proprietor of the "Yet Far Low' Chop Suey Restaurant, Tulare St. and China Alley, Fresno." Survey of Race Relations, Hoover Institution on War, Revolution and Peace Collection, Stanford University, n.d.

Johnson, David. "Communication, Class, and Consciousness in Late Imperial China." In *Popular Culture in Late Imperial China*, ed. David Johnson et al. 34–72. Berkeley: University of California Press, 1985.

Jung, Marshall. *Chinese American Family Therapy: A New Model for Clinicians*. San Francisco: Jossey-Bass Publishers, 1998.

Kim, Elaine H. *Asian American Literature: An Introduction to the Writings and Their Social Context*. Philadelphia: Temple University Press, 1982.

———. "Asian Americans and Popular Culture." In *Dictionary of Asian American History*, ed. Kim Hyung-Chan, 99–114. Chicago: University of Chicago Press, 1986.

———. " 'Bad Women': Asian American Visual Artists Hanh Thi Pham, Hung Liu, and Yong Soon Min." In *Making More Waves: New Writing by Asian American Women*, edited by Elaine H. Kim, Lilia V. Villanueva, and Asian Women United of California, 184–94. Boston: Beacon Press, 1997.

Kin, Huie. *Reminiscences*. Peiping: San Yu Press, 1909.

Kingston, Maxine Hong. *China Men*. New York: Alfred A. Knopf, 1980.

———. *The Woman Warrior, Memoirs of a Girlhood among Ghosts*. New York: Vintage Books, 1976.

Kitano, Harry L., and Roger Daniels. *Asian Americans: Emerging Minorities*. 2d ed. Englewood Cliffs, N.J.: Prentice Hall, 1995.

Kitano, Harry L., Wai-Tsang Yeung, Lynn Chai, and Herbert Hatanaka. "Asian American Interracial Marriage." *Journal of Marriage and the Family* 46 (February 1984): 179–90.

Kuo, Chia-ling. *Social and Political Change in New York's Chinatown: The Role of Voluntary Associations*. New York: Praeger, 1977.

Kwong, Peter. *Chinatown, New York: Labor and Politics, 1930–1950*. New York: Monthly Review Press, 1979.

———. "Chinese Staff and Workers' Association: A Model for Organizing in the Changing Economy?" In *New American Destinies: A Reader in Contem-*

porary Asian and Latino Immigration, ed. Darrell Y. Hamamoto and Rodolfo D. Torres, 183–89. New York: Routledge, 1997.

———. *Forbidden Workers: Illegal Chinese Immigrants and American Labor.* New York: New Press, 1997.

———. *The New Chinatown.* Rev. ed. New York: Hill and Wang, 1996.

Lai Chun-Chuen. *Remarks of the Chinese Merchants of San Francisco upon Governor Bigler's Message.* San Francisco: Whitton, Towne, 1855.

Lai, Him Mark. "Chinese Organizations in America Based on Locality or Origin and/or Dialect-Group Affiliation, 1940s–1990s." In *Chinese America: History and Perspectives 1996,* 19–92. San Francisco: Chinese Historical Society of America, 1996.

———. "The Guangdong Historical Background, with Emphasis on the Development of the Pearl River Delta Region." In *Chinese America: History and Perspectives 1991,* 75–99. San Francisco: Chinese Historical Society of America, 1991.

———. "Historical Development of the Chinese Consolidated Benevolent Association/*Huiguan* System." In *Chinese America: History and Perspectives, 1987,* 13–51. San Francisco: Chinese Historical Society of America, 1987.

———. "The Kuomintang in Chinese American Communities Before World War II." In *Entry Denied: Exclusion and the Chinese Community in America, 1882–1943,* edited by Sucheng Chan, 170–212. Philadelphia: Temple University Press, 1991.

———. "To Bring Forth a New China, to Build a Better America: The Chinese Marxist Left in America to 1960s." In *Chinese America: History and Perspectives 1992,* 3–82. San Francisco: Chinese Historical Society of America, 1992.

Lai, Him Mark, Joe Huang, and Don Wong. *The Chinese of America, 1785–1980.* San Francisco: Chinese Culture Center, 1980.

Lai, Him Mark, Genny Lim, and Judy Yung. *Island: Poetry and History of Chinese Immigrants on Angel Island, 1910–1940.* San Francisco: Hoc Doi, 1986.

Lam, Julie Shuk-yee. "The Chinese Digest, 1935–1940." In *Chinese America: History and Perspectives 1989,* 119–37. San Francisco: Chinese Historical Society of America, 1989.

Lee, Elisa. "Silicon Valley Study Finds Asian Americans Hitting the Glass Ceiling." *Asian Week,* October 8, 1993.

Lee, Joann Faung Jean, ed. *Asian Americans: Oral Histories of First to Fourth Generation Americans from China, the Philippines, Japan, India, the Pacific Islands, Vietnam, and Cambodia.* New York: New Press, 1992.

Lee, Rose Hum. *The Chinese in the United States of America.* Hong Kong: Hong Kong University Press, 1960.

———. *The Growth and Decline of Chinese Communities in the Rocky Mountain Region.* New York: Arno Press, 1978.

—————. "The Recent Immigrant Chinese Families of the San Francisco–Oakland Area." *Marriage and Family Living* 18 (February 1956): 14–24.

Lee, Sharon M., and Keiko Yamanaka. "Patterns of Asian American Intermarriage and Marital Assimilation." *Journal of Comparative Family Studies* 21 (Summer 1990): 287–305.

Legge, James, ed. *The Chinese Classics*, 5 vols. Oxford: Clarendon Press, 1893–1895.

Leong, Andrew. "The Struggle over Parcel C: How Boston's Chinatown Won a Victory in the Fight Against Institutional Expansion and Environmental Racism." *Amerasia Journal* 21, no. 3 (Winter 1995/1996): 99–119.

Leong, Russell, ed. *Asian American Sexualities: Dimensions of the Gay and Lesbian Experience*. New York: Routledge, 1996.

Leung, Sin Jang. "A Laundryman Sings the Blues." In *Chinese America: History and Perspectives 1991*. Translated by Marlon K. Hom, 3–24. San Francisco: Chinese Historical Society of America, 1991.

Li, Peter S. "Fictive Kinship, Conjugal Tie and Kinship Chain among Chinese Immigrants in the United States." *Journal of Comparative Family Studies* 8 (Spring 1977): 47–63.

Light, Ivan H. *Ethnic Enterprise in America: Business and Welfare among Chinese, Japanese, and Blacks*. Berkeley: University of California Press, 1972.

—————. "From Vice District to Tourist Attraction: The Moral Career of American Chinatowns, 1880–1940." *Pacific Historical Review* 43 (August 1974): 367–94.

Lim, Genny, ed. *The Chinese American Experience: Papers from the Second National Conference on Chinese American Studies*. San Francisco: Chinese Historical Society of America and the Chinese Culture Foundation of San Francisco, 1980.

Ling, Amy. *Between Worlds: Women Writers of Chinese Ancestry*. New York: Pergamon Press, 1990.

Ling, Huping. *Surviving on the Gold Mountain: A History of Chinese American Women and Their Lives*. Albany: State University of New York Press, 1998.

Ling, Jinqi. "Identity Crisis and Gender Politics: Reappropriating Asian American Masculinity." In *An Interethnic Companion to Asian American Literature*, ed. King-kok Cheung, 312–27. New York: Cambridge University Press, 1997.

—————. *Narrating Nationalisms: Ideology and Form in Asian American Literature*. New York: Oxford University Press, 1998.

Loewen, James W. *The Mississippi Chinese: Between Black and White*. Cambridge, Mass.: Harvard University Press, 1971.

Loo, Chalsa, and Paul Ong. "Slaying Demons with a Sewing Needle: Feminist Issues for Chinatown's Women." *Berkeley Journal of Sociology* 27 (1982): 77–88.

Loo, Chalsa M. *Chinatown: Most Time, Hard Time*. New York: Praeger, 1991.

Louie, Miriam Ching. "Immigrant Asian Women in Bay Area Garment Shops: 'After Sewing, Laundry, Cleaning, and Cooking, I Have No Breath Left to Sing.' " *Amerasia Journal* 18, no. 1 (1992): 1–26.

Louis, Kit King. "A Study of American-born and American-reared Chinese in Los Angeles." Master's thesis, University of Southern California, 1931.

Low, Victor. *The Unimpressible Race: A Century of Educational Struggle by the Chinese in San Francisco*. San Francisco: East/West Publishing, 1982.

Lowe, Lydia. "Chinese Immigrant Workers and Community-based Labor Organizing in Boston: Paving the Way." *Amerasia Journal* 18, no. 1 (1992): 39–48.

Lowe, Pardee. *Father and Glorious Descendant*. Boston: Little, Brown, 1943.

Lum, Philip A. "The Creation and Demise of San Francisco Chinatown Freedom Schools: One Response to Desegregation." *Amerasia Journal* 5, no. 1 (1978): 57–73.

Lyman, Stanford. *The Asian in the West*. Reno, Nev.: Desert Research Institute, 1970.

———. *Chinese Americans*. New York: Random House, 1974.

Mathews, Linda. "When Being Best Isn't Good Enough: Why Yat-pang Au Won't Be Going to Berkeley." *Los Angeles Times Magazine*, July 19, 1987, 22–28.

McClain, Charles J. *In Search of Equality: The Chinese Struggle Against Discrimination in Nineteenth-Century America*. Berkeley: University of California Press, 1994.

McClain, Charles J., and Laurence Wu McClain. "The Chinese Contribution to the Development of American Law." In *Entry Denied: Exclusion and the Chinese Community in America, 1882–1943*, edited by Sucheng Chan, 3–24. Philadelphia: Temple University Press, 1991.

McCunn, Ruthanne Lum. *Chinese American Portraits: Personal Histories 1828–1988*. San Francisco: Chronicle Books, 1988.

McKee, Delber L. "The Chinese Boycott of 1905–1906. Reconsidered: The Role of Chinese Americans." *Pacific Historical Review* 55 (May 1986): 165–91.

Mar, Don. "Another Look at the Enclave Economy Thesis: Chinese Immigrants in the Ethnic Labor Market." *Amerasia Journal* 17, no. 3 (1991): 5–21.

Mar, Don, and Marlene Kim. "Historical Trends." In *The State of Asian Pacific America: Economic Diversity, Issues & Policies*, edited by Paul Ong, 13–30. Los Angeles: LEAP Asian Pacific American Public Policy Institute and UCLA Asian American Studies Center, 1994.

Marchetti, Gina. *Romance and the "Yellow Peril": Race, Sex, and Discursive Strategies in Hollywood Fiction*. Berkeley: University of California Press, 1993.

Mark, Diane Mei Lin, and Ginger Chih. *A Place Called Chinese America*. San Francisco: Organization of Chinese Americans, 1982.

Mei, June. "Socioeconomic Origins of Emigration: Guangdong to California, 1850–1882." In *Labor Immigration under Capitalism: Asian Workers in the United States Before World War II*, edited by Lucie Cheng and Edna Bonacich, 219–47. Berkeley: University of California Press, 1984.

Meskill, John, ed. *An Introduction to Chinese Civilization*. New York: Columbia University Press, 1973.

Miller, Stuart Creighton. *The Unwelcome Immigrant: The American Image of the Chinese, 1785–1882.* Berkeley: University of California Press, 1969.

Minnick, Sylvia Sun. *Sam Fow: The San Joaquin Chinese Legacy.* Fresno, Calif.: Panorama Publishing, 1988.

Moy, James S. *Marginal Sights: Staging the Chinese in America.* Iowa City: University of Iowa Press, 1993.

Nee, Victor G., and Brett de Bary Nee. *Longtime Californ': A Documentary Study of an American Chinatown.* New York: Pantheon Books, 1973.

Ng, Franklin. "Maya Lin and the Vietnam Veterans Memorial." In *Chinese America: History and Perspectives 1994,* 201–22. San Francisco: Chinese Historical Society of America, 1994.

———. "The Sojourner, Return Migration, and Immigration History." In *Chinese America: History and Perspectives 1987,* 53–71. San Francisco: Chinese Historical Society of America, 1987.

Ng, Wing-Cheung. "An Evaluation of the Labor Market Status of Chinese Americans." *Amerasia Journal* 4, no. 2 (1977): 101–22.

Ng, Wing Chung. "Scholarship on Post–World War II Chinese Societies in North America: A Thematic Discussion." In *Chinese America: History and Perspectives 1992,* 177–210. San Francisco: Chinese Historical Society of America, 1992.

Okihiro, Gary Y. *Margins and Mainstreams: Asians in American History and Culture.* Seattle: University of Washington Press, 1994.

"The Old Oriental Warehouse in San Francisco." *Bulletin of the Chinese Historical Society of America* 25 (November 1990): 1–3.

Ong, Paul. "Chinatown Unemployment and the Ethnic Labor Market." *Amerasia Journal* 11, no. 1 (1984): 35–54.

———. "Chinese Labor in Early San Francisco: Racial Segmentation and Industrial Expansion." *Amerasia Journal* 8, no. 1 (1981): 69–92.

———, ed. *The State of Asian Pacific America: Economic Diversity, Issues & Policies: A Public Policy Report.* Los Angeles: LEAP Asian Pacific American Public Policy Institute and UCLA Asian American Studies Center, 1994.

Ong, Paul, and Evelyn Blumenberg. "Scientists and Engineers." In *New American Destinies: A Reader in Contemporary Asian and Latino Immigration,* edited by Darrell Y. Hamamoto and Rodolfo D. Torres, 163–81. New York: Routledge, 1997.

Ong, Paul, Edna Bonacich, and Lucie Cheng, eds. *The New Asian Immigration in Los Angeles and Global Restructuring.* Philadelphia: Temple University Press, 1994.

Ong, Paul, and Suzanne J. Hee, "Economic Diversity." In *The Story of Asian Pacific America: Economic Diversity, Issues, and Policies,* edited by Paul Ong, 31–56. Los Angeles: LEAP Asian Pacific American Public Policy Institute and UCLA Asian American Studies Center, 1994.

Ong, Paul, and Suzanne J. Hee. "The Growth of Asian Pacific America Population:

Twenty Million in 2020." In *The State of Asian Pacific America: Policy Issues to the Year 2020*, 11–24. Los Angeles: LEAP Asian Pacific American Public Policy Institute and UCLA Asian American Studies Center, 1993).

Ong, Paul, and Don Nakanishi. "Becoming Citizens, Becoming Voters: The Naturalization and Political Participation of Asian Pacific Immigrants." In *The State of Asian Pacific America: Reframing the Immigration Debate*, edited by Bill Ong Hing and Ronald Lee, 275–305. Los Angeles: LEAP Asian Pacific American Policy Institute and UCLA Asian American Studies Center, 1996.

Peffer, George Anthony. "Forbidden Families: Emigration Experiences of Chinese Women under the Page Law, 1875–1882." *Journal of American Ethnic History* 6 (Fall 1986): 28–46.

Pomerantz, Linda. "The Chinese Bourgeoisie and the Anti-Chinese Movement in the United States, 1850–1905." *Amerasia Journal* 11, no. 1 (1984): 1–34.

Pozzetta, George E. "The Chinese Encounter with Florida, 1865–1920." In *Chinese America: History and Perspectives 1989*, 43–57. San Francisco: Chinese Historical Society of America, 1989.

Report of the San Francisco Chinese Community Citizens' Survey and Fact Finding Committee. San Francisco: H. J. Carle & Sons, 1969.

Riddle, Ronald. *Flying Dragons, Flowing Streams: Music in the Life of San Francisco's Chinese.* Westport, Conn.: Greenwood Press, 1983.

Rohe, Randall E. "After the Gold Rush: Chinese Mining in the Far West, 1850–1890." *Montana: The Magazine of Western History* 32 (Autumn 1980): 2–19.

Root, Maria P. "Multi-racial Asians: Models of Ethnic Identity." *Amerasia Journal* 23, no. 1 (1997): 29–41.

Rudolph, Frederick. "Chinamen in Yankeedom: Anti-Unionism in Massachusetts in 1870." *American Historical Review* 53 (October 1947): 1–29.

Rumbaut, Rubén G. "Origins and Destinies: Immigration to the United States Since World War II." In *New American Destinies: A Reader in Contemporary Asian and Latino Immigration*, edited by Darrell Y. Hamamoto and Rodolfo D. Torres, 15–45. New York: Routledge, 1997.

Saito, Leland T. "Asian Americans and Latinos in San Gabriel Valley, California: Ethnic Political Cooperation and Redistricting 1990–92." *Amerasia Journal* 19, no. 2 (1993): 55–68.

Salyer, Lucy E. *Laws Harsh as Tigers: Chinese Immigrants and the Shaping of Modern Immigration Law.* Chapel Hill: University of North Carolina Press, 1995.

Sato, Gayle K. Fujita. "The Island Influence on Chinese American Writers: Wing Tek Lum, Darrell H. Y. Lum, and Eric Chock." *Amerasia Journal* 16, no. 2 (1990): 17–33.

Saxton, Alexander. *The Indispensable Enemy: Labor and the Anti-Chinese Movement in California.* Berkeley: University of California Press, 1971.

Schwendinger, Robert J. *Ocean of Bitter Dreams: Maritime Relations Between China and the United States, 1850–1915.* Tucson, Ariz.: Westernlore Press, 1988.

Shinagawa, Larry Hajime. "The Impact of Immigration on the Demography of Asian Pacific Americans." In *The State of Asian Pacific America: Reframing the Immigration Debate*, ed. Bill Ong Hing and Ronald Lee, 66–90. Los Angeles:

LEAP Asian Pacific American Public Policy Institute and UCLA Asian American Studies Center, 1996.

Shinagawa, Larry H., and Gin Yong Pang. "Asian American Pan-Ethnicity and Intermarriage." *Amerasia Journal* 22, no. 2 (1996): 127–52.

———. "Marriage Patterns of Asian Americans in California, 1980." *Mellen Studies in Sociology* 3 (1990): 225–82.

Smith, Richard J. *China's Cultural Heritage: The Qing Dynasty, 1644–1912.* 2nd ed. Boulder, Colo.: Westview Press, 1994.

Sollenberger, Richard T. "Chinese American Child-rearing Practices and Juvenile Delinquency." *Journal of Social Psychology* 74 (1968): 13–23.

Spence, Jonathan D. *The Search for Modern China.* New York: W. W. Norton, 1990.

Spickard, Paul R. "What I Must Be? Asian Americans and the Question of Multiethnic Identity." *Amerasia Journal* 23, no. 1 (1997): 43–60.

The State of Asian Pacific America: Policy Issues to the Year 2020. Los Angeles: LEAP Asian Pacific American Public Policy Institute and UCLA Asian American Studies Center, 1993.

"Success Story of One Minority Group in the U.S." *U.S. News and World Report,* December 26, 1966, 73–78.

Sue, Sam. "Growing Up in Mississippi." In *Asian Americans: Oral Histories of First to Fourth Generation Americans from China, the Philippines, Japan, India, the Pacific Islands, Vietnam, and Cambodia,* ed. Joann Faung Jean Lee, 3–9. New York: New Press, 1992.

Sue, Stanley, and Sumie Okazaki. "Asian-American Educational Achievements: A Phenomenon in Search of an Explanation." *American Psychologist* 46, no. 8 (1990): 913–20.

Sue, Stanley, and Derald W. Sue. "Chinese American Personality and Mental Health." In *Roots: An Asian-American Reader,* edited by Amy Tachiki et al., 72–81. Los Angeles: Continental Graphics, 1971.

Sung, Betty Lee. *The Adjustment Experience of Chinese Immigrant Children in New York City.* New York: Center for Migration Studies, 1987.

———. "Intermarriage among the Chinese in New York City." In *Chinese America: History and Perspectives 1987,* 101–17. San Francisco: Chinese Historical Society of America, 1987.

———. *Mountain of Gold: The Story of the Chinese in America.* New York: Macmillan, 1967.

Tajima, Renee E. "Lotus Blossoms Don't Bleed: Images of Asian Women." In *Making Waves: An Anthology of Writings by and about Asian American Women,* ed. Asian Women United of California, 308–17. Boston: Beacon Press, 1989.

———. "Moving the Image: Asian American Independent Filmmaking 1970–1990." In *Moving the Image: Independent Asian American Media Arts,* edited by Russell Leong, 10–33. Los Angeles: UCLA Asian American Studies Center and Visual Communications, Southern California Asian American Studies Central, 1991.

Takaki, Ronald. *Pau Hana: Plantation Life and Labor in Hawaii.* Honolulu: University of Hawaii Press, 1983.

———. *Strangers from a Different Shore: A History of Asian Americans.* Boston: Penguin Books, 1989.

———. "They Also Came: The Migration of Chinese and Japanese Women to Hawaii and the Continental United States." In *Chinese America: History and Perspectives 1990,* 3–20. San Francisco: Chinese Historical Society of America, 1990.

Tan, Mely Giok-lan. *The Chinese in the United States: Social Mobility and Assimilation.* Taipei, Taiwan: Orient Cultural Service, 1973.

Tchen, John Kuo Wei. "New York Chinese: The Nineteenth-Century Pre-Chinatown Settlement." In *Chinese America: History and Perspectives 1990,* 157–92. San Francisco: Chinese Historical Society of America, 1990.

———. "Staging Orientalism and Occidentalism: Chang and Eng Bunker and Phineas T. Barnum." In *Chinese America: History and Perspectives 1996,* 93–132. San Francisco: Chinese Historical Society of America, 1996.

Tong, Benson. *Unsubmissive Women: Chinese Prostitutes in Nineteenth-Century San Francisco.* Norman: University of Oklahoma Press, 1994.

Torok, John Hayakawa. " 'Interest Convergence' and the Liberalization of Discriminatory Immigration and Naturalization Laws Affecting Asians, 1943–1965." In *Chinese America: History and Perspectives 1995,* 1–28. San Francisco: Chinese Historical Society of America, 1995.

Tsai, Shih-shan Henry. *China and the Overseas Chinese in the United States, 1868–1911.* Fayetteville: University of Arkansas Press, 1983.

———. *The Chinese Experience in America.* Bloomington: Indiana University Press, 1986.

Tseng, Timothy. "Chinese Protestant Nationalism in the United States, 1880–1927." *Amerasia Journal* 22, no. 1 (1996): 31–56.

Tseng, Yen-fen. "Suburban Ethnic Economy: Chinese Business Communities in Los Angeles." Ph.D. diss., University of California at Los Angeles, 1994.

Tu Wei-ming. "Cultural China: The Periphery as the Center." In *The Living Tree: The Changing Meaning of Being Chinese Today,* edited by Tu Wei-ming, 1–34. Stanford, Calif.: Stanford University Press, 1994.

Uba, Laura. *Asian Americans: Personality Patterns, Identity, and Mental Health.* New York: Guilford Press, 1994.

U.S. Bureau of the Census. *Survey of Minority-Owned Business Enterprises: Asian Americans, American Indians, and Others.* Washington, D.C.: Department of Commerce, 1987.

U.S. Commission on Civil Rights. *Civil Rights Issues Facing Asian Americans in the 1990s.* Washington, D.C.: U.S. Government Printing Office, 1992.

————. *Recent Activities against Citizens and Residents of Asian Descent.* Washington, D.C.: Clearinghouse Publication no. 88, 1986.

Wang, L. Ling-chi. "Lau V. Nichols: History of a Struggle for Equal and Quality Education." *Amerasia Journal* 2, no. 2 (1974): 16–45.

————. "Roots and the Changing Identity of the Chinese in the United States." In *The Living Tree: The Changing Meaning of Being Chinese Today,* edited by Tu Wei-ming, 185–212. Stanford, Calif.: Stanford University Press, 1994.

Wang, Xinyang. "Economic Opportunity, Artisan Leadership, and Immigrant Workers' Labor Militancy: Italian and Chinese Workers in New York City, 1890–1970." *Labor History* 37 (Fall 1996): 480–99.

Wei, William. "The Anti-Chinese Movement in Colorado: Interethnic Competition and Conflict on the Eve of Exclusion." In *Chinese America: History and Perspectives 1995,* 179–198. San Francisco: Chinese Historical Society of America, 1995.

————. *The Asian American Movement.* Philadelphia: Temple University Press, 1993.

Weinstein, Robert A. "North from Panama, West to the Orient: The Pacific Mail Steamship Company." *California History* 57 (Spring 1978): 46–57.

Weiss, Melford S. *Valley City: A Chinese Community in America.* Cambridge, Mass.: Schenkman, 1974.

Wenquan. "Chinatown Literature During the Last Ten Years (1939–1949)." Trans. Marlon K. Hom. *Amerasia Journal* 9, no. 1 (1982): 75–100.

Wong, Bernard P. *Chinatown: Economic Adaptation and Ethnic Identity of the Chinese.* New York: Holt, Rinehart, & Winston, 1982.

————. *Ethnicity and Entrepreneurship: The New Chinese Immigrants in the San Francisco Bay Area.* Boston: Allyn and Bacon, 1998.

————. *Patronage, Brokerage, Entrepreneurship and the Chinese Community of New York.* New York: AMS Press, 1988.

Wong, Charles Choy, and Kenneth Klein. "False Papers, Lost Lives." In *Origins and Destinations: 41 Essays on Chinese America,* edited by Chinese Historical Society of Southern California and UCLA Asian American Studies Center, 355–74. Los Angeles: Chinese Historical Society of Southern California and UCLA Asian American Studies Center, 1994.

Wong, Diane Yen-Mei with Dennis Hayashi. "Behind, Unmarked Doors: Developments in the Garment Industry." *In Making Waves: An Anthology of Writings by and about Asian American Women,* ed. Asian Women United of California, 159–71. Boston: Beacon Press, 1989.

Wong, Eugene Franklin. *On Visual Media Racism: Asians in the American Motion Pictures.* New York: Arno Press, 1978.

Wong, Jade Snow. *Fifth Chinese Daughter.* New York: Harper & Row, 1950.

Wong, K. Scott. " 'The Eagle Seeks a Helpless Quarry': Chinatown, the Police, and the Press—The 1903 Boston Chinatown Raid Revisited." *Amerasia Journal* 22, no. 3 (1996): 81–103.

Wong, Morrison G. "The Chinese-American Family." In *Ethnic Families in America: Patterns and Variations*, 4th ed., edited by Charles H. Mindel, Robert W. Habenstein, and Roosevelt Wright, Jr., 284–310. Upper Saddle River, N.J.: Prentice Hall, 1998.

———. "Chinese Americans." In *Asian Americans: Contemporary Trends and Issues*, edited by Pyong Gap Min, 58–94. Thousand Oaks, Calif.: Sage Publications, 1995.

———. "A Look at Intermarriage among the Chinese in the United States in 1980." *Sociological Perspectives* 32, no. 1 (1989): 87–107.

Wong, Sau-ling Cynthia. "Autobiography as Guided Chinatown Tour? Maxine Hong Kingston's *The Woman Warrior* and the Chinese-American Autobiographical Controversy." In *Multicultural Autobiography: American Lives*, ed. James Robert Payne, 248–71. Knoxville: University of Tennessee Press, 1992.

———. "Chinese American Literature." In *An Interethnic Companion to Asian American Literature*, edited by King-kok Cheung, 39–61. New York: Cambridge University Press, 1997.

———. "Tales of Postwar Chinatown: Short Stories of *The Bud*, 1947–1948." *Amerasia Journal* 14, no. 2 (1988): 61–79.

Wong, Victoria. "Square and Circle Club: Women in the Public Sphere." In *Chinese America: History and Perspectives 1994*, 127–53. San Francisco: Chinese Historical Society, 1994.

Woo, Wesley. "Chinese Protestants in the San Francisco Bay Area." In *Entry Denied: Exclusion and the Chinese Community in America, 1882–1943*, edited by Sucheng Chan, 213–45. Philadelphia: Temple University Press, 1991.

Wu, Cheng-tsu, ed. *Chink! A Documentary History of Anti-Chinese Prejudice in America*. New York: World Publishing, 1972.

Wu Ching Chao. "Chinatowns: A Study of Symbiosis and Assimilation." Ph.D diss., University of Chicago, 1928.

Wu, William F. *The Yellow Peril: Chinese Americans in American Fiction, 1850–1940*. Hamden, Conn.: Archon Books, 1982.

Wu Xingci, and Li Zhen. "*Gum San Haak* in the 1980s: A Study on Chinese Emigrants Who Return to Taishan County for Marriage." *Amerasia Journal* 14, no. 2 (1988): 21–35.

Yang, C. K. "The Role of Religion in Chinese Society." In *An Introduction to Chinese Civilization*, ed. John Meskill, 643–74. New York: Columbia University Press, 1973.

Yoo, David. "For Those Who Have Eyes to See: Religious Sightings in Asian America." *Amerasia Journal* 22, no. 1 (1996): xiii–xxii.

Yu, Renqui. *To Save China, To Save Ourselves: The Chinese Hand Laundry Alliance of New York*. Philadelphia: Temple University Press, 1992.

Yuan, D. Y. "Chinatown and Beyond: The Chinese Population in Metropolitan New York." *Phylon* 27, no. 4 (1966): 320–31.

Yung, Judy. *Chinese Women of America: A Pictorial History.* Seattle: University of Washington Press, 1986.

———. *Unbound Feet: A Social History of Chinese Women in San Francisco.* Berkeley: University of California Press, 1995.

Zhang, Qingsong. "The Origins of the Chinese Americanization Movement: Wong Chin Foo and the Chinese Equal Rights League." In *Claiming America: Constructing Chinese American Identities During the Exclusion Era,* edited by K. Scott Wong and Sucheng Chan, 41–63. Philadelphia: Temple University Press, 1998.

Zhang, Wei-hua. "Fred Ho and Jon Jang: Profiles of Two Chinese American Jazz Musicians." In *Chinese America: History and Perspectives 1994,* 175–200. San Francisco: Chinese Historical Society of America, 1994.

Zhou, Min. *Chinatown: The Socioeconomic Potential of an Urban Enclave.* Philadelphia: Temple University Press, 1992.

Zhu, Liping. *A Chinaman's Chance: The Chinese on the Rocky Mountain Mining Frontier.* Niwot: University Press of Colorado, 1997.

Zia, Helen. "Violence in Our Communities: Where Are the Asian Women?" In *Making More Waves: New Writing by Asian American Women,* edited by Elaine H. Kim, Lilia V. Villanueva, and Asian Women United of California, 207–14. Boston: Beacon Press, 1997.

Zo Kil-Young. *Chinese Immigration into the United States, 1850–1880.* New York: Arno Press, 1979.

Index

About the Author

BENSON TONG is Assistant Professor of History in the Department of History at Wichita State University, Wichita, Kansas. He is the author of *Unsubmissive Women: Chinese Prostitutes in Nineteenth-Century San Francisco* (1994) and *Susan La Flesche Picotte, M.D.: Omaha Reformer and Tribal Leader* (1999).